PLANNING GUIDE

TO ACCOMPANY

SOCIOLOGY AND YOU

PREPARED BY

CINDY JOY WOOD

I. **SEMESTER COURSE**
   A. **Traditional (18 weeks)** 1
   B. **Block (9 weeks)** 93

II. **TWO-SEMESTER COURSE**
   A. **Traditional (36 weeks)** 141
   B. **Block (18 weeks)** 323

 **Glencoe
McGraw-Hill**

New York, New York
Columbus, Ohio
Chicago, Illinois
Peoria, Illinois
Woodland Hills, California

Planning Guide
Sociology and You

Semester course – Traditional (18 weeks – 90 days)

Resource Key

TWE   Teacher's Wrap Edition
TRB   Teacher's Resource Box

Select the activities best suited to your students' needs and abilities.

Chapter 1
AN INVITATION TO SOCIOLOGY

Day 1

Week of _____

Day 1 of 4

Content:	Unit 1 Intro., Ch. 1 Intro., and Sec. 1: The Sociological Perspective (pp. 2-13)
Objective:	Students will understand the importance of the sociological imagination and will describe uses of the sociological perspective.
Act. Type:	Demonstration, Class Discussion, Class Activity, Independent Practice
Introduction:	Use one of the strategies described in the Ch. 1 Lead-Off Activity (TWE pp. 4-5).
Instruction:	Have students read and discuss Using Your Sociological Imagination (TWE p. 5).
	Do Demonstration-Sociological Imagination (TWE p. 12).
	Do Demonstration-Societal vs. Individual Responsibilities (TWE pp. 6-7).
	Have students do Demonstration-Perspectives (TWE p. 8).
	Read and discuss Reteaching – The Sociological Perspective (TWE p. 9).
	Ask students to answer the questions in Another Time – Native American's Speech (TWE p. 10).
Close:	Assign chapter project (see Chapter Assessment: Sociology Projects and Technology Activities, pp. 33-34) to be presented to the class prior to final chapter evaluation.
	Assign Chapter 1 Vocabulary Activity (see *Unit 1 Booklet*, TRB), due the day of the chapter review.
	Ask students to read Sec. 2: The Origins of Sociology (pp. 14-22).

Notes and Comments: _____

_____

_____

_____

_____

_____

Day 2   Block Schedule   Week of _____

Day 2 of 4

Content:	Ch. 1, Sec. 2: The Origins of Sociology (pp. 14-22)
Objective:	Students will outline the contributions of the major pioneers of sociology.
Act. Type:	Class Discussion, Class Activity, Independent Practice, Cooperative Learning, Role-playing, Presentation
Introduction:	Do Using the Section Preview (TWE p. 14).
Instruction:	Discuss More About...August Comte (TWE p. 14).
	Ask students to do Interdisciplinary Activity – Current Events (TWE p. 14).
	Discuss More About...Emile Durkheim (TWE p. 16).
	Discuss More About...Sociology in America (TWE p. 15)
	Ask students to complete Ch. 1 Graphic Organizer (*Unit 1 Booklet*, TRB).
	Discuss More About...Jane Addams (TWE p. 19).
	Ask students to do activity described in Biography-W.E.B. DuBois (TWE p. 22).
	Read and discuss Focus on Research (pp. 20-21).
Close:	Ask students to read Sec. 3: Theoretical Perspectives (pp. 23-31).
	Remind students that chapter presentations are due the following class session.

Notes and Comments: _____

_____

_____

_____

_____

_____

_____

_____

AN INVITATION TO SOCIOLOGY

Day 3

Week of _____

Day 3 of 4

Content:	Ch. 1, Sec. 3: Theoretical Perspectives (pp. 23-31), Chapter 1 Presentations
Objective:	Students will understand the theoretical perspective of the historic interpretations of human social development and will present projects and activities summarizing objective/s learned in the chapter.
Act. Type:	Class Discussion, Class Activity, Independent Practice, Cooperative Learning, Demonstration, Presentations
Introduction:	Have students do Demonstration-The Chairs Game (TWE p. 24).
	Introduce the terms *perception* and *perspective* as in Using the Illustration (TWE p. 23).
Instruction:	Ask students to interpret the map in World View (TWE p. 24).
	Do Using Problem-Solving Skills-Conflict Perspective (TWE p. 27).
	Have students work in groups to do activity in Careers in Sociology (TWE pp. 28-29).
	Have students do presentations (See TWE Chapter Assessment: Sociology Projects and Technology Activities, pp. 33-34).
Close:	Discuss and have students answer questions in Tech Trends (TWE pp. 28-29).
	Assign Chapter 1 Learning Goals Outline (see *Unit 1 Booklet*, TRB), due the day of the chapter evaluation.
	Remind students to study for the chapter evaluation.

Notes and Comments: _____

_____

_____

_____

_____

_____

Day 4

Week of _____

Day 4 of 4

Content:	Ch. 1 Assessment (pp. 32-34) and Evaluation
Objective:	Students will review for evaluation of the concepts learned in this chapter.
Act. Type:	Class Discussion, Class Activity, Independent Practice, Cooperative Learning, Demonstration, Experiment, Debate, Role-playing, Presentation
Introduction:	Review Chapter 1 Vocabulary Activity homework (see *Unit 1 Booklet*, TRB).
Instruction:	Do Chapter Assessment as needed (TWE pp. 32-34).
Evaluate:	To evaluate the students' comprehension of the chapter, administer Chapter 1 Test A or B. You may want to use the Alternative Assessment found in the Teacher's Edition.
Close:	Discuss Enrichment Reading (pp. 35).
	Assign Chapter 2 Intro, (pp. 36-37) and Sec. 1: Research Methods (pp. 38-49).

Notes and Comments: _____

_____

_____

_____

_____

_____

_____

_____

_____

_____

_____

Chapter 2

SOCIOLOGISTS DOING RESEARCH

Day 5

Week of _____

Day 1 of 4

Content: Ch. 2 Intro. (pp. 36-37) and Ch. 2, Sec. 1: Research Methods (pp. 38-49)

Objective: Students will understand the importance of sociological research and will describe the major quantitative and qualitative research methods used by sociologists.

Act. Type: Class Discussion, Class Activity, Independent Practice, Demonstration

Introduction: Have students do Lead-Off Activity (TWE pp. 36-37).

Instruction: Read and discuss Using Your Sociological Imagination (TWE p. 37).

Do Demonstration-Quantitative Research (TWE p. 38).

Have students learn mnemonic in Reinforcing Vocabulary (TWE p. 38).

Do Demonstration-Qualitative Research (TWE p. 39).

Do Demonstration-Surveys (TWE p. 40).

Close: Ask students to do On-Demand Writing (TWE p. 44).

Assign Chapter 2 Vocabulary Activity (see *Unit 1 Booklet*, TRB), due the day of the chapter review.

Assign chapter project (Chapter Assessment: Sociology Projects and Technology Activities, TWE pp. 64-65) to be presented to the class prior to final chapter evaluation.

Ask students to read Sec. 2: Causation in Science (pp. 50-55).

Notes and Comments: _____

_____

_____

_____

_____

_____

_____

_____

Day 6   Week of _____

Day 2 of 4

Content:	Ch. 2, Skills at a Glance (pp. 46-49) and Ch. 2, Sec. 2: Causation in Science (pp. 50-55)
Objective:	Students will use geographic and other tools to collect, analyze, and interpret sociological data and will discuss basic research concepts, including variables and correlations and the standards for proving a cause-and-effect relationship.
Act. Type:	Class Discussion, Class Activity, Independent Practice, Cooperative Learning, Demonstration
Introduction:	Discuss More About the Census (TWE p. 46).
	Discuss Addressing Current Social Issues (TWE p. 42).
	Have students do Cooperative Learning Activity-School Census Survey (TWE pp. 42-43).
Instruction:	Introduce Working with the Data-Skills at a Glance (TWE p. 46).
	Do Skills at a Glance, (pp. 46-49, answers in TWE pp. 47, 49).
	Ask students to interpret the map in World View (TWE p. 51).
	Have students do Paired Learning Activity (TWE p. 55).
	Assign Doing Sociology: Focus on Research (see TRB).
Close:	Read and answer questions for Another Time – Reason and Science (TWE p. 54.
	Ask students to read Sec. 3: Procedures and Ethics in Research (pp. 56-61).
	Remind students that chapter presentations are due the following class session.

Notes and Comments: _____

_____

_____

_____

_____

_____

SOCIOLOGISTS DOING RESEARCH

Day 7   Week of _____

Day 3 of 4

Content:	Ch. 2, Sec. 3: Procedures and Ethics in Research (pp. 56-61), and Chapter 2 Presentations (pp. 36-62)
Objective:	Students will discuss ethics in sociological research and will present projects and activities summarizing objective/s learned in the chapter.
Act. Type:	Class Discussion, Class Activity, Independent Practice, Cooperative Learning, and Presentations
Introduction:	Discuss Focus on Research (pp. 56-57, see TWE p. 56 for Teaching Strategy).
	*Optional - Invite a psychologist in to do Encouraging Citizenship Activity (TWE p. 57).
Instruction:	Assign groups to do Encouraging Citizenship Activity (TWE pp. 58-59).
	Read and discuss Using Decision-Making Skills-Dr. Peter Publish (TWE pp. 60-61).
	Do Ch. 2 Student Journal Prompts (*see Unit 1 Booklet,* TRB).
	Have students do presentations (See TWE, Chapter Assessment: Sociology Projects and Technology Activities, pp. 64-65).
Close:	Discuss Tech Trends (p. 60).
	Assign Chapter 2 Learning Goals Outline (see *Unit 1 Booklet*, TRB), due the day of the chapter evaluation.
	Remind students to study for the chapter evaluation.

Notes and Comments: _____

_____

_____

_____

_____

_____

_____

Chapter 2

SOCIOLOGISTS DOING RESEARCH

Day 8

Week of _____

Day 4 of 4

Content:	Ch. 2 Assessment (pp. 63-65) and Evaluation
Objective:	Students will review for evaluation of the concepts learned in this chapter.
Act. Type:	Class Discussion, Class Activity, Independent Practice, Cooperative Learning
Introduction:	Review Chapter 2 Vocabulary Activity homework (see *Unit 1 Booklet,* TRB).
Instruction:	Do Chapter Assessment as needed (TWE pp. 63-65).
Evaluate:	To evaluate the students' comprehension of the chapter, administer Chapter 2 Test A or B. You may want to use the Alternative Assessment found in the TRB. A test for Unit 1 is also available in the TRB.
Close:	Discuss Sociology Today (TWE p. 62).
	Read and discuss Enrichment Reading (TWE pp. 66-67).
	Assign Unit 2, Chapter 3 Intro. (pp. 68-71) and Sec. 1: The Basis of Culture.

Notes and Comments: _____

_____

_____

_____

_____

_____

_____

_____

_____

_____

_____

_____

Chapter 3

CULTURE

Day 9

Day 1 of 6

Content: Unit 2 Intro, Ch. 3 Intro. (pp. 68-71) and Ch. 3, Sec. 1: The Basis of Culture (pp. 72-75)

Objective: Students will understand the importance of culture in society and will name the essential components of culture.

Act. Type: Class Discussion, Class Activity, Independent Practice, Cooperative Learning, Debate, Role-playing

Introduction: Ask students to do Lead-Off Activity (TWE pp. 70-71).

Read and discuss Using Your Sociological Imagination (TWE p. 71).

Instruction: Do activity in Using Conflict Resolution Skills (TWE p. 72).

Lead students in informal debate in Using Problem-Solving Skills (TWE p. 73).

Have students do Role Play (TWE p. 75).

Close: Assign Chapter 3 Vocabulary Activity (see *Unit 2 Booklet*, TRB), due the day of the chapter review.

Assign chapter project (see Chapter Assessment: Sociology Projects and Technology Activities, pp. 104-105) to be presented to the class prior to final chapter evaluation.

Ask students to read Sec. 2: Language and Culture (pp. 77-78).

Notes and Comments: _____

_____

_____

_____

_____

_____

_____

_____

CULTURE

Day 10

Week of _____

Day 2 of 6

Content:	Ch. 3, Sec. 2: Language and Culture (pp. 76-80)
Objective:	Students will describe how language and culture are related and will explain the hypothesis of linguistic relativity.
Act. Type:	Class Discussion, Class Activity, Independent Practice, Demonstration
Introduction:	Discuss Another Time (TWE p. 76).
	Ask students to do On-Demand Writing (TWE p. 76).
Instruction:	Introduce Using the Section Preview (TWE p. 77).
	Do Demonstration-Knowing Your Culture (TWE p. 77).
	Discuss Working with the Quote (TWE p. 78).
	Do Demonstration-Keeping the Time (TWE p. 78).
	Ask students to do Demonstration-The Importance of Language (TWE p. 79).
	Discuss Teaching Strategy (TWE p. 79).
	Read and discuss Sociology Today-Cultural Relativism (TWE p. 80).
Close:	Discuss Making Connections to Other Cultures (TWE p. 80).
	Ask students to read Sec. 3: Norms and Values (pp. 81-91).

Notes and Comments: _____

_____

_____

_____

_____

_____

_____

_____

CULTURE

Day 11

Week of _____

Day 3 of 6

Content:	Ch. 3, Sec. 3: Norms and Values (pp. 81-91)
Objective:	Students will identify various types of norms and how conformity to those norms is encouraged and will understand that cultural values vary in different locations.
Act. Type:	Class Discussion, Class Activity, Independent Practice, Cooperative Learning, Demonstration, Experiment, Debate, Role-playing
Introduction:	Do Using the Section Preview (TWE p. 81).
Instruction:	*Optional - Use Teaching Strategy-*The Gods Must Be Crazy* (TWE p. 82).
	Assign Learning Styles-Bodily-Kinesthetic (TWE p. 84).
	Ask students to interpret the map in World View (TWE p. 85).
	Ask students to do Cooperative Learning Activity (TWE pp. 86-87).
	Have students do Cooperative Learning Activity(TWE p. 90).
Close:	Ask students to read Sec. 4: Beliefs and Material Culture (pp. 92-94) and Ch. 3, Sec. 5: Cultural Diversity and Similarity – Cultural Change; Cultural Diversity (pp. 95-98).
	Ask students to do Learning Styles-Interpersonal/Linguistic (TWE p. 85).

Notes and Comments: _____

_____

_____

_____

_____

_____

_____

Chapter 3 — CULTURE

Day 12   Week of _____

Content:	Ch. 3, Sec. 4: Beliefs and Material Culture (pp. 92-94) and Ch. 3, Sec. 5: Cultural Diversity and Similarity – Cultural Change; Cultural Diversity (pp. 95-98)
Objective:	Students will distinguish between nonmaterial, material, ideal, and real culture and will discuss how cultural diversity is promoted within a society.
Act. Type:	Class Discussion, Class Activity, Independent Practice, Cooperative Learning, Experiment
Introduction:	Discuss student-designed projects from Learning Styles-Interpersonal/ Linguistic (TWE p. 85).
Instruction:	Have students do Paired-Learning Activity (TWE p. 92).
	Discuss Observation – Ideal and Real Culture (TWE p. 94).
	Present and discuss Using Problem-Solving Skills (TWE p. 95).
	Discuss and do Survey (TWE pp. 96-97 and/or TWE p. 98).
	Read and discuss Focus on Research-How Do Schools and Parents Fail Teens? (TWE pp. 96-97).
Close:	As needed, have students do the Ch. 3 Increasing Your Reading Comprehension worksheet in the *Unit 2 Booklet*, TRB.
	Ask students to read Sec. 5: Cultural Diversity and Similarity – Ethnocentrism; Cultural Universals (pp. 98-102).
	Remind students that chapter presentations are due the following class session.

Notes and Comments: _____

_____

_____

_____

_____

_____

Chapter 3

CULTURE

Day 13

Day 5 of 6

Content:	Ch. 3, Sec. 5: Cultural Diversity and Similarity – Ethnocentrism; Cultural Universals (pp. 98-102), and Chapter 3 Presentations (pp. 70-102)
Objective:	Students will compare and contrast cultural norms among subculture groups and will present projects and activities summarizing objective/s learned in the chapter.
Act. Type:	Class Discussion, Class Activity, Independent Practice, Cooperative Learning, Debate, and Presentations
Introduction:	Discuss Reinforcing Vocabulary-Ethnocentrism (TWE p. 100).
Instruction:	Ask student to do Cooperative Learning Activity (TWE p. 100).
	Have students interpret the map in Snapshot of America (TWE p. 101).
	Discuss and have students analyze the graph in Working with the Data-Fig. 3.5 (TWE p. 102).
	Read and discuss Tech Trends-Star Wars and the Internet (TWE p. 99).
	Have students do presentations (See TWE, Ch. Assessment: Sociology Projects and Technology Activities, pp. 104-105).
Close:	Assign Chapter 3 Learning Goals Outline (see *Unit 2 Booklet*, TRB), due the day of the chapter evaluation.
	Remind students to study for the chapter evaluation.

Notes and Comments: _____

_____

_____

_____

_____

_____

_____

Day 14

Week of _____

Day 6 of 6

Content: Ch. 3 Assessment (pp. 103-105) and Evaluation

Objective: Students will review for evaluation of the concepts learned in this chapter.

Act. Type: Class Discussion, Class Activity, Independent Practice, Cooperative Learning, Demonstration, Experiment, Debate, Role-playing, Presentation

Introduction: Review Chapter 3 Vocabulary Activity homework (see *Unit 2 Booklet*, TRB).

Instruction: Do Chapter Assessment as needed (TWE pp. 103-105).

Evaluate: To evaluate the students' comprehension of the chapter, administer Chapter 3 Test A or B. You may want to use the Alternative Assessment found in the TRB.

Close: Discuss Enrichment Reading (TWE pp. 106-107).

Assign Chapter 4 intro. (pp. 108-109) and Sec. 1: The Importance of Socialization (pp. 110-114).

Notes and Comments: _____

_____

_____

_____

_____

_____

_____

_____

_____

_____

_____

Chapter 4 — SOCIALIZATION

Day 15

Week of _____

Day 1 of 5

Content:	Ch. 4 Intro. (pp. 108-109) and Ch. 4, Sec. 1: The Importance of Socialization (pp. 110-114)
Objective:	Students will understand the importance of socialization and the role socialization plays in human development.
Act. Type:	Class Discussion, Class Activity, Independent Practice, Cooperative Learning, Demonstration, Debate, Presentation
Introduction:	Do Lead-Off Activity (TWE pp. 108-109).
	Read and discuss Using Your Sociological Imagination (TWE p. 109).
Instruction:	Do demonstration in Using the Section Preview (TWE p. 110).
	Use Teaching Strategy (TWE p. 110).
	Ask students to do Interdisciplinary Activity-Animal Research Debate (TWE p. 111).
	Read and discuss Tech Trends (TWE p. 112).
	Ask students to do Learning Styles-Logical-Mathematical (TWE p. 112).
Close:	Assign Chapter 4 Vocabulary Activity (see *Unit 2 Booklet*, TRB), due the day of the chapter review.
	Assign chapter project (see TWE pp. 134-135, Chapter Assessment: Sociology Projects and Technology Activities) to be presented to the class prior to final chapter evaluation.
	Ask students to read Sec. 2: Socialization and the Self (pp. 115-119).

Notes and Comments: _____

_____

_____

_____

_____

_____

_____

Chapter 4

SOCIALIZATION

Day 16

Week of _____

Day 2 of 5

Content:	Ch. 4, Sec. 2: Socialization and the Self (pp. 115-119)
Objective:	Students will compare and contrast the functionalist, conflict, and symbolic interactionist perspectives on socialization.
Act. Type:	Class Discussion, Class Activity, Independent Practice, Cooperative Learning, Experiment
Introduction:	Do Using the Section Preview (TWE p. 115).
Instruction:	Discuss Points to Stress (TWE p. 116).
	Ask students to do On-Demand Writing-Self-Concept (TWE p. 116).
	Ask students to do Working with the Table -Fig. 4.1 (TWE p. 117).
	Do Learning Styles-Musical/Interpersonal (TWE p. 118).
	Discuss Points to Stress (TWE p. 118).
	Use Reteaching (TWE p. 118) for emphasis.
Close:	Discuss Pulling It All Together (TWE p. 119).
	Ask students to read Sec. 3: Agents of Socialization (pp. 120-127).

Notes and Comments: _____

_____

_____

_____

_____

_____

_____

_____

_____

Chapter 4

SOCIALIZATION

Day 17

Week of _____

Day 3 of 5

Content:	Ch. 4, Sec. 3: Agents of Socialization (pp. 120-127)
Objective:	Students will analyze the roles of the family and school in socializing young people and will evaluate mass media techniques used to influence perceptions, attitudes, and behaviors of individuals and groups.
Act. Type:	Class Discussion, Class Activity, Demonstration, Cooperative Learning, Presentation
Introduction:	Read and discuss Another Time (TWE p. 120).
Instruction:	Introduce socialization in the family as in Using the Section Preview (TWE p. 121).
	Share More About...School Socialization (TWE p. 122).
	Share Making Connections to Other Cultures (TWE p. 123).
	Ask students to do Cooperative Learning Activity (TWE p. 121).
	Do Interdisciplinary Activity-Culture Studies (TWE pp. 124-125).
Close:	Introduce "Writing on the Wall" described in Learning Styles-Visual (TWE pp. 122-123).
	Ask students to read Sec. 4: Processes of Socialization (pp. 128-132).
	Remind students that chapter presentations are due the following class session.

Notes and Comments: _____

_____

_____

_____

_____

_____

_____

SOCIALIZATION

Day 18

Week of _____

Day 4 of 5

Content:	Ch. 4, Sec. 4: Processes of Socialization (pp. 128-132), and Ch. 4 Presentations (pp. 108-132)
Objective:	Students will discuss processes for socialization in adulthood and will present projects and activities summarizing objective/s learned in the chapter.
Act. Type:	Class Discussion, Class Activity, Independent Practice, Role Play Presentations
Introduction:	Follow-up on Interdisciplinary Activity-Culture Studies (TWE pp. 124-125) from previous session.
Instruction:	Read and discuss Sociology Today-Struggling Through the Teen Years (TWE pp. 126-127).
	Ask students to interpret the map in Snapshot of America (TWE p. 129).
	Read and do Focus on Research (TWE p. 130-131).
	Ask students to do Role Play (TWE p. 131).
	Have students do presentations (See TWE, Chapter Assessment: Sociology Projects and Technology Activities, pp. 134-135).
	Have students do On-Demand Writing (TWE p. 130).
Close:	Assign Chapter 4 Learning Goals Outline (see *Unit 2 Booklet*, TRB), due the day of the chapter evaluation.
	Remind students to study for the chapter evaluation.

Notes and Comments: _____

_____

_____

_____

_____

_____

_____

Chapter 4

SOCIALIZATION

Day 19

Week of _____

Day 5 of 5

Content:	Ch. 4 Assessment (pp. 133-135) and Evaluation
Objective:	Students will review for evaluation of the concepts learned in this chapter.
Act. Type:	Class Discussion, Class Activity, Independent Practice, Cooperative Learning, Demonstration, Experiment, Debate, Role-playing, Presentation
Introduction:	Review Chapter 4 Vocabulary Activity homework (see *Unit 2 Booklet*, TRB).
Instruction:	Do Chapter Assessment as needed (TWE pp. 133-135).
Evaluate:	To evaluate the students' comprehension of the chapter, administer Chapter 4 Test A or B. You may want to use the Alternative Assessment found in the TRB.
Close:	Discuss Enrichment Reading (TWE pp. 136-137).
	Assign Chapter 5, intro. (pp. 138-139) and Ch. 5, Sec. 1: Social Structure and Status (pp. 140-143).

Notes and Comments: _____

_____

_____

_____

_____

_____

_____

_____

_____

_____

_____

Chapter 5

SOCIAL STRUCTURE AND SOCIETY

Day 20 Week of _____

Day 1 of 6

Content:	Ch. 5 Intro. (pp. 138-139) and Ch. 5, Sec. 1: Social Structure and Status (pp. 140-143)
Objective:	Students will understand the effects of social structure and will explain what sociologists mean by social structure and how statuses are related to it.
Act. Type:	Class Discussion, Class Activity, Independent Practice, Cooperative Learning, Demonstration, Role-playing, Presentation
Introduction:	Direct students in Lead-Off Activity (TWE p. 138).
	Read and discuss Using Your Sociological Imagination (TWE p. 139).
Introduction:	Do Demonstration (TWE p. 140).
	Have students do Role Play activity (TWE p. 141).
Close:	Introduce and assign Teaching Strategy-Act.#5 from Ch. Rev (TWE p. 167).
	Assign Chapter 5 Vocabulary Activity (see *Unit 2 Booklet*, TRB), due the day of the chapter review.
	Assign chapter project(see Chapter Assessment: Sociology Projects and Technology Activities) to be presented to the class prior to final chapter evaluation.
	Ask students to read Sec. 2: Social Structure and Roles (pp. 144-151).

Notes and Comments: _____

_____

_____

_____

_____

_____

_____

_____

_____

Chapter 5
SOCIAL STRUCTURE AND SOCIETY

Day 21

Day 2 of 6

Content:	Ch. 5, Sec. 2: Social Structure and Roles (pp. 144-151)
Objective:	Students will discuss how roles are related to social structure and will define and explain how to manage role conflict and role strain.
Act. Type:	Class Discussion, Class Activity, Independent Practice, Cooperative Learning, Demonstration, Role-playing, Presentation
Introduction:	Follow up on Teaching Strategy-Act.#5 from Ch. Assessment.
Instruction:	Read and discuss Focus on Research (TWE pp. 144-145).
	Ask students to do On-Demand Writing (TWE p. 145).
	Ask students to do Demonstration (TWE p. 146).
	Ask students to do Role Play (TWE p. 149).
	Ask students to interpret the map in Snapshot of America (TWE p. 149).
	Conduct Survey (TWE p. 150).
	Read and discuss Sociology Today (TWE p. 152).
Close:	Assign Learning Styles-Linguistic/Spatial (TWE p. 147).
	Ask students to read Sec. 3: Preindustrial Societies (pp. 153-157).

Notes and Comments: _____

_____

_____

_____

_____

_____

_____

_____

Day 22   Week of _____

Day 3 of 6

Content:	Ch. 5, Sec. 3: Preindustrial Societies (pp. 153-157)
Objective:	Students will describe the means of subsistence in preindustrial societies.
Act. Type:	Class Discussion, Class Activity, Demonstration, Presentation, Independent Practice, Cooperative Learning
Introduction:	Show video as described in Using the Section Preview (TWE p. 153).
Instruction:	Do Demonstration (TWE p. 153).
	*Optional - Do Interdisciplinary Activity (TWE p. 154).
	Discuss Using the Illustration-Timeline (TWE p. 155).
Close:	Assign Learning Styles-Artistic (TWE p. 155) as appropriate.
	Ask students to read Sec. 4: Industrial and Postindustrial Societies – Basic Features of Industrial Societies; A Conversation with Two Sociologists (pp. 158-162).

Notes and Comments: _____

_____

_____

_____

_____

_____

_____

_____

_____

 **Chapter 5**

SOCIAL STRUCTURE AND SOCIETY

Day 23   Week of _____

Day 4 of 6

Content:	Ch. 5, Sec. 4: Industrial and Postindustrial Societies – Basic Features of Industrial Societies; A Conversation with Two Sociologists (pp. 158-162)
Objective:	Students will describe changes that take place when agricultural societies become industrial societies and will explain the contributions of early sociologists who wrote about preindustrial and industrial societies.
Act. Type:	Class Discussion, Class Activity, Cooperative Learning, Role-playing, Presentation
Introduction:	Read and discuss Another Place (TWE p. 158).
Instruction:	Ask student to do Role Play (TWE p. 160).
	Discuss and do activity in Using Decision-Making Skills (TWE p. 162).
	Ask students to do Learning Styles-Bodily/Kinesthetic (TWE p. 159).
Close:	Discuss World View (TWE p. 161).
	Ask students to read Sec. 4: Industrial and Postindustrial Societies – Major Features of Postindustrial Society; Social Instability in Postindustrial Society (pp. 162-163).
	Remind students that chapter presentations are due the following class session.

Notes and Comments: _____

_____

_____

_____

_____

_____

_____

_____

Chapter 5

SOCIAL STRUCTURE AND SOCIETY

Day 24

Week of _____

Day 5 of 6

Content:	Ch. 5, Sec. 4: Industrial and Postindustrial Societies – Major Features of Postindustrial Society; Social Instability in Postindustrial Society (pp. 162-163) and Ch. 5 Presentations (pp. 138-164)
Objective:	Students will analyze changes resulting from industrialization and will present projects and activities summarizing objective/s learned in the chapter.
Act. Type:	Class Discussion, Class Activity, Cooperative Learning, and Presentation
Introduction:	Discuss Pulling It All Together (TWE p. 163).
Instruction:	Share information in Points to Stress (TWE p. 162).
	Use Reteaching suggestion (TWE p. 162) as needed.
	*Optional - Do Encouraging Citizenship activity (TWE p. 163).
	Read and discuss Tech Trends (TWE p. 164).
	Have students do Cooperative Learning Activity (TWE p. 164).
	Have students do presentations (See TWE Chapter Assessment: Sociology Projects and Technology Activities, pp. 166-167).
Close:	Assign Chapter 5 Learning Goals Outline (see *Unit 2 Booklet*, TRB), due the day of the chapter evaluation.
	Remind students to study for the chapter evaluation.

Notes and Comments: _____

_____

_____

_____

_____

_____

_____

_____

Chapter 5   SOCIAL STRUCTURE AND SOCIETY

Day 25

Week of _____

Day 6 of 6

Content:	Ch. 5, Assessment and Evaluation
Objective:	Students will review for evaluation of the concepts learned in this chapter.
Act. Type:	Class Discussion, Class Activity, Independent Practice, Cooperative Learning, Demonstration, Experiment, Debate, Role-playing, Presentation
Introduction:	Review Chapter 5 Vocabulary Activity homework (see *Unit 2 Booklet*, TRB).
Instruction:	Do Chapter Assessment as needed (TWE pp. 165-166)
Evaluate:	To evaluate the students' comprehension of the chapter, administer Chapter 5 Test A or B. You may want to use the Alternative Assessment found in the TRB.
Close:	Discuss Enrichment Reading (TWE pp. 168-169).
	Assign Chapter 6, intro. (pp. 170-171) and Ch. 6, Sec. 1: Primary and Secondary Groups – Groups, Categories, and Aggregates; Primary Groups (pp. 172-174)

Notes and Comments: _____

_____

_____

_____

_____

_____

_____

_____

_____

_____

_____

Chapter 6

GROUPS AND FORMAL ORGANIZATIONS

Day 26

Day 1 of 5

Content:	Ch. 6 Intro. (pp. 170-171) and Ch. 6, Sec. 1: Primary and Secondary Groups – Groups, Categories, and Aggregates; Primary Groups (pp. 172-174)
Objective:	Students will understand the effects of group membership and will compare the roles of group membership in primary groups.
Act. Type:	Class Discussion, Class Activity, Independent Practice
Introduction:	Introduce Lead-Off Activity (TWE p. 170).
	Read and discuss Using Your Sociological Imagination (TWE p. 171).
Introduction:	Ask students to do On-Demand Writing (TWE p. 172).
	Discuss Using the Illustration (TWE p. 172).
	Share and discuss More About...Gender Interaction (TWE p. 173).
Close:	Assign Chapter 6 Vocabulary Activity (see *Unit 2 Booklet*, TRB), due the day of the chapter review.
	Assign chapter project (see TWE pp. 198-199, Chapter Assessment: Sociology Projects and Technology Activities) to be presented to the class prior to final chapter evaluation.
	Ask students to read Sec. 1: Primary and Secondary Groups – Secondary Groups (pp. 174-175) and Sec. 2: Other Groups and Networks (pp. 177-179).

Notes and Comments: _____

_____

_____

_____

_____

_____

_____

_____

28

Chapter 6

GROUPS AND FORMAL ORGANIZATIONS

Day 27

Week of _____

Day 2 of 5

Content:	Ch. 6, Sec. 1: Primary and Secondary Groups – Secondary Groups (pp. 174-175) and Ch. 6, Sec. 2: Other Groups and Networks (pp. 177-179)
Objective:	Students will compare the roles of group membership in secondary groups and will explain the purposes of reference groups and social networks.
Act. Type:	Class Discussion, Class Activity, Independent Practice, Cooperative Learning, Demonstration, Presentation
Introduction:	Do activity as described in Making Connections to Other Cultures (TWE p. 174).
Instruction:	Ask students to do Observation (TWE p. 174).
	Conduct Survey-Primary and Secondary Groups (TWE p. 175).
	Brainstorm as in Using the Section Preview (TWE p. 177).
	Discuss Using the Illustration (TWE p. 178).
	Facilitate students in doing Cooperative Learning Activity (TWE p. 177).
	Do Observation (TWE p. 178).
Close:	Ask students to read Sec. 3: Types of Social Interaction (pp. 180-186).

Notes and Comments: _____

_____

_____

_____

_____

_____

_____

_____

_____

Chapter 6

GROUPS AND FORMAL ORGANIZATIONS

Day 28   Week of _____

Day 3 of 5

Content:	Ch. 6, Sec. 3: Types of Social Interaction (pp. 180-186)
Objective:	Students will discuss how these interactions affect the members of groups and will compare and contrast coercion and conformity.
Act. Type:	Class Discussion, Class Activity, Independent Practice, Cooperative Learning, Demonstration, Experiment, Debate
Introduction:	Do Using Problem-Solving Skills (TWE p. 179).
Instruction:	Use Using the Section Preview (TWE p. 181).
	As students to do Cooperative Learning Activity (TWE p. 181).
	Lead students in doing the Encouraging Citizenship Activity (TWE p. 183).
	Have students do Demonstration (TWE p. 184).
	Discuss Using the Illustration (TWE p. 185).
	Discuss Sociology Today (TWE p. 180).
Close:	Assign Learning Styles-Intrapersonal/Linguistic (TWE p. 186).
	Ask students to read Sec. 4: Formal Organizations (pp. 190-196).
	Remind students that chapter presentations are due the following class session.

Notes and Comments: _____

_____

_____

_____

_____

_____

_____

_____

_____

 **Chapter**
6

GROUPS AND FORMAL ORGANIZATIONS

Day 29

Week of _____

Day 4 of 5

Content:	Ch. 6, Sec. 4: Formal Organizations (pp. 190-196) and Ch. 6 Presentations (pp. 170-196)
Objective:	Students will discuss the use of power and its effect on the roles of group membership in formal organizations and will present projects and activities summarizing objective/s learned in the chapter.
Act. Type:	Class Discussion, Class Activity, Independent Practice, Demonstration, and Presentations
Introduction:	Read and discuss Tech Trends (TWE p. 187).
Instruction:	Lead Observation (TWE pp. 190-191).
	With students, do Demonstration (TWE p. 193).
	Read and discuss Focus on Research (TWE pp. 188-189).
	Have students do presentations (See TWE, Chapter Assessment: Sociology Projects and Technology Activities, pp. 198-199).
Close:	Discuss Snapshot of America (TWE p. 193).
	Assign Chapter 6 Learning Goals Outline (see *Unit 2 Booklet*, TRB), due the day of the chapter evaluation.
	Remind students to study for the chapter evaluation.

Notes and Comments: _____

_____

_____

_____

_____

_____

_____

_____

Chapter 6

GROUPS AND FORMAL ORGANIZATIONS

Day 30

Day 5 of 5

Content: Ch. 6, Assessment (pp. 197-199) and Evaluation

Objective: Students will review for evaluation of the concepts learned in this chapter.

Act. Type: Class Discussion, Class Activity, Independent Practice, Cooperative Learning, Demonstration, Experiment, Debate, Role-playing, Presentation

Introduction: Review Chapter 6 Vocabulary Activity homework (see *Unit 2 Booklet*, TRB).

Instruction: Do Chapter Assessment as needed (TWE pp. 197-199).

Evaluate: To evaluate the students' comprehension of the chapter, administer Chapter 6 Test A or B. You may want to use the Alternative Assessment found in the TRB.

Close: Discuss Enrichment Reading (TWE pp. 200-201).

Assign Chapter 7, intro. (pp. 202-203) and Ch. 7, Sec. 1: Deviance and Social Control (pp. 204-208).

Notes and Comments: _____

_____

_____

_____

_____

_____

_____

_____

_____

_____

_____

Chapter 7

DEVIANCE AND SOCIAL CONTROL

Day 31

Day 1 of 6

Content:	Ch. 7 Intro. (pp. 202-203) and Ch. 7, Sec. 1: Deviance and Social Control (pp. 204-208)
Objective:	Students will identify the major types of social control.
Act. Type:	Class Discussion, Class Activity, Independent Practice, Demonstration, Debate
Introduction:	Have students do Lead-Off Activity (TWE pp. 202-203).
	Read and discuss Using Your Sociological Imagination (TWE p. 203).
Introduction:	Share and discuss Using the Section Preview (TWE p. 204).
	Review and discuss Working with the Data-Fig. 7.1 (TWE p. 204).
	Discuss and do activity/ies in Using Conflict-Resolution Skills (TWE pp. 204-205) or Observation (TWE p. 207).
	Ask students to interpret the map in Snapshot of America (TWE p. 206).
Close:	Discuss Another Time (TWE p. 208).
	Assign Chapter 7 Vocabulary Activity (see *Unit 2 Booklet*, TRB), due the day of the chapter review.
	Assign chapter project (see TWE pp. 235, Chapter Assessment: Sociology Projects and Technology Activities) to be presented to the class prior to final chapter evaluation.
	Ask students to read Sec. 2: Functionalism and Deviance (pp. 209-212).

Notes and Comments: _____

_____

_____

_____

_____

_____

_____

Day 32

Week of _____

Day 2 of 6

Content:	Ch. 7, Sec. 2: Functionalism and Deviance (pp. 209-212)
Objective:	Students will explain the positive and negative consequences of deviance and will differentiate the major functional theories of deviance.
Act. Type:	Class Discussion, Class Activity, Cooperative Learning, Independent Practice, Debate, Role-playing
Introduction:	Introduce Using the Section Preview (TWE p. 209).
Instruction:	Ask students to do Role Play (TWE p. 209).
	Share More About Strain Theory (TWE p. 210).
	Share and discuss Controversy and Debate (TWE p. 210).
	Review and discuss Working with the Data-Fig. 7.2 (TWE p. 211).
	Ask students to do On-Demand Writing (TWE p. 210).
Close:	Ask students to read Sec. 3: Symbolic Interactionism and Deviance (pp. 213-217) and Ch. 7, Sec. 4: Conflict Theory and Deviance (pp. 218-221).

Notes and Comments: _____

_____

_____

_____

_____

_____

_____

_____

_____

34

Chapter 7   DEVIANCE AND SOCIAL CONTROL

Day 33

Week of _____

Day 3 of 6

Content:	Ch. 7, Sec. 3: Symbolic Interactionism and Deviance (pp. 213-217) and Ch. 7, Sec. 4: Conflict Theory and Deviance (pp. 218-221)
Objective:	Students will compare and contrast cultural transmission theory and labeling theory, will discuss the conflict theory view of deviance, and will discuss the relationship between minorities, white-collar crime, and the judicial system.
Act. Type:	Class Discussion, Class Activity, Independent Practice, Cooperative Learning, Debate, Demonstration, Experiment
Introduction:	Read and discuss Sociology Today (TWE p. 213).
Instruction:	Share More About...Deviance and Labeling Theory (TWE p. 215).
	Use Teaching Strategy-the Labeling Game (TWE p. 216).
	Discuss and assign Controversy and Debate (TWE p. 219).
	Facilitate Cooperative Learning Activity (TWE p. 218).
	Lead students in Cooperative Learning Activity (TWE p. 219).
	Ask students to do Reinforcing Vocabulary (TWE p. 220).
	Discuss and do Paired Learning Activity (TWE p. 220).
Close:	Assign Interdisciplinary Activity-Creative Writing (TWE p. 217).
	Ask students to read Sec. 5: Crime and Punishment (pp. 222-232).

Notes and Comments: _____

_____

_____

_____

_____

_____

_____

Chapter 7 DEVIANCE AND SOCIAL CONTROL

Day 34   Week of _____

Day 4 of 6

Content:	Ch. 7, Sec. 5: Crime and Punishment (pp. 222-232)
Objective:	Students will identify the meaning of crime statistics, especially as related to juvenile delinquency and will describe four approaches to crime control.
Act. Type:	Class Discussion, Class Activity, Independent Practice, Demonstration, Cooperative Learning, Presentation
Introduction:	Read and discuss Focus on Research (TWE pp. 222-223).
Instruction:	Introduce Using the Section Preview (TWE p. 224).
	Do Demonstration (TWE pp. 224-225).
	Review and discuss Working with the Data-Fig.7.6 (TWE p. 225).
	Facilitate Cooperative Learning Activity (TWE p. 226).
	Read and discuss Making Connections to Other Cultures (TWE p. 227).
	If possible, use Teaching Strategy (TWE p. 228) or Careers in Sociology (TWE p. 229) to invite a guest speaker to visit your class.
	Read and discuss Tech Trends (TWE p. 228).
	Have students do On-Demand Writing (TWE p. 227).
Close:	Remind students that chapter presentations are due the following class session.

Notes and Comments: _____

_____

_____

_____

_____

_____

_____

_____

Chapter 7
DEVIANCE AND SOCIAL CONTROL

Day 35

Week of _____

Day 5 of 6

Content:	Chapter 7 (pp. 202-232) Presentations
Objective:	Students will present projects and activities summarizing objective/s learned in the chapter.
Act. Type:	Class Activity, Role-playing, and Presentation
Introduction:	Ask students to Role Play (TWE p. 231).
Instruction:	Have students do presentations (See TWE Chapter Assessment: Sociology Projects and Technology Activities, p. 235.)
Close:	Assign Chapter 7 Learning Goals Outline (see *Unit 2 Booklet*, TRB), due the day of the chapter evaluation.
	Remind students to study for the chapter evaluation.

Notes and Comments: _____

_____

_____

_____

_____

_____

_____

_____

_____

_____

_____

_____

_____

_____

Chapter 7   DEVIANCE AND SOCIAL CONTROL

Day 36

Week of _____

Day 6 of 6

Content:	Ch. 7, Assessment (pp. 233-235) and Evaluation
Objective:	Students will review for evaluation of the concepts learned in this chapter.
Act. Type:	Class Discussion, Class Activity, Independent Practice, Cooperative Learning, Demonstration, Experiment, Debate, Role-playing, Presentation
Introduction:	Review Chapter 7 Vocabulary Activity homework (see *Unit 2 Booklet*, TRB).
Instruction:	Do Chapter Assessment as needed (TWE pp. 233-235).
Evaluate:	To evaluate the students' comprehension of the chapter, administer Chapter 7 Test A or B. You may want to use the Alternative Assessment found in the TRB. A test for Unit 2 is also available in the TRB.
Close:	Discuss Enrichment Reading (TWE pp. 236-237).
	Assign Unit 3, Chapter 8 Intro. (pp. 238-241) and Ch. 8, Sec. 1: Dimensions of Stratification (pp. 242-249).

Notes and Comments: _____

_____

_____

_____

_____

_____

_____

_____

_____

_____

_____

_____

Chapter 8

SOCIAL STRATIFICATION

Day 37

Day 1 of 6

Content:	Unit 3, Chapter 8 Intro. (pp. 238-241) and Ch. 8, Sec. 1: Dimensions of Stratification (pp. 242-249).
Objective:	Students will understand how the economic dimension of social stratification affects human motivation and will analyze the relationships among social class and other culture group membership and political power.
Act. Type:	Class Discussion, Class Activity, Independent Practice, Demonstration, Cooperative Learning, Debate
Introduction:	Use Lead-Off Activity (TWE p. 240-241).
	Read and discuss Using Your Sociological Imagination (TWE p. 241).
Instruction:	Do activity found in Learning Styles-Bodily-Kinesthetic/Interpersonal (TWE p. 242).
	Ask students to do On-Demand Writing (TWE p. 244).
	Discuss Using the Illustration and Reinforcing Vocabulary (TWE p. 246).
	Facilitate Cooperative Learning Activity (TWE pp. 246-247).
Close:	Discuss and assign Another Time (TWE p. 249).
	Assign Chapter 8 Vocabulary Activity (see *Unit 3 Booklet*, TRB), due the day of the chapter review.
	Assign chapter project (see TWE p. 271, Chapter Assessment: Sociology Projects and Technology Activities) to be presented to the class prior to final chapter evaluation.
	Ask students to read Sec. 2: Explanations of Stratification (pp. 250-253).

Notes and Comments: _____

_____

_____

_____

_____

_____

Chapter 8 — SOCIAL STRATIFICATION

Day 38   Week of _____

Day 2 of 6

Content:	Ch. 8, Sec. 2: Explanations of Stratification (pp. 250-253)
Objective:	Students will state the differences between the functionalist, conflict, and symbolic interactionist approaches to social stratification.
Act. Type:	Class Discussion, Class Activity, Debate, Role-playing
Introduction:	Share Using the Section Preview (TWE p. 250).
Instruction:	Ask students to Role Play (TWE p. 250).
	Share and discuss Controversy and Debate (TWE p. 251).
	Review and discuss Working with the Data-Fig. 8.4 (TWE p. 252).
Close:	Discuss Focus on Research and Using Problem-Solving Skills (TWE p. 253).
	Ask students to read Sec. 3: Social Classes in America (pp. 254-257).

Notes and Comments: _____

_____

_____

_____

_____

_____

_____

_____

_____

_____

_____

_____

SOCIAL STRATIFICATION

Day 39

Week of _____

Day 3 of 6

Content: Ch. 8, Sec. 3: Social Classes in America (pp. 254-257)

Objective: Students will compare cultural values associated with socioeconomic stratification of the upper, middle, working, and underclasses.

Act. Type: Class Discussion, Class Activity, Independent Practice, Cooperative Learning, Demonstration

Introduction: Do activity/demonstration described in Using the Section Preview (TWE p. 254).

Instruction: Ask students to conduct a Survey (TWE p. 254).

Share More About...Social Mobility (TWE p. 255).

Assign Increasing Your Reading Comprehension (see TRB) as needed.

Share Points to Stress (TWE p. 256).

If possible, use Teaching Strategy (TWE p. 256).

Have students do Using Decision-Making Skills activity (TWE p. 258).

Close: Assign On-Demand Writing (TWE p. 257).

Ask students to read Sec. 4: Poverty in America (pp. 258-264).

Notes and Comments: _____

_____

_____

_____

_____

_____

_____

_____

Chapter 8

SOCIAL STRATIFICATION

Day 40

Week of _____

Day 4 of 6

Content:	Ch. 8, Sec. 4: Poverty in America (pp. 258-264)
Objective:	Students will discuss the measurement and extent of poverty in the United States and will evaluate commitment to poverty programs in the United States.
Act. Type:	Class Discussion, Class Activity, Independent Practice, Cooperative Learning, Debate
Introduction:	Use the Internet to do Using the Section Preview (TWE p. 259).
Instruction:	Ask the students to do Paired Learning Activity (TWE p. 259).
	Discuss Points to Stress (TWE p. 259).
	Discuss and do Using Problem-Solving Skills activity (TWE pp. 260-261).
	Lead discussion in Controversy and Debate (TWE p. 260).
	Ask students to do Encouraging Citizenship Activity (TWE p. 263).
Close:	Discuss and assign Sociology Today – Parenting Across Class Lines (TWE p. 258).
	Ask students to read Sec. 5: Social Mobility (pp. 265-268).
	Remind students that chapter presentations are due the following class session.

Notes and Comments: _____

_____

_____

_____

_____

_____

_____

_____

_____

SOCIAL STRUCTURE

Day 41

Day 5 of 6

Content:	Ch. 8, Sec. 5: Social Mobility and Ch. 5 Presentations (pp. 242-268)
Objective:	Students will analyze the influence of motivation on socioeconomic consequences and will present projects and activities summarizing objective/s learned in the chapter.
Act. Type:	Class Discussion, Class Activity, Independent Practice, Cooperative Learning, Demonstration, and Presentations
Introduction:	Do demonstration in Using the Section Preview (TWE p. 265).
Instruction:	Facilitate Cooperative Learning Activity (TWE p. 268).
	Read and discuss Tech Trends (TWE p. 264).
	Have students do presentations (See TWE, Chapter Assessment: Sociology Projects and Technology Activities, p. 271).
Close:	Assign Learning Styles-Intrapersonal/Spatial (TWE p. 265).
	Assign Chapter 8 Learning Goals Outline (see *Unit 3 Booklet*, TRB), due the day of the chapter evaluation.
	Remind students to study for the chapter evaluation.

Notes and Comments: _____

_____

_____

_____

_____

_____

_____

_____

_____

_____

Day 42

Week of _____

Day 6 of 6

Content:	Ch. 8, Assessment (pp. 269-271) and Evaluation
Objective:	Students will review for evaluation of the concepts learned in this chapter.
Act. Type:	Class Discussion, Class Activity, Independent Practice, Cooperative Learning, Demonstration, Experiment, Debate, Role-playing, Presentation
Introduction:	Review Chapter 8 Vocabulary Activity homework (see *Unit 3 Booklet*, TRB).
Instruction:	Do Chapter Assessment as needed (TWE pp. 269-271).
Evaluate:	To evaluate the students' comprehension of the chapter, administer Chapter 8 Test A or B. You may want to use the Alternative Assessment found in the TRB.
Close:	Discuss Enrichment Reading (TWE pp. 272-273).
	Assign Chapter 9, intro. (pp. 274-275) and Sec. 1: Minority, Race, and Ethnicity (pp. 276-279).

Notes and Comments: _____

_____

_____

_____

_____

_____

_____

_____

_____

_____

_____

Day 43

Week of _____

Day 1 of 5

Content:	Ch. 9 Intro. (pp. 274-275) and Sec. 1: Minority, Race, and Ethnicity (pp. 276-279)
Objective:	Students will compare various U.S. subculture groups such as ethnic and national origin and will describe what sociologists mean by minority, race, and ethnicity.
Act. Type:	Class Discussion, Class Activity, Independent Practice, Demonstration, Cooperative Learning
Introduction:	Use Lead-Off Activity (TWE p. 274-275).
	Read and discuss Using Your Sociological Imagination (TWE p. 275).
Introduction:	Use Teaching Strategy (TWE p. 276).
	Ask students to do Survey (TWE p. 276).
	Review and discuss Working with the Data (TWE p. 278).
Close:	Do Making Connections to Other Cultures (TWE p. 278).
	Assign chapter project (see TWE pp. 305, Chapter Assessment: Sociology Projects and Technology Activities) to be presented to the class prior to final chapter evaluation.
	Assign Chapter 9 Vocabulary Activity (see *Unit 3 Booklet*, TRB), due the day of the chapter review.
	Ask students to read Sec. 2: Racial and Ethnic Relations (pp. 280-283).

Notes and Comments: _____

_____

_____

_____

_____

_____

_____

Chapter 9

INEQUALITIES OF RACE AND ETHNICITY

Day 44

Day 2 of 5

Content:	Ch. 9, Sec. 2: Racial and Ethnic Relations
Objective:	Students will discuss patterns of racial and ethnic relations.
Act. Type:	Class Discussion, Class Activity, Independent Practice, Cooperative Learning, Demonstration
Introduction:	Read and discuss Another Place – The Travelling People (TWE p. 279).
Instruction:	Discuss Using the Section Preview (TWE p. 280).
	Ask students to do Using Problem-Solving Skills (TWE pp. 280-281).
	Do Pulling It All Together activity (TWE p. 282).
Close:	Read and discuss Sociology Today – Bridging the Digital Divide (TWE p. 283).
	Ask students to read Sec. 3: Theories of Prejudice and Discrimination (pp. 284-289).

Notes and Comments: _____

_____

_____

_____

_____

_____

_____

_____

_____

_____

_____

_____

_____

46

INEQUALITIES OF RACE AND ETHNICITY

Day 45

Week of _____

Day 3 of 5

Content:	Ch. 9, Sec. 3: Theories of Prejudice and Discrimination (pp. 284-289)
Objective:	Students will discuss the difference between prejudice and discrimination and will compare and contrast the perspectives of the three theories.
Act. Type:	Class Discussion, Class Activity, Independent Practice, Cooperative Learning, Debate
Introduction:	Read and debate Using the Section Preview (TWE p. 284).
Instruction:	Discuss Open-Response Question (TWE p. 284).
	Have students do the Survey (TWE p. 284).
	Do Learning Styles-Visual/Spatial activity (TWE pp. 286-287).
	Use the second Teaching Strategy (TWE p. 286).
	Ask students to interpret the map in Snapshot of America (TWE p. 287).
	Review and discuss Working with the Data (TWE p. 288).
Close:	Read and discuss Tech Trends-Spinning a Web of Hate (TWE p. 289).
	Ask students to read Sec. 4: Minority Groups in the United States (pp. 290-301).

Notes and Comments: _____

_____

_____

_____

_____

_____

_____

_____

_____

INEQUALITIES OF RACE AND ETHNICITY

Day 46

Week of _____

Day 4 of 5

Content:	Ch. 9, Sec. 4: Minority Groups in the United States (pp. 290-301)
Objective:	Students will compare cultural socialization, norms, values, motivation, and communication between subculture groups.
Act. Type:	Class Discussion, Class Activity, Independent Practice, Cooperative Learning, Demonstration, Experiment, Debate, Role-playing, Presentation
Introduction:	Do demonstration activity in Using the Section Preview (TWE p. 290).
Instruction:	Ask students to do Demonstration (TWE p. 290).
	Introduce and assign Learning Styles – Interpersonal (TWE pp. 292-293) and Learning Styles-Visual (TWE p. 295).
	Have students research and debate Controversy and Debate-Casinos and Gambling (TWE p. 296).
	Discuss information in the first Teaching Strategy (TWE p. 297).
Close:	Read and discuss Focus on Research (TWE pp. 298-299).
	Assign Chapter 9 Learning Goals Outline (see *Unit 3 Booklet*, TRB), due the day of the chapter evaluation.
	Remind students that chapter presentations are due the following class session.
	Also remind students to study for the chapter evaluation.

Notes and Comments: _____

_____

_____

_____

_____

_____

_____

48

Chapter 9

INEQUALITIES OF RACE AND ETHNICITY

Day 47

Week of _____

Day 5 of 5

Content:	Ch. 9 Presentations (pp. 274-301), Assessment (pp. 302-305) and Evaluation
Objective:	Students will present projects and activities summarizing objective/s learned in the chapter and will review for evaluation of the concepts learned in this chapter.
Act. Type:	Class Activity and Presentation
Introduction:	Review Chapter 9 Vocabulary Activity homework (see *Unit 3 Booklet*, TRB).
Instruction:	Have students do presentations (See TWE, Chapter Assessment: Sociology Projects and Technology Activities, p. 305).
	Do Chapter Assessment as needed (TWE pp. 302-305)
Evaluate:	To evaluate the students' comprehension of the chapter, administer Chapter 9 Test A or B. You may want to use the Alternative Assessment found in the TRB.
Close:	Discuss Enrichment Reading (TWE pp. 306-307).
	Assign Chapter 10, intro. (pp. 308-309) and Sec. 1: Sex and Gender Identity (pp. 310-315).

Notes and Comments: _____

_____

_____

_____

_____

_____

_____

_____

_____

Chapter 10

INEQUALITIES OF GENDER AND AGE

Day 48

Week of _____

Day 1 of 6

Content:	Ch. 10 Intro. (pp. 308-309) and Ch. 10, Sec. 1: Sex and Gender Identity (pp. 310-315)
Objective:	Students will compare various U.S. subculture groups such as gender and age, distinguish the concepts of sex, gender, and gender identity, and discuss the research findings regarding gender and behavior.
Act. Type:	Class Discussion, Class Activity, Independent Practice, Cooperative Learning, Demonstration, Experiment, Presentation
Introduction:	Use Lead-Off Activity (TWE p. 308).
	Do Demonstration (TWE p. 309).
	Read and discuss Using Your Sociological Imagination (TWE p. 309).
Instruction:	Use Teaching Strategy to make assignment (TWE p. 310).
	Have students do Cooperative Learning Activity (TWE pp. 310-311).
Close:	Assign chapter project (see TWE pp. 340-341, Chapter Assessment: Sociology Projects and Technology Activities) to be presented to the class prior to final chapter evaluation.
	Assign Chapter 10 Vocabulary Activity (see *Unit 3 Booklet*, TRB), due the day of the chapter review.
	Ask students to read Sec. 2: Theoretical Perspectives on Gender (pp. 316-320).

Notes and Comments: _____

_____

_____

_____

_____

_____

50

Chapter 10 — INEQUALITIES OF GENDER AND AGE

Day 49

Week of _____

Day 2 of 6

Content:	Ch. 10, Sec. 2: Theoretical Perspectives on Gender (pp. 316-320)
Objective:	Students will outline the perspectives on gender taken by the three theories.
Act. Type:	Class Discussion, Class Activity, Independent Practice, Demonstration
Introduction:	Read and discuss Another Time-Manly Hearted Woman (TWE p. 315).
	Do Demonstration-Gender Roles (TWE p. 318-319).
	Discuss Using the Section Preview (TWE p. 316).
Instruction:	Ask students to do On-Demand Writing (TWE p. 316).
	If possible, ask students to do Demonstration (TWE p. 317).
	Ask students to interpret the map in World View (TWE p. 318).
	Review and discuss Working with the Data (TWE p. 319).
Close:	Ask students to read Sec. 3: Gender Inequality (pp. 320-329).
	Assign Observation (TWE p. 322).

Notes and Comments: _____

_____

_____

_____

_____

_____

_____

_____

_____

_____

Chapter 10 INEQUALITIES OF GENDER AND AGE

Day 50

Week of _____

Day 3 of 6

Content:	Ch. 10, Sec. 3: Gender Inequality (pp. 320-329)
Objective:	Students will describe the occupational, economic, legal, and political status of women in the United States.
Act. Type:	Class Discussion, Class Activity, Independent Practice, Cooperative Learning, Debate, Role-playing
Introduction:	Discuss results from Observation assignment (TWE p. 322).
Instruction:	Read and discuss Sociology Today-Gender-Based Hierarchy (TWE p. 321).
	Review and discuss Working with the Data (TWE p. 323), (TWE p. 324), and (TWE p. 325).
	Use activity in Controversy and Debate (TWE p. 324).
	Review and discuss Working with the Data (TWE p. 326) and (TWE p. 327).
	Have students do role-plays as in Teaching Strategy (TWE p. 327).
	Ask students to do Paired-Learning Activity (TWE p. 328).
Close:	Read and discuss Tech Trends-Men, Women, and the Internet (TWE p. 329).
	Ask students to read Sec. 4: Ageism (pp. 330-332) and Ch. 10, Sec. 5: Inequality in America's Elderly Population – Elderly People as a Minority Group; Economics of the Elderly (pp. 333-336).

Notes and Comments: _____

_____

_____

_____

_____

_____

_____

_____

Day 51

Week of _____

Day 4 of 6

Content:	Ch. 10, Sec. 4: Ageism (pp. 330-332) and Ch. 10, Sec. 5: Inequality in America's Elderly Population – Elderly People as a Minority Group; Economics of the Elderly (pp. 333-336)
Objective:	Students will distinguish between age stratification and ageism and will describe the economic status of the elderly in the United States.
Act. Type:	Class Discussion, Class Activity, Independent Practice, Cooperative Learning
Introduction:	Ask students to do Cooperative Learning Activity (TWE p. 329).
Instruction:	Review and discuss Working with the Data (TWE p. 331).
	Do Internet activity in Using the Section Preview (TWE p. 333).
	Read and discuss Focus on Research (TWE pp. 334-335).
	Discuss and ask students to do On-Demand Writing (TWE pp. 334-335).
Close:	Discuss and assign Using Problem-Solving Skills (TWE p. 332).
	Discuss and assign Learning Styles-Musical/Interpersonal (TWE p. 337).
	Ask students to read Sec. 5: Inequality in America's Elderly Population – Political Power and the Elderly (pp. 337-338).
	Remind students that chapter presentations are due the following class session.

Notes and Comments: _____

_____

_____

_____

_____

_____

_____

_____

Day 52

Week of _____

Day 5 of 6

Content:	Ch. 10, Sec. 5: Inequality in America's Elderly Population – Political Power and the Elderly (pp. 337-338) and Ch. 10 Presentations (pp. 308-338)
Objective:	Students will describe the legal and political status of the elderly in the United States and will present projects and activities summarizing objective/s learned in the chapter.
Act. Type:	Class Discussion, Class Activity, Independent Practice, Demonstration, and Presentations
Introduction:	Discuss results from Learning Styles-Musical/Interpersonal activity (TWE p. 337).
Instruction:	Discuss Open-Response Question (TWE p. 336).
	Ask students to interpret the map in Snapshot of America (TWE p. 337).
	Ask students to do On-Demand Writing (TWE p. 336).
	Review and discuss Working with the Data (TWE p. 338).
	Have students do presentations (See TWE, Chapter Assessment: Sociology Projects and Technology Activities, pp. 340-341).
Close:	Assign Chapter 10 Learning Goals Outline (see *Unit 3 Booklet*, TRB), due the day of the chapter evaluation.
	Remind students to study for the chapter evaluation.

Notes and Comments: _____

_____

_____

_____

_____

_____

_____

54

Chapter 10 — INEQUALITIES OF GENDER AND AGE

Day 53

Week of _____

Day 6 of 6

Content:	Ch. 10 Assessement (pp. 339-341) and Evaluation
Objective:	Students will review for evaluation of the concepts learned in this chapter.
Act. Type:	Class Discussion, Class Activity, Independent Practice, Cooperative Learning, Demonstration, Experiment, Debate, Role-playing, Presentation
Introduction:	Review Chapter 10 Vocabulary Activity homework (see *Unit 3 Booklet*, TRB).
Instruction:	Do Chapter Assessment as needed (TWE pp. 339-341).
Evaluate:	To evaluate the students' comprehension of the chapter, administer Chapter 10 Test A or B. You may want to use the Alternative Assessment found in the TRB.
Close:	Discuss Enrichment Reading (TWE pp. 342-343).
	Ask students to do On-Demand Writing (TWE p. 313).
	Assign Unit 4 Intro., Chapter 11 intro. (pp. 344-347) and Sec. 1: Family and Marriage Across Cultures – Defining the Family; Two Basic Types of Families; Patterns of Family Structure (pp. 348-351).

Notes and Comments: _____

_____

_____

_____

_____

_____

_____

_____

_____

_____

Chapter 11

THE FAMILY

Day 54

Day 1 of 5

Content:	Ch. 11 Intro. (pp. 344-347) and Ch. 11, Sec. 1: Family and Marriage Across Cultures – Defining the Family; Two Basic Types of Families; Patterns of Family Structure (pp. 348-351)
Objective:	Students will understand how the social institution of family meets basic needs in society and will summarize the functions of the social institution of the family.
Act. Type:	Class Discussion, Class Activity, Independent Practice, Demonstration, Presentation
Introduction:	Use Lead-Off Activity (TWE p. 346). Read and discuss Using Your Sociological Imagination (TWE p. 347).
Instruction:	Ask students to do Cooperative Learning Activity (TWE p. 348). Ask students to write in response to Open-Response Question (TWE p. 348).
Close:	Do Learning Styles-Visual (TWE p. 350). Assign chapter project (see Chapter Assessment: Sociology Projects and Technology Activities) to be presented to the class prior to final chapter evaluation. Assign Chapter 11 Vocabulary Activity (see *Unit 4 Booklet*, TRB), due the day of the chapter review. Ask students to read Sec. 1: Family and Marriage Across Cultures – Marriage Arrangements; Choosing a Mate (pp. 351-355) and Ch. 11, Sec. 2: Theoretical Perspectives and the Family (pp. 356-361)

Notes and Comments: _____

_____

_____

_____

_____

_____

56

Chapter 11

THE FAMILY

Day 55

Week of _____

Day 2 of 5

Content:	Ch. 11, Sec. 1: Family and Marriage Across Cultures – Marriage Arrangements; Choosing a Mate (pp. 351-355); and Ch. 11, Sec. 2: Theoretical Perspectives and the Family (pp. 356-361)
Objective:	Students will describe norms for marriage arrangements and will compare and contrast views of the family proposed by the three major perspectives.
Act. Type:	Class Discussion, Class Activity, Independent Practice, Cooperative Learning, Demonstration, Experiment, Debate
Introduction:	Use Teaching Strategy (TWE p. 351).
Instruction:	Ask students to interpret the map in World View (TWE p. 353).
	Have students do Cooperative Learning Activity (TWE pp. 354-355).
	Do activity in Working with the Data (TWE p. 358).
	Do Controversy and Debate (TWE p. 359).
	Read and discuss Another Time-Courtship and Marriage Among the Hopi (TWE p. 356).
Close:	Assign On-Demand Writing (TWE p. 353).
	Ask students to read Sec. 3: Family and Marriage in the United States (pp. 362-369) and Ch. 11, Sec. 4: Changes in Marriage and Family – Blended Families; Single-Parent Families; Childless Marriages; Dual-Employed Marriages (pp. 370-375).

Notes and Comments: _____

_____

_____

_____

_____

_____

_____

Chapter 11

THE FAMILY

Day 56

Week of _____

Day 3 of 5

Content:	Ch. 11, Sec. 3: Family and Marriage in the United States (pp. 362-369) and Ch. 11, Sec. 4: Changes in Marriage and Family – Blended Families; Single-Parent Families; Childless Marriages; Dual-Employed Marriages (pp. 370-375)
Objective:	Students will outline the extent and causes of divorce and family violence in the United States and will describe alternatives to the traditional nuclear family structure.
Act. Type:	Class Discussion, Class Activity, Independent Practice, Cooperative Learning, Demonstration, Debate, Role-playing
Introduction:	Have students do Using Decision-Making Skills (TWE pp. 360-361).
Instruction:	Read and discuss Sociology Today (TWE p. 362).
	Do Demonstration (TWE p. 369).
	Review and discuss Working with the Data (TWE p. 364 and p. 368).
	Ask students to interpret the map in Snapshot of America (TWE p. 365).
	Have students do Cooperative Learning Activity (TWE pp. 366-367).
	Read and discuss Tech Trends-Technology and the Family (TWE p. 370).
Close:	Do Cooperative Learning Activity (TWE p. 374).
	Ask students to read Sec. 4: Changes in Marriage and Family – Cohabitation; Same Sex Domestic Partners; Single Life; Boomerang Kids; Looking Forward (pp. 375-380).
	Remind students that chapter presentations are due the following class session.

Notes and Comments: _____

_____

_____

_____

_____

Chapter 11

THE FAMILY

Day 57

Day 4 of 5

Content:	Ch. 11, Sec. 4: Changes in Marriage and Family – Cohabitation; Same Sex Domestic Partners; Single Life; Boomerang Kids; Looking Forward (pp. 375-380) and Ch. 11 Presentations (pp. 346-380)
Objective:	Students will evaluate the importance of the social institution of the family in the United States and will present projects and activities summarizing objective/s learned in the chapter.
Act. Type:	Class Discussion, Class Activity, Independent Practice, Cooperative Learning, Debate, and Presentations
Introduction:	Have students do Learning Styles activity (TWE p. 375).
Instruction:	Share More About...Lasting Marriages and More About...Happy Marriages (TWE p. 378)
	Ask students to do On-Demand Writing (TWE pp. 378-379).
	Read and discuss Focus on Research (TWE pp. 376-377).
	Have students do presentations (See TWE, Chapter Assessment: Sociology Projects and Technology Activities, pp. 382-383).
Close:	Assign Chapter 11 Learning Goals Outline (see *Unit 4 Booklet*, TRB), due the day of the chapter evaluation.
	Remind students to study for the chapter evaluation.

Notes and Comments: _____

_____

_____

_____

_____

_____

Day 58

Week of _____

Day 5 of 5

Content:	Ch. 11 Assessment (pp. 381-383)
Objective:	Students will review for evaluation of the concepts learned in this chapter.
Act. Type:	Class Discussion, Class Activity, Independent Practice, Cooperative Learning, Demonstration, Experiment, Debate, Role-playing, Presentation
Introduction:	Review Chapter 11 Vocabulary Activity homework (see *Unit 4 Booklet*, TRB).
Instruction:	Do Chapter Assessment as needed (TWE pp. 381-383).
Evaluate:	To evaluate the students' comprehension of the chapter, administer Chapter 11 Test A or B. You may want to use the Alternative Assessment found in the TRB.
Close:	Discuss Enrichment Reading (TWE pp. 384-385).
	Assign Chapter 12, intro. (pp. 386-387) and Sec. 1: Development and Structure of Education.

Notes and Comments: _____

_____

_____

_____

_____

_____

_____

_____

_____

_____

_____

_____

Chapter

12

EDUCATION

Day 59   Week of _____

Day 1 of 4

Content:	Ch. 12 Intro. (pp. 386-387) and Sec. 1: Development and Structure of Education (pp. 388-395)
Objective:	Students will understand how the social institution of education meets basic needs in society, will discuss schools as bureaucracies, and alternative forms of education.
Act. Type:	Class Discussion, Class Activity, Independent Practice, Cooperative Learning, Demonstration, Debate, Presentation
Introduction:	Use Lead-Off Activity (TWE pp. 386-387).
	Read and discuss Using Your Sociological Imagination (TWE p. 387) with guest speaker, if possible.
Instruction:	Ask students to do the Survey (TWE p. 389).
	Do Controversy and Debate (TWE p. 390).
	Read and discuss Another Time-Understanding Freedom and Education in America (TWE p. 392).
	Have students do the Cooperative Learning Activity (TWE p. 393).
Close:	Assign students to do the Paired-Learning Activity (TWE p. 392).
	Assign chapter project (see Chapter Assessment: Sociology Projects and Technology Activities) to be presented to the class prior to final chapter evaluation.
	Ask students to read Sec. 2: Functionalist Perspective (pp. 396-399) and Sec. 3: Conflict Perspective.

Notes and Comments: _____

_____

_____

_____

_____

_____

Chapter 12

EDUCATION

Day 60

Week of _____

Day 2 of 4

Content:	Ch. 12, Sec. 2: Functionalist Perspective (pp. 396-399) and Ch. 12, Sec. 3: Conflict Perspective (pp. 400-407)
Objective:	Students will summarize the functions of the social institution of education, evaluate the merit-based nature of public education, and educational equality.
Act. Type:	Class Discussion, Class Activity, Independent Practice, Experiment, Role-playing, Debate, Presentation
Introduction:	Do the activity in Using the Section Preview (TWE p. 396).
Instruction:	Read and discuss Sociology Today (TWE p. 399).
	Show video as described in Using the Section Preview (TWE p. 400).
	Ask students to do Using Conflict Resolution Skills (TWE pp. 400-401).
	Share and discuss More About...College Entrance Exams (TWE p. 401).
	Do Learning Styles-Linguistic/Bodily-Kinesthetic (TWE pp. 402-403).
	Ask students to interpret the map in Snapshot of America-School Expenditures (TWE p. 404).
	Do Role Play activity (TWE p. 407).
Close:	Assign On-Demand Writing (TWE pp. 398-399).
	Assign Chapter 12 Vocabulary Activity (see *Unit 4 Booklet*, TRB), due the day of the chapter review.
	Ask students to read Sec. 4: Symbolic Interactionism (pp. 409-415).
	Remind students that chapter presentations are due the following class session.

Notes and Comments: _____

_____

_____

_____

_____

Chapter 12

EDUCATION

Day 61

Day 3 of 4

Content:	Ch. 12, Sec. 4: Symbolic Interactionism (pp. 409-415) and Ch. 12 Presentations (pp. 386-415)
Objective:	Students will evaluate the importance of the social institution of education in the United States and will present projects and activities summarizing objective/s learned in the chapter.
Act. Type:	Class Discussion, Class Activity, Independent Practice, Demonstration, Experiment, Debate, and Presentations
Introduction:	Introduce research project in Using the Section Preview (TWE p. 409).
Instruction:	Do Demonstration (TWE pp. 410-411).
	Do Controversy and Debate (TWE p. 410).
	Review and discuss Working with the Data (TWE p. 411).
	Read and discuss Focus on Research (TWE pp. 414-415).
	Read and discuss Tech Trends (TWE p. 408).
	Have students do presentations (See TWE, Chapter Assessment: Sociology Projects and Technology Activities, pp. 418-419)
Close:	Have students do On-Demand Writing (TWE p. 412).
	Assign Chapter 12 Learning Goals Outline (see *Unit 4 Booklet*, TRB), due the day of the chapter evaluation.
	Remind students to study for the chapter evaluation.

Notes and Comments: _____

_____

_____

_____

_____

_____

Chapter 12

Day 62

Week of _____

Day 4 of 4

Content:	Ch. 12, Assessment (pp. 416-419) and Evaluation
Objective:	Students will review for evaluation of the concepts learned in this chapter.
Act. Type:	Class Discussion, Class Activity, Independent Practice, Cooperative Learning, Demonstration, Experiment, Debate, Role-playing, Presentation
Introduction:	Review Chapter 12 Vocabulary Activity homework (see *Unit 4 Booklet*, TRB).
Instruction:	Do Chapter Assessment as needed (TWE pp. 416-419).
Evaluate:	To evaluate the students' comprehension of the chapter, administer Chapter 12 Test A or B. You may want to use the Alternative Assessment found in the TRB.
Close:	Discuss Enrichment Reading (TWE pp. 420-421).
	Assign Chapter 13, Intro. (pp. 422-423) and Sec. 1: Power and Authority.

Notes and Comments: _____

_____

_____

_____

_____

_____

_____

_____

_____

_____

_____

_____

64

Chapter 13

POLITICAL AND ECONOMIC INSTITUTIONS

Day 63

Day 1 of 6

Content:	Ch. 13 Intro. (pp. 422-423) and Sec. 1: Power and Authority (pp. 424-431)
Objective:	Students will understand how the political and economic social institutions meet basic needs in society, will identify three forms of authority, and will discuss differences among democracy, totalitarianism, and authoritarianism.
Act. Type:	Class Discussion, Class Activity, Independent Practice, Role-playing, Debate, Presentation, Simulation, Cooperative Learning, Demonstration
Introduction:	Use Lead-Off Activity (TWE pp. 422-423).
	Read and discuss Using Your Sociological Imagination (TWE p. 423).
Instruction:	Do Demonstration (TWE pp. 424-425).
	Do Learning Styles activity (TWE pp. 426-427).
	Ask students to interpret the map in World View (TWE p. 429).
	Have students write and share On-Demand Writing (TWE p. 429).
Close:	Review and discuss Working with the Data (TWE p. 430).
	Assign Another Place-China's One-Child Policy (TWE p. 432).
	Assign Chapter 13 Vocabulary Activity (see *Unit 4 Booklet*, TRB), due the day of the chapter review.
	Assign chapter project (see Chapter Assessment: Sociology Projects and Technology Activities) to be presented to the class prior to final chapter evaluation.
	Ask students to read Sec. 2: Political Power in American Society (pp. 433-439).

Notes and Comments: _____

_____

_____

_____

_____

_____

POLITICAL AND ECONOMIC INSTITUTIONS

Day 64

Week of _____

Day 2 of 6

Content:	Ch. 13, Sec. 2: Political Power in American Society (pp. 433-439)
Objective:	Students will explain how voting is an exercise of power and will evaluate the importance of political social institutions in the United States.
Act. Type:	Class Discussion, Class Activity, Independent Practice, Cooperative Learning, Presentation
Introduction:	Discuss assignment Another Place-China's One-Child Policy (TWE p. 432).
Instruction:	Discuss Using the Section Preview (TWE p. 433).
	Review and discuss Working with the Data (TWE p. 435).
	Have students do Net Worthy activities (TWE p. 434).
	Review and discuss Working with the Data (TWE p. 437).
	Use Teaching Strategy (TWE p. 437).
	Review and discuss Working with the Data (TWE p. 438).
	Do Interdisciplinary Activity (TWE pp. 436-437).
Close:	Ask students to interpret the map in Snapshot of America (TWE p. 436).
	Ask students to read Sec. 3: Economic Systems (pp. 440-444) and Sec. 4: The Modern Corporation (pp. 446-449).

Notes and Comments: _____

_____

_____

_____

_____

_____

_____

_____

POLITICAL AND ECONOMIC INSTITUTIONS

Day 65

Week of _____

Day 3 of 6

Content:	Ch. 13, Sec. 3: Economic Systems (pp. 440-444) and Sec. 4: The Modern Corporation (pp. 446-449)
Objective:	Students will list characteristics of capitalism and socialism and will analyze the influence of corporations on economic decisions.
Act. Type:	Class Discussion, Class Activity, Independent Practice, Cooperative Learning
Introduction:	Pre-assess by Using the Section Preview (TWE p. 440).
Instruction:	Review and discuss Working with the Data (TWE p. 442).
	Share More About...Socialism (TWE p. 442).
	Have students do Cooperative Learning Activity (TWE p. 446).
	Compare results from above with Making Connections to Other Cultures (TWE p. 447).
	Review and discuss Working with the Data (TWE p. 447).
Close:	Assign Sociology Today-Employee Rights (TWE p. 448).
	Ask students to read Sec. 5: Work in the Modern Economy (pp. 450-456).

Notes and Comments: _____

_____

_____

_____

_____

_____

_____

_____

Day 66

Week of _____

Day 4 of 6

Content:	Ch. 13, Sec. 5: Work in the Modern Economy (pp. 450-456)
Objective:	Students will analyze the influence of cultural values on economic behavior and will evaluate the importance of economic social institutions in the United States.
Act. Type:	Class Discussion, Class Activity, Independent Practice, Demonstration, Cooperative Learning, Presentation
Introduction:	Discuss assignment Sociology Today-Employee Rights (TWE p. 448).
Instruction:	Discuss Using the Section Preview (TWE p. 450).
	Get student participation using Teaching Strategy (TWE p. 450).
	Read and discuss Focus on Research (TWE pp. 452-453).
	Discuss Reteaching (TWE p. 455).
	Do Demonstration (TWE p. 456).
	Have students do Observation (TWE pp. 452-453).
Close:	Review and discuss Working with the Data (TWE p. 451).
	Ask students to do Survey (TWE pp. 450-451).
	Remind students that chapter presentations are due the following class session.

Notes and Comments: _____

_____

_____

_____

_____

_____

_____

_____

_____

Chapter 13

POLITICAL AND ECONOMIC INSTITUTIONS

Day 67

Week of _____

Day 5 of 6

Content:	Chapter 13 Presentations (pp. 422-455)
Objective:	Students will present projects and activities summarizing objective/s learned in the chapter.
Act. Type:	Class Activity and Presentation
Introduction:	Read and discuss Tech Trends (TWE p. 445).
Instruction:	Have students do presentations (See TWE, Chapter Assessment: Sociology Projects and Technology Activities, p. 459.)
Close:	Assign Chapter 13 Learning Goals Outline (see *Unit 4 Booklet*, TRB), due the day of the chapter evaluation.
	Remind students to study for the chapter evaluation.

Notes and Comments: _____

_____

_____

_____

_____

_____

_____

_____

_____

_____

_____

_____

Day 68   Week of _____

Day 6 of 6

Content:	Ch. 13 Assessment (pp. 457-459) and Evaluation
Objective:	Students will review for evaluation of the concepts learned in this chapter.
Act. Type:	Class Discussion, Class Activity, Independent Practice, Cooperative Learning, Demonstration, Experiment, Debate, Role-playing, Presentation
Introduction:	Review Chapter 13 Vocabulary Activity homework (see *Unit 4 Booklet*, TRB).
Instruction:	Do Chapter Assessment as needed (TWE pp. 457-459).
Evaluate:	To evaluate the students' comprehension of the chapter, administer Chapter 13 Test A or B. You may want to use the Alternative Assessment found in the TRB.
Close:	Discuss Enrichment Reading (TWE pp. 460-461).
	Assign Chapter 14 Intro. (pp. 462-463) and Sec. 1: Religion and Society.

Notes and Comments: _____

_____

_____

_____

_____

_____

_____

_____

_____

_____

_____

_____

Chapter 14

RELIGION

Day 69

Week of _____

Day 1 of 5

Content: Ch. 14 Intro. (pp. 462-463) and Sec. 1: Religion and Society (pp. 464-466)

Objective: Students will understand how social institutions of religion meet basic needs in society and will explain the sociological meaning of religion.

Act. Type: Class Discussion, Class Activity, Independent Practice, Demonstration, Debate

Introduction: Use Lead-Off Activity (TWE pp. 462-463).

Read and discuss Using Your Sociological Imagination (TWE p. 463).

Introduction: Share Using the Section Preview (TWE p. 464).

Do Demonstration (TWE p. 464).

Discuss More About...Studying Religion (TWE p. 464).

Have students do Demonstration (TWE p. 465).

Close: Read and discuss Another Place-Religion at War (TWE p. 466).

Assign chapter project (Chapter Assessment: Sociology Projects and Technology Activities) to be presented to the class prior to final chapter evaluation.

Assign Chapter 14 Vocabulary Activity (see *Unit 4 Booklet*, TRB), due the day of the chapter review.

Ask students to read Sec. 2: Theoretical Perspectives (pp. 467-473).

Notes and Comments: _____

_____

_____

_____

_____

_____

_____

_____

Day 70

Week of _____

Day 2 of 5

Content:	Ch. 14, Sec. 2: Theoretical Perspectives (pp. 467-473)
Objective:	Students will describe the sociological functions of religion and will analyze the relationship between cultural values and religion.
Act. Type:	Class Discussion, Class Activity, Independent Practice, Cooperative Learning, Demonstration
Introduction:	Discuss Careers in Sociology (TWE pp. 466-467).
Instruction:	Ask students to do On-Demand Writing (TWE pp. 468-469).
	Discuss and compare Working with the Data (TWE p. 468) and World View (TWE p. 469).
	Introduce Demonstration (TWE p. 472).
	Share and discuss More About...Marx (TWE p. 470).
	Have students do On-Demand Writing (TWE pp. 470-471).
	Discuss both Open-Response Questions (TWE p. 472).
	Have students do Cooperative Learning Activity (TWE p. 473).
Close:	Assign Tech Trends (TWE p. 474).
	Ask students to read Sec. 3: Religious Organization and Religiosity (pp. 475-480); and Sec. 4: Religion in the United States.

Notes and Comments: _____

_____

_____

_____

_____

_____

_____

Day 71

Week of _____

Day 3 of 5

Content:	Ch. 14, Sec. 3: Religious Organization and Religiosity (pp. 475-480); and Sec. 4: Religion in the United States (pp. 481-488)
Objective:	Students will discuss the meaning and nature of religiosity and will analyze the relationship between secularization and religion in the United States.
Act. Type:	Class Discussion, Class Activity, Independent Practice, Cooperative Learning, Demonstration, Role-playing
Introduction:	Discuss Tech Trends (TWE p. 474).
Instruction:	Have students do Encouraging Citizenship Activity (TWE p. 476).
	Facilitate Cooperative Learning Activity (TWE pp. 478-479).
	Read and discuss Sociology Today (TWE pp. 476-477).
	Introduce and have students do the Survey (TWE p. 482).
	Discuss results of the Survey (TWE p. 482).
	Review and discuss Working with the Data (TWE p. 485) and (TWE p. 486).
	Have students do Using Decision-Making Skills (TWE pp. 486-487).
Close:	Assign On-Demand Writing (TWE p. 477).
	Discuss Learning Styles (TWE p. 488).
	Remind students that chapter presentations are due the following class session.

Notes and Comments: _____

_____

_____

_____

_____

_____

Day 72

Week of _____

Day 4 of 5

Content:	Ch. 14 Presentations (pp. 462-488)
Objective:	Students will present projects and activities summarizing objective/s learned in the chapter.
Act. Type:	Class Activity and Presentation
Introduction:	Read and discuss Focus on Research (TWE p. 484).
Instruction:	Have students do presentations (See Chapter Assessment: Sociology Projects and Technology Activities, p. 491).
Close:	Assign Chapter 14 Learning Goals Outline (see *Unit 4 Booklet*, TRB), due the day of the chapter evaluation.
	Remind students to study for the chapter evaluation.

Notes and Comments: _____

_____

_____

_____

_____

_____

_____

_____

_____

_____

_____

_____

_____

PLANNING GUIDE 74

Chapter 14

RELIGION

Day 73

Week of _____

Day 5 of 5

Content:	Ch. 14 Assessment (pp. 489-491) and Evaluation
Objective:	Students will review for evaluation of the concepts learned in this chapter.
Act. Type:	Class Discussion, Class Activity, Independent Practice, Cooperative Learning, Demonstration, Experiment, Debate, Role-playing, Presentation
Introduction:	Review Chapter 14 Vocabulary Activity homework (see *Unit 4 Booklet*, TRB).
Instruction:	Do Chapter Assessment as needed (TWE pp. 489-491).
Evaluate:	To evaluate the students' comprehension of the chapter, administer Chapter 14 Test A or B. You may want to use the Alternative Assessment found in the TRB.
Close:	Discuss Enrichment Reading (TWE p. 492-493).
	Assign Chapter 15, Intro. (pp. 494-495) and Ch. 15, Sec. 1: The Nature of Sport (pp. 496-501).

Notes and Comments: _____

_____

_____

_____

_____

_____

_____

_____

_____

_____

_____

Chapter 15 — SPORT

Day 74

Day 1 of 3

Content: Ch. 15 Intro. (pp. 494-495) and Ch. 15, Sec. 1: The Nature of Sport (pp. 496-501)

Objective: Students will understand how social institutions of sport meet basic needs in society and will justify sport as an American institution.

Act. Type: Class Discussion, Class Activity, Independent Practice, Cooperative Learning, Experiment

Introduction: Use Lead-Off Activity (TWE pp. 494-495).

Read and discuss Using Your Sociological Imagination (TWE p. 495).

Instruction: Discuss Using the Section Preview and Using the Illustration (TWE p. 496).

Discuss and graph Open-Response Questions (TWE pp. 497-498).

Ask students to do Learning Styles (TWE p. 496).

Close: Assign Using Decision-Making Skills (TWE pp. 500-501).

Assign chapter project (Chapter Assessment: Sociology Projects and Technology Activities) to be presented to the class prior to final chapter evaluation.

Ask students to read Ch. 15, Sec. 2: Theoretical Perspectives and Sport (pp. 502-511) and Sec. 3: Social Issues in Sport (pp. 512-518).

Notes and Comments: _____

_____

_____

_____

_____

_____

_____

_____

_____

Day 75

Week of _____

Day 2 of 3

Content:	Ch. 15, Sec. 2: Theoretical Perspectives and Sport (pp. 502-511) and Sec. 3: Social Issues in Sport (pp. 512-518).
Objective:	Students will compare and contrast sport in America from functionalist, conflict, and symbolic interactionist perspectives, define the relationship between American sport and social mobility, and cite evidence of sexism and racism in American sport.
Act. Type:	Class Discussion, Class Activity, Independent Practice, Cooperative Learning, Debate
Introduction:	Discuss assignment Using Decision-Making Skills (TWE pp. 500-501).
Instruction:	Read and discuss Focus on Research (TWE pp. 510-511).
	Have students do Cooperative Learning Activity (TWE pp. 510-511).
	Show video from Using the Section Preview (TWE p. 512).
	Have students take the Survey (TWE pp. 512-513).
	Review and discuss Working with the Data (TWE pp. 513-514).
	Ask students to interpret the map in Snapshot of America (TWE p. 516).
Close:	Read and discuss Sociology Today (TWE p. 519).
	Assign Chapter 15 Learning Goals Outline or Chapter 15 Vocabulary Activity (see *Unit 4 Booklet*, TRB), due the day of the chapter evaluation.
	Remind students to study for the chapter evaluation.
	Also remind students that chapter presentations are due the following class session.

Notes and Comments: _____

_____

_____

_____

_____

Chapter 15

Day 76

Week of _____

Day 3 of 3

Content:	Ch. 15 Presentations (pp. 494-519), Chapter Assessment (pp. 520-523), and Evaluation
Objective:	Students will present projects and activities summarizing objective/s learned in the chapter and will review for evaluation of the concepts learned in this chapter.
Act. Type:	Class Discussion, Class Activity, Independent Practice, Cooperative Learning, Demonstration, Experiment, Debate, Role-playing, Presentations
Introduction:	Review Chapter 15 homework (see *Unit 4 Booklet*, TRB). Read and discuss Tech Trends-Mass Media and Sports (TWE p. 502). Do Chapter Assessment as needed (TWE pp. 520-523).
Instruction:	Have students do presentations (See TWE, Chapter Assessment: Sociology Projects and Technology Activities, pp. 522-523).
Evaluate:	To evaluate the students' comprehension of the chapter, administer Chapter 15 Test A or B. You may want to use the Alternative Assessment found in the TRB.
Close:	Read and discuss Careers in Sociology (TWE pp. 518-519).

Notes and Comments: _____

_____

_____

_____

_____

_____

_____

_____

_____

_____

PLANNING GUIDE

78

Copyright © by The McGraw-Hill Companies, Inc

Day 77   Week of _____

SPECIAL PROJECT PLANNING DAY

Content:	*Doing Sociology: Focus on Research*
Objective:	Students will plan and carry out a complete research project, including presentation of results.
Act. Type:	Class Discussion, Class Activity, Independent Practice, Cooperative Learning, Demonstration, Experiment, Debate, Role-playing, Presentation
Introduction:	Assign student research projects. (See TRB, *Doing Sociology: Focus on Research),* Research Projects 10-15.
Instruction:	Allow students to work with partners/groups to plan research projects.
Close:	Discuss timeline for research project presentation-students will make presentations the last class session.

Notes and Comments: _____

_____

_____

_____

_____

_____

_____

_____

_____

_____

_____

_____

Chapter 15

SPORT

Day 78   Week of _____

SPECIAL PROJECT PLANNING DAY

Content: *Doing Sociology: Focus on Research*

Objective: Students will plan and carry out a complete research project, including presentation of results.

Act. Type: Class Discussion, Class Activity, Independent Practice, Cooperative Learning, Demonstration, Experiment, Debate, Role-playing, Presentation

Introduction: Discuss reading from Culture Studies: The Sociological Perspective (see TRB).

Instruction: Allow students to work with partners/groups to plan research projects.

Close: Assign Unit 5, Chapter 16, Intro, (pp. 526-529).

Notes and Comments: _____

_____

_____

_____

_____

_____

_____

_____

_____

_____

_____

_____

Chapter 16 — POPULATION AND URBANIZATION

Day 79

Week of _____

Day 1 of 6

Content:	Ch. 16 Intro. (pp. 526-529)
Objective:	Students will understand the importance of urbanization resulting in changes in American institutions.
Act. Type:	Class Discussion, Class Activity, Independent Practice
Introduction:	Use Lead-Off Activity (TWE pp. 528-529).
Instruction:	Read and discuss Using Your Sociological Imagination (TWE p. 529).
	Assign chapter project (see Chapter Assessment: Sociology Projects and Technology Activities) to be presented to the class prior to final chapter evaluation.
Close:	Ask students to read Sec. 1: The Dynamics of Demography (pp. 530-535).

Notes and Comments: _____

_____

_____

_____

_____

_____

_____

_____

_____

_____

_____

_____

_____

Chapter 16 — POPULATION AND URBANIZATION

Day 80

Week of _____

Day 2 of 6

Content: Ch. 16, Sec. 1: The Dynamics of Demography (pp. 530-535)

Objective: Students will evaluate cause and effect on American institutions due to population and urbanization changes.

Act. Type: Class Discussion, Class Activity, Independent Practice, Cooperative Learning, Demonstration

Introduction: Discuss Using the Section Preview (TWE p. 530).

Instruction: Share and have students draw graphic representations of information in Teaching Strategy (TWE p. 530).

Ask students to do Demonstration (TWE pp. 530-531).

Ask students to interpret the map in Snapshot of America (TWE p. 532).

Conduct a Survey (TWE pp. 532-533).

Read and discuss Another Place (TWE p. 535).

Close: Assign Chapter 16 Vocabulary Activity (see *Unit 5 Booklet*, TRB), due the day of the chapter review.

Ask students to read Sec. 2: World Population (pp. 536-546).

Notes and Comments: _____

_____

_____

_____

_____

_____

_____

_____

_____

Chapter 16 POPULATION AND URBANIZATION

Day 81

Week of _____

Day 3 of 6

Content:	Ch. 16, Sec. 2: World Population (pp. 536-546)
Objective:	Students will evaluate cause and effect on global institutions due to population and urbanization changes and will predict world population trends.
Act. Type:	Class Discussion, Class Activity, Independent Practice, Cooperative Learning, Demonstration
Introduction:	Do activity in Using the Section Preview (TWE p. 536).
Instruction:	Have students do Demonstration (TWE pp. 536-537).
	Review and discuss Working with the Data (TWE pp. 537-538).
	Do Demonstration (TWE pp. 538-539).
	Use demonstration in Teaching Strategy (TWE p. 541).
	Have students do Using Conflict-Resolution Skills (TWE pp. 540-541).
	Ask students to do Cooperative Learning Activity (TWE pp. 542-543).
	Share More About...Population Control (TWE p. 543).
Close:	Have students do On-Demand Writing (TWE pp. 544-545).
	Ask students to read Sec. 3: The Urban Transition (pp. 547-554) and Ch. 16, Sec. 4: Urban Ecology (pp. 556-560).

Notes and Comments: _____

_____

_____

_____

_____

_____

_____

_____

Day 82

Week of _____

Day 4 of 6

Content:	Ch. 16, Sec. 3: The Urban Transition (pp. 547-554) and Ch. 16, Sec. 4: Urban Ecology (pp. 556-560)
Objective:	Students will trace the development of preindustrial and modern cities and will compare and contrast four theories of city growth.
Act. Type:	Class Discussion, Class Activity, Independent Practice, Demonstration, Role-playing, Presentation, Cooperative Learning
Introduction:	Read and discuss Sociology Today (TWE p. 547).
Instruction:	Do activity in Using the Section Preview (TWE p. 548).
	Have students do Role Play (TWE pp. 548-549).
	Ask students to interpret the map in World View (TWE p. 550).
	Ask students to do On-Demand Writing (TWE pp. 554-555).
	Do transparency activity in Using the Section Preview (TWE pp. 556).
	Discuss Open-Response Question (TWE p. 556).
	Have students do Learning Styles (TWE pp. 556-557).
	Facilitate Cooperative Learning Activity (TWE pp. 558-559).
Close:	Discuss Careers in Sociology (TWE pp. 552-553).
	Assign Tech Trends (TWE p. 555).
	Remind students that chapter presentations are due the following class session.

Notes and Comments: _____

_____

_____

_____

_____

_____

Day 83

Week of _____

Day 5 of 6

Content:	Ch. 16 (pp. 528-560) Presentations
Objective:	Students will present projects and activities summarizing objective/s learned in the chapter.
Act. Type:	Class Activity and Presentation
Introduction:	Read and discuss Focus on Research (TWE p. 558).
Instruction:	Have students do presentations (See TWE, Chapter Assessment: Sociology Projects and Technology Activities, pp. 562-563).
Close:	Assign Chapter 16 Learning Goals Outline (see *Unit 5 Booklet*, TRB), due the day of the chapter evaluation.
	Remind students to study for the evaluation.

Notes and Comments: _____

_____

_____

_____

_____

_____

_____

_____

_____

_____

_____

_____

_____

Chapter 16   POPULATION AND URBANIZATION

Day 84

Day 6 of 6

Content: Ch. 16 Assessment (pp. 561-563) and Evaluation

Objective: Students will review for evaluation of the concepts learned in this chapter.

Act. Type: Class Discussion, Class Activity, Independent Practice, Cooperative Learning, Demonstration, Experiment, Debate, Role-playing, Presentation

Introduction: Review Chapter 16 Vocabulary Activity homework (see *Unit 5 Booklet*, TRB).

Instruction: Do Chapter Assessment as needed (TWE pp. 561-563).

Evaluate: To evaluate the students' comprehension of the chapter, administer Chapter 16 Test A or B. You may want to use the Alternative Assessment found in the TRB.

Close: Discuss Enrichment Reading (TW pp. 564-565).

Assign Chapter 17 Intro. (pp. 566-567) and Ch. 17, Sec. 1: Social Change (pp. 568-575).

Notes and Comments: _____

_____

_____

_____

_____

_____

_____

_____

_____

_____

_____

PLANNING GUIDE   **86**

Chapter 17

SOCIAL CHANGE AND COLLECTIVE BEHAVIOR

Day 85

Week of _____

Day 1 of 5

Content:	Ch. 17 Intro. (pp. 566-567) and Ch. 17, Sec. 1: Social Change (pp. 568-575)
Objective:	Students will understand the relevance and importance of social change, basic sociological principles related to social change, and the impact of scientific and technological discoveries evidenced by social change.
Act. Type:	Class Discussion, Class Activity, Independent Practice, Cooperative Learning, Role-playing
Introduction:	Introduce Lead-Off Activity (TWE pp. 566-567).
Instruction:	Discuss results of Lead-Off Activity (TWE pp. 566-567).
	Review and discuss Working with the Data (TWE p. 569).
	Introduce and have students do Learning Styles (TWE p. 568).
	Share More About...the Internet (TWE p. 570).
	Ask students to interpret map in World View (TWE p. 574).
	Ask students to do Learning Styles activity (TWE pp. 572-573).
	Read and discuss Another Time (TWE p. 573).
Close:	Assign chapter project (Chapter Assessment: Sociology Projects and Technology Activities) to be presented to the class prior to final chapter evaluation.
	Assign Chapter 17 Vocabulary Activity (see *Unit 5 Booklet*, TRB), due the day of the chapter review.
	Ask students to read Sec. 2: Theoretical Perspectives on Social Change (pp. 576-580) and Sec. 3: Collective Behavior (pp. 581-589).
	Introduce and assign Paired Learning Activity (TWE pp. 574-575).

Notes and Comments: _____

_____

_____

_____

_____

Chapter 17

SOCIAL CHANGE AND COLLECTIVE BEHAVIOR

Day 86

Week of _____

Day 2 of 5

Content: Ch. 17, Sec. 2: Theoretical Perspectives on Social Change (pp. 576-580) and Ch. 17, Sec. 3: Collective Behavior (pp. 581-589)

Objective: Students will describe social change as viewed by the functionalist, conflict, and symbolic interactionist perspective and will analyze social problems within and across groups.

Act. Type: Class Discussion, Class Activity, Independent Practice, Cooperative Learning, Demonstration, Role-playing, Presentation

Introduction: Discuss results from Paired Learning Activity (TWE pp. 574-575).

Instruction: Discuss Focus on Research (TWE pp. 576-577).

Ask students to do On-Demand Writing (TWE pp. 576-577).

Review and discuss Working with the Data (TWE p. 579).

Have students do Role Play (TWE p. 581).

Discuss Using the Section Preview (TWE p. 581).

Use Teaching Strategy (TWE p. 583).

Have students do On-Demand Writing (TWE pp. 586-587).

Close: Do Demonstration (TWE p. 580).

Read and discuss Sociology Today (TWE p. 584).

Ask students to read Sec. 4: Social Movements (pp. 590-596).

Assign students to prepare questions for guest speakers from Working with the Data (TWE p. 594).

Notes and Comments: _____

_____

_____

_____

_____

Chapter 17

SOCIAL CHANGE AND COLLECTIVE BEHAVIOR

Day 87

Week of _____

Day 3 of 5

Content:	Ch. 17, Sec. 4: Social Movements (pp. 590-596)
Objective:	Students will identify types of social movements and will compare and contrast theories of social movements.
Act. Type:	Class Discussion, Class Activity, Independent Practice, Cooperative Learning, Presentation
Introduction:	Read and discuss Tech Trends (TWE p. 590).
Instruction:	Have students do Using Decision-Making Skills (TWE pp. 590-591).
	Review and discuss Working with the Data (TWE p. 592).
	Discuss Reinforcing Vocabulary (TWE p. 592).
	Use Teaching Strategy (TWE p. 593).
	Discuss Working with the Data (TWE p. 594)
Close:	Remind students that chapter presentations are due the following class session.

Notes and Comments: _____

_____

_____

_____

_____

_____

_____

_____

_____

_____

_____

_____

Chapter 17

SOCIAL CHANGE AND COLLECTIVE BEHAVIOR

Day 88

Week of _____

Day 4 of 5

Content:	Ch. 17 (pp. 566-596) Presentations
Objective:	Students will present projects and activities summarizing objective/s learned in the chapter.
Act. Type:	Class Activity and Presentation
Introduction:	Have students interpret the map in Snapshot of America (TWE p. 595).
Instruction:	Have students do presentations (See TWE, Chapter Assessment: Sociology Projects and Technology Activities, pp. 598-599).
Close:	Assign Chapter 17 Learning Goals Outline (see *Unit 5 Booklet*, TRB), due the day of the chapter evaluation.
	Remind students to study for the chapter evaluation.

Notes and Comments: _____

_____

_____

_____

_____

_____

_____

_____

_____

_____

_____

_____

_____

SOCIAL CHANGE AND COLLECTIVE BEHAVIOR

Day 89

Week of _____

Day 5 of 5

Content:	Ch. 17 Assessment (pp. 597-599) and Evaluation
Objective:	Students will review for evaluation of the concepts learned in this chapter.
Act. Type:	Class Discussion, Class Activity, Independent Practice, Cooperative Learning, Demonstration, Experiment, Debate, Role-playing, Presentation
Introduction:	Review Chapter 17 Vocabulary Activity homework (see *Unit 5 Booklet*, TRB).
Instruction:	Do Chapter Assessment as needed (TWE pp. 597-599).
Evaluate:	To evaluate the students' comprehension of the chapter, administer Chapter 17 Test A or B. You may want to use the Alternative Assessment found in the TRB. There is also a final exam for your use, in the TRB.
Close:	Discuss Enrichment Reading (TWE pp. 600-601).
	Remind students that final presentations are due the following class session.

Notes and Comments: _____

_____

_____

_____

_____

_____

_____

_____

_____

_____

_____

_____

Chapter 17

SOCIAL CHANGE AND COLLECTIVE BEHAVIOR

Day 90

Week of _____

SPECIAL PROJECT PRESENTATION DAY

Content:	*Doing Sociology: Focus on Research*
Objective:	Students will present results of research projects.
Act. Type:	Class Discussion, Class Activity, Independent Practice, Cooperative Learning, Demonstration, Experiment, Debate, Role-playing, Presentation
Introduction:	Discuss reading from Culture Studies: The Sociological Perspective (see TRB).
Instruction:	Allow time for students to present research projects.
Close:	Give feedback on presentations.

Notes and Comments: _____

_____

_____

_____

_____

_____

_____

_____

_____

_____

_____

_____

_____

_____

_____

Planning Guide
Sociology and You

Semester course – Block (9 weeks – 45 days)

Resource Key

TWE   Teacher's Wrap Edition
TRB   Teacher's Resource Box

Select the activities best suited to your students' needs and abilities.

Chapter 1

AN INVITATION TO SOCIOLOGY

Day 1   Block Schedule   Week of _____

Content: Unit 1 Intro., Ch. 1 Intro., Sec. 1: The Sociological Perspective (pp. 2-13), and Sec. 2: The Origins of Sociology (pp. 14-22)

Objective: Students will understand the importance of the sociological imagination, describe uses of the sociological perspective, and outline the contributions of the major pioneers of sociology.

Act. Type: Demonstration, Class Discussion, Class Activity, Independent Practice, Cooperative Learning, Role-playing, Presentation

Introduction: Use one of the strategies described in the Ch. 1 Lead-Off Activity (TWE pp. 4-5).

Instruction: Have students read and discuss Using Your Sociological Imagination (TWE p. 5).

     Do Demonstration-Sociological Imagination (TWE p. 12).

     Discuss More About...August Comte (TWE p. 14).

     Discuss More About...Emile Durkheim (TWE p. 16).

     Discuss More About...Jane Addams (TWE p. 19).

     Ask students to do activity described in Biography-W.E.B. DuBois (TWE p. 22).

     Ask students to complete Ch. 1 Graphic Organizer (*Unit 1 Booklet*, TRB).

     Read and discuss Focus on Research (pp. 20-21).

Close: Assign Chapter 1 Vocabulary Activity (see *Unit 1 Booklet*, TRB).

     Ask students to read Sec. 3: Theoretical Perspectives (pp. 23-31).

Notes and Comments: _____

_____

_____

_____

_____

_____

Chapter 1   AN INVITATION TO SOCIOLOGY

Day 2	**Block Schedule** **Week of** _____

Content:	Ch. 1, Sec. 3: Theoretical Perspectives (pp. 23-31) and Ch. 1, Assessment (pp. 32-34)
Objective:	Students will understand the theoretical perspective of the historic interpretations of human social development and will review for evaluation of the concepts learned in this chapter.
Act. Type:	Class Discussion, Class Activity, Independent Practice, Cooperative Learning, Demonstration, Presentations
Introduction:	Introduce the terms *perception* and *perspective* as in Using the Illustration (TWE p. 23).
Instruction:	Ask students to interpret the map in World View (TWE p. 24).
	Do Using Problem-Solving Skills-Conflict Perspective (TWE p. 27).
	Assign groups to do activity in Careers in Sociology (TWE pp. 28-29).
	Review Chapter 1 Vocabulary Activity homework (see *Unit 1 Booklet*, TRB).
	Do Chapter Assessment as needed (TWE pp. 32-34).
Close:	Discuss and have students answer questions in Tech Trends (TWE pp. 28-29).
	Assign Chapter 1 Learning Goals Outline (see *Unit 1 Booklet*, TRB), due the day of the chapter evaluation.
	Remind students to study for the chapter evaluation.
	Assign Chapter 2 Intro, (pp. 36-37) and Sec. 1: Research Methods (pp. 38-49).

Notes and Comments: _____

_____

_____

_____

_____

_____

_____

AN INVITATION TO SOCIOLOGY
AND
SOCIOLOGISTS DOING RESEARCH

Day 3	**Block Schedule**	**Week of** _____

Content: Ch. 1 Evaluation; Ch. 2 Intro. (pp. 36-37) and Ch. 2, Sec. 1: Research Methods (pp. 38-49)

Objective: Students will be evaluated on the concepts learned in Chapter 1. Students will understand the importance of the sociological research and will describe the major quantitative and qualitative research methods used by sociologists.

Act. Type: Class Discussion, Class Activity, Independent Practice, Demonstration

Evaluate: To evaluate the students' comprehension of the chapter, administer Chapter 1 Test A or B. You may want to use the Alternative Assessment found in the TRB.

Introduction: Discuss Enrichment Reading (pp. 35).

Instruction: Have students do Lead-Off Activity (TWE pp. 36-37).

Read and discuss Using Your Sociological Imagination (TWE p. 37).

Do Demonstrations-Quantitative Research (TWE p. 38) and Qualitative Research (TWE p. 39).

Close: Ask students to do On-Demand Writing (TWE p. 44).

Assign Chapter 2 Vocabulary Activity (see *Unit 1 Booklet*, TRB), due the day of the chapter review.

Assign chapter project (see Chapter Assessment: Sociology Projects and Technology Activities, TWE pp. 64-65) to be presented to the class prior to final chapter evaluation.

Ask students to read Sec. 2: Causation in Science (pp. 50-55) and Sec. 3: Procedures and Ethics in Research (pp. 56-61).

Notes and Comments: _____

_____

_____

_____

_____

_____

Chapter 2
SOCIOLOGISTS DOING RESEARCH

Day 4   **Block Schedule**   **Week of** _____

Content:	Ch. 2, Skills at a Glance (pp. 46-49), Ch. 2, Sec. 2: Causation in Science (pp. 50-55), and Ch. 2, Sec. 3: Procedures and Ethics in Research (pp. 56-61)
Objective:	Students will use geographic and other tools to collect, analyze, and interpret sociological data, will discuss basic research concepts, including variables and correlations and the standards for proving a cause-and-effect relationship, and will discuss ethics in sociological research.
Act. Type:	Class Discussion, Class Activity, Independent Practice, Cooperative Learning, Demonstration
Introduction:	Discuss More About the Census (TWE p. 46).
	Discuss Addressing Current Social Issues (TWE p. 42).
	Do Cooperative Learning Activity-School Census Survey (TWE pp. 42-43).
Instruction:	Have students do Cooperative Learning Activity-Statistics Review (pp. 46-47).
	Do Skills at a Glance, (pp. 46-49, answers in TWE pp. 47, 49).
	*Optional – Invite a psychologist in to do Encouraging Citizenship Activity (TWE p. 57).
	Do Ch. 2 Student Journal Prompts (*see Unit 1 Booklet*, TRB).
	Read and answer questions for Another Time – Reason and Science (TWE p. 54).
Close:	Discuss Tech Trends (p. 60).
	Assign Chapter 2 Learning Goals Outline (see *Unit 1 Booklet*, TRB), due the day of the chapter evaluation.
	Remind students that chapter presentations are due the following class session.
	Also remind students to study for the chapter evaluation.

Notes and Comments: _____

_____

_____

Day 5   **Block Schedule**   Week of _____

Content: Ch. 2 Presentations (pp. 36-62), Ch. 2 Assessment (pp. 63-65) and Evaluation

Objective: Students will present projects and activities summarizing objective/s learned in the chapter. Students will review for evaluation of the concepts learned.

Act. Type: Class Discussion, Class Activity, Independent Practice, Cooperative Learning, Presentations

Introduction: Have students do presentations (See TWE, Chapter Assessment: Sociology Projects and Technology Activities, pp. 64-65).

Instruction: Review Chapter 2 Vocabulary Activity homework (see *Unit 1 Booklet,* TRB).

Do Chapter Assessment as needed (TWE pp. 63-65).

Evaluate: To evaluate the students' comprehension of the chapter, administer Chapter 2 Test A or B. You may want to use the Alternative Assessment found in the TRB. A test for Unit 1 is also available in the TRB.

Close: Discuss Sociology Today (TWE p. 62).

Discuss Enrichment Reading (TWE pp. 66-67).

Assign Unit 2, Chapter 3 Intro. (pp. 68-71), Sec. 1: The Basis of Culture and Ch. 3, Sec. 2: Language and Culture (pp. 76-80)

Notes and Comments: _____

_____

_____

_____

_____

_____

_____

_____

CULTURE

Day 6   **Block Schedule**   **Week of** _____

Content:	Unit 2 Intro, Ch. 3 Intro. (pp. 68-71), Ch. 3, Sec. 1: The Basis of Culture (pp. 72-75) and Ch. 3, Sec. 2: Language and Culture (pp. 76-80)
Objective:	Students will understand the importance of culture in society, will name the essential components of culture, and will describe how language and culture are related and will explain the hypothesis of linguistic relativity.
Act. Type:	Class Discussion, Class Activity, Independent Practice, Cooperative Learning, Debate, Role-playing, Demonstration
Introduction:	Ask students to do Lead-Off Activity (TWE pp. 70-71).
Instruction:	Do activity in Using Conflict Resolution Skills (TWE p. 72).
	Lead students in informal debate in Using Problem-Solving Skills (TWE p. 73).
	Ask students to do On-Demand Writing (TWE p. 76).
	Do Demonstrations—Knowing Your Culture (TWE p. 77) and Keeping the Time (TWE p. 78).
	Ask students to do Demonstration-The Importance of Language (TWE p. 79).
	Read and discuss Sociology Today-Cultural Relativism (TWE p. 80).
Close:	Assign Chapter 3 Vocabulary Activity (see *Unit 2 Booklet*, TRB), due the day of the chapter review.
	Ask students to read Sec. 3: Norms and Values (pp. 81-91), Ch. 3, Sec. 4: Beliefs and Material Culture (pp. 92-94) and Ch. 3, Sec. 5: Cultural Diversity and Similarity (pp. 95-102).
	Assign chapter project (see *Performance Assessments*, TRB) to be presented to the class prior to final chapter evaluation.
	Ask students to do Learning Styles-Interpersonal/Linguistic (TWE p. 85).

Notes and Comments: _____

_____

_____

_____

Chapter 3

CULTURE

Day 7 **Block Schedule** **Week of** _____

Content: Sec. 3: Norms and Values (pp. 81-91), Sec. 4: Beliefs and Material Culture (pp. 92-94) and Sec. 5: Cultural Diversity and Similarity (pp. 95-102).

Objective: Students will identify various types of norms and how conformity to those norms is encouraged, distinguish between nonmaterial, material, ideal, and real culture, and discuss how cultural diversity is promoted within a society.

Act. Type: Class Discussion, Class Activity, Independent Practice, Cooperative Learning, Demonstration, Experiment, Debate, Role-playing

Introduction: *Optional - Use Teaching Strategy-*The Gods Must Be Crazy* (TWE p. 82).

Instruction: Discuss student-designed projects from Learning Styles-Interpersonal/ Linguistic (TWE p. 85).

Ask students to enact scenarios in Learning Styles-Bodily-Kinesthetic (TWE p. 84).

Have students do Paired-Learning Activity (TWE p. 92).

Discuss and do activities in Survey (TWE pp. 96-97) and/or Survey (TWE p. 98).

Ask student to do Cooperative Learning Activity (TWE p. 100).

Have students interpret the map in Snapshot of America (TWE p. 101).

Discuss and have students analyze the graph in Working with the Data-Fig. 3.5 (TWE p. 102).

Close: As needed, have students do the Ch. 3 Increasing Your Reading Comprehension worksheet in the *Unit 2 Booklet*, TRB.

Assign Chapter 3 Learning Goals Outline (see *Unit 2 Booklet*, TRB), due the day of the chapter evaluation.

Remind students that chapter presentations are due the following class session.

Also remind students to study for the chapter evaluation.

Notes and Comments: _____

_____

_____

_____

Day 8 **Block Schedule** **Week of** _____

Content:	Ch. 3 Presentations (pp. 70-102), Assessment (pp. 103-105), and Evaluation
Objective:	Students will present projects and activities summarizing objective/s learned in Chapter 3, and will review for evaluation of the concepts learned in this chapter.
Act. Type:	Class Discussion, Class Activity, Independent Practice, Cooperative Learning, Demonstration, Experiment, Debate, Role-playing, Presentations
Introduction:	Read and discuss Tech Trends-Star Wars and the Internet (TWE p. 99).
Instruction:	Have students do presentations (See TWE, Chapter Assessment: Sociology Projects and Technology Activities, pp. 104-105).
	Review Chapter 3 Vocabulary Activity homework (see *Unit 2 Booklet*, TRB).
	Do Chapter Assessment as needed (TWE pp. 103-105).
Evaluate:	To evaluate the students' comprehension of the chapter, administer Chapter 3 Test A or B. You may want to use the Alternative Assessment found in the TRB.
Close:	Discuss Enrichment Reading (TWE pp. 106-107).
	Assign Chapter 4 intro. (pp. 108-109), Sec. 1: The Importance of Socialization (pp. 110-114), and Sec. 2: Socialization and the Self (pp. 115-119).

Notes and Comments: _____

_____

_____

_____

_____

_____

_____

_____

_____

102

Chapter 4

SOCIALIZATION

Day 9	Block Schedule	Week of _____

Content: Ch. 4 Intro. (pp. 108-109), Ch. 4, Sec. 1: The Importance of Socialization (pp. 110-114), and Sec. 2: Socialization and the Self (pp. 115-119)

Objective: Students will understand the importance of socialization and the role socialization plays in human development and will compare and contrast the functionalist, conflict, and symbolic interactionist perspectives on socialization.

Act. Type: Class Discussion, Class Activity, Independent Practice, Cooperative Learning, Demonstration, Experiment, Debate, Presentation

Introduction: Do Lead-Off Activity (TWE pp. 108-109).

Read and discuss Using Your Sociological Imagination (TWE p. 109).

Instruction: Do demonstration in Using the Section Preview (TWE p. 110).

Do Interdisciplinary Activity-Animal Research Debate (TWE p. 111).

Read and discuss Tech Trends (TWE p. 112).

Ask students to do Learning Styles-Logical-Mathematical (TWE p. 112).

Ask students to do On-Demand Writing-Self-Concept (TWE p. 116).

Ask students to do Working with the Table–Fig. 4.1 (TWE p. 117).

Do Learning Styles-Musical/Interpersonal (TWE p. 118).

Close: Assign Chapter 4 Vocabulary Activity (see *Unit 2 Booklet*, TRB), due the day of the chapter review.

Ask students to read Sec. 3: Agents of Socialization (pp. 120-127) and Sec. 4: Processes of Socialization (pp. 128-132).

Notes and Comments: _____

_____

_____

_____

_____

_____

Chapter 4

SOCIALIZATION

Day 10   **Block Schedule**   Week of _____

Content: Ch. 4, Sec. 3: Agents of Socialization (pp. 120-127) and Ch. 4, Sec. 4: Processes of Socialization (pp. 128-132)

Objective: Students will analyze the roles of the family and school in socializing young people, will evaluate mass media techniques used to influence perceptions, attitudes, and behaviors of individuals and groups, and will discuss processes for socialization in adulthood.

Act. Type: Class Discussion, Class Activity, Demonstration, Cooperative Learning, Independent Practice, Role Play, Presentation

Introduction: Introduce socialization as in Using the Section Preview (TWE p. 121).

Instruction: Share More About...School Socialization (TWE p. 122).

Ask students to do Cooperative Learning Activity (TWE p. 121).

Do Interdisciplinary Activity-Culture Studies (TWE pp. 124-125).

Read and discuss Sociology Today (TWE pp. 126-127).

Ask students to interpret the map in Snapshot of America (TWE p. 129).

Read and do Focus on Research (TWE p. 130-131).

Ask students to do Role Play (TWE p. 131).

Have students do On-Demand Writing (TWE p. 130).

Close: Introduce "Writing on the Wall" described in Learning Styles-Visual (TWE pp. 122-123).

Assign Chapter 4 Learning Goals Outline (see *Unit 2 Booklet*, TRB), due the day of the chapter evaluation.

Remind students to study for the chapter evaluation.

Notes and Comments: _____

_____

_____

_____

_____

Day 11   Block Schedule   Week of _____

Content: Ch. 4, Assessment (pp. 133-135) and Evaluation; Ch. 5 Intro. (pp. 138-139) and Ch. 5, Sec. 1: Social Structure and Status (pp. 140-143)

Objective: Students will review for evaluation of the concepts learned in Chapter 4.

Students will understand the effects of social structure and will explain what sociologists mean by social structure and how statuses are related to it.

Act. Type: Class Discussion, Class Activity, Independent Practice, Cooperative Learning, Demonstration, Role-playing, Presentation

Introduction: Follow-up on Interdisciplinary Activity-Culture Studies (TWE pp. 124-125) from previous session.

Review Chapter 4 Vocabulary Activity homework (see *Unit 2 Booklet*, TRB).

Do Chapter Assessment as needed (TWE pp. 133-135).

Evaluate: To evaluate the students' comprehension of the chapter, administer Chapter 4 Test A or B. You may want to use the Alternative Assessment found in the TRB.

Instruction: Direct students in Lead-Off Activity (TWE p. 138).

Do Demonstration (TWE p. 140).

Have students do Role Play activity (TWE p. 141).

Close: Discuss Enrichment Reading (TWE pp. 136-137).

Assign Chapter 5, intro. (pp. 138-139) and Ch. 5, Sec. 1: Social Structure and Status (pp. 140-143). Ask students to read Sec. 2: Social Structure and Roles (pp. 144-151), Ch. 5, Sec. 3: Preindustrial Societies (pp. 153-157), and Sec. 4: Industrial and Postindustrial Societies (pp. 158-163).

Introduce and assign Teaching Strategy-Act.#5 from Ch. Assessment.

Assign Chapter 5 Vocabulary Activity (see *Unit 2 Booklet*, TRB), due the day of the chapter review.

Notes and Comments: _____

_____

_____

_____

Chapter 5

SOCIAL STRUCTURE AND SOCIETY

| **Day 12** | **Block Schedule** | **Week of** _____ |

Content: Ch. 5, Sec. 2: Social Structure and Roles (pp. 144-151), Ch. 5, Sec. 3: Preindustrial Societies (pp. 153-157), Ch. 5, Sec. 4: Industrial and Postindustrial Societies

Objective: Students will discuss how roles are related to social structure and will define and explain how to manage role conflict and role strain; will describe changes that take place when agricultural societies become industrial societies, and analyze changes resulting from industrialization.

Act. Type: Class Discussion, Class Activity, Independent Practice, Cooperative Learning, Demonstration, Role-playing, Presentation

Introduction: Follow up on Teaching Strategy-Act.#5 from Ch. Assessment.

Instruction: Read and discuss Focus on Research (TWE pp. 144-145).

Ask students to interpret the map in Snapshot of America (TWE p. 149).

Conduct Survey (TWE p. 150).

Show video as described in Using the Section Preview (TWE p. 153).

Ask students to do Paired Learning Activity (TWE p. 156).

Discuss and do activity in Using Decision-Making Skills (TWE p. 162).

Discuss and ask students to do Learning Styles-Bodily/Kinesthetic (TWE p. 159).

Read and discuss Tech Trends (TWE p. 164).

Have students do Cooperative Learning Activity (TWE p. 164).

Close: Assign Learning Styles-Linguistic/Spatial (TWE p. 147) or Learning Styles-Artistic (TWE p. 155) as appropriate.

Assign Chapter 5 Learning Goals Outline (see *Unit 2 Booklet*, TRB), due the day of the chapter evaluation.

Assign Chapter 6, intro. (pp. 170-171) and Ch. 6, Sec. 1: Primary and Secondary Groups (pp. 172-175).

Remind students to study for the chapter evaluation.

Notes and Comments: _____

_____

_____

106

SOCIAL STRUCTURE AND SOCIETY
AND
GROUPS AND FORMAL ORGANIZATIONS

Chapter

5 & 6

Day 13   Block Schedule   Week of _____

Content: Ch. 5 Assessment and Evaluation, and Ch. 6 Intro. (pp. 170-171) and Ch. 6, Sec. 1: Primary and Secondary Groups (pp. 172-175)

Objective: Students will review for evaluation of the concepts learned in Chapter 5. Students will understand the effects of group membership and will compare the roles of group membership in primary groups and secondary groups.

Act. Type: Class Discussion, Class Activity, Independent Practice, Cooperative Learning, Demonstration, Experiment, Debate, Role-playing, Presentation

Introduction: Review Chapter 5 Vocabulary Activity homework (see *Unit 2 Booklet*, TRB).

Do Chapter Assessment as needed.

Evaluate: To evaluate the students' comprehension of the chapter, administer Chapter 5 Test A or B. You may want to use the Alternative Assessment found in the TRB.

Instruction: Introduce Lead-Off Activity (TWE p. 170).

Ask students to do On-Demand Writing (TWE p. 172).

Do Making Connections to Other Cultures (TWE p. 174).

Ask students to do Observation (TWE p. 174).

Conduct Survey-Primary and Secondary Groups (TWE p. 175).

Close: Discuss Enrichment Reading (TWE pp. 168-169).

Assign Chapter 6 Vocabulary Activity (see *Unit 2 Booklet*, TRB), due the day of the chapter review.

Ask students to read Sec. 2: Other Groups and Networks (pp. 177-179), Sec. 3: Types of Social Interaction (pp. 180-186), and Sec. 4: Formal Organizations (pp. 190-196).

Notes and Comments: _____

_____

_____

_____

_____

Day 14   Block Schedule   Week of _____

Content: Ch. 6, Sec. 2: Other Groups and Networks (pp. 177-179), Sec. 3: Types of Social Interaction (pp. 180-186), Sec. 4: Formal Organizations (pp. 190-196)

Objective: Students will explain the purposes of reference groups and social networks, discuss how these interactions affect the members of groups, compare and contrast coercion and conformity, and discuss the use of power and its effect on the roles of group membership in formal organizations.

Act. Type: Class Discussion, Class Activity, Independent Practice, Cooperative Learning, Demonstration, Experiment, Debate, Presentation

Introduction: Brainstorm as in Using the Section Preview (TWE p. 177).

Instruction: Facilitate students in doing Cooperative Learning Activity (TWE p. 177).

Do Using Problem-Solving Skills (TWE p. 179).

Ask students to do Cooperative Learning Activity (TWE p. 181).

Lead students in doing the Encouraging Citizenship Activity (TWE p. 183).

Read and discuss Tech Trends (TWE p. 187).

Lead Observation (TWE pp. 190-191).

Read and discuss Focus on Research (TWE pp. 188-189).

Close: Assign Learning Styles-Intrapersonal/Linguistic (TWE p. 186).

Assign Chapter 6 Learning Goals Outline (see *Unit 2 Booklet*, TRB), due the day of the chapter evaluation.

Assign Chapter 7, intro. (pp. 202-203) and Ch. 7, Sec. 1: Deviance and Social Control (pp. 204-208).

Remind students to study for the chapter evaluation.

Notes and Comments: _____

_____

_____

_____

_____

GROUPS AND FORMAL ORGANIZATIONS
AND
DEVIANCE AND SOCIAL CONTROL

Day 15	**Block Schedule**	**Week of** _____

Content: Ch. 6 Assessment (pp. 197-199) and Evaluation; Ch. 7 Intro. (pp. 202-203) and Ch. 7, Sec. 1: Deviance and Social Control (pp. 204-208)

Objective: Students will review for evaluation of the concepts learned in Chapter 6 and identify the major types of social control.

Act. Type: Class Discussion, Class Activity, Independent Practice, Cooperative Learning, Demonstration, Experiment, Debate, Role-playing, Presentation

Introduction: Review Chapter 6 Vocabulary Activity homework (see *Unit 2 Booklet*, TRB).

Do Chapter Assessment as needed (TWE pp. 197-199).

Evaluate: To evaluate the students' comprehension of the chapter, administer Chapter 6 Test A or B. You may want to use the Alternative Assessment found in the TRB.

Instruction: Have students do Lead-Off Activity (TWE pp. 202-203).

Read and discuss Using Your Sociological Imagination (TWE p. 203).

Discuss and do activity/ies in Using Conflict-Resolution Skills (TWE pp. 204-205) or Observation (TWE p. 207).

Ask students to interpret the map in Snapshot of America (TWE p. 206).

Close: Discuss Enrichment Reading (TWE pp. 200-201).

Assign Chapter 7 Vocabulary Activity (see *Unit 2 Booklet*, TRB), due the day of the chapter review.

Assign chapter project (see TWE pp. 235, Chapter Assessment: Sociology Projects and Technology Activities) to be presented to the class prior to final chapter evaluation.

Ask students to read Sec. 2: Functionalism and Deviance (pp. 209-212), Ch. 7, Sec. 3: Symbolic Interactionism and Deviance (pp. 213-217), and Ch. 7, Sec. 4: Conflict Theory and Deviance (pp. 218-221).

Notes and Comments: _____

_____

_____

_____

DEVIANCE AND SOCIAL CONTROL

Day 16	**Block Schedule**	**Week of** _____

Content: Ch. 7, Sec. 2: Functionalism and Deviance (pp. 209-212), Sec. 3: Symbolic Interactionism and Deviance (pp. 213-217), and Sec. 4: Conflict Theory and Deviance (pp. 218-221)

Objective: Students will explain the positive and negative consequences of deviance, differentiate the major functional theories of deviance, compare and contrast cultural transmission theory and labeling theory, discuss the conflict theory view of deviance, and discuss the relationship between minorities, white-collar crime, and the judicial system.

Act. Type: Class Discussion, Class Activity, Cooperative Learning, Independent Practice, Debate, Role-playing, Demonstration, Experiment

Introduction: Introduce Using the Section Preview (TWE p. 209).

Instruction: Ask students to do Role Play (TWE p. 209).

Review and discuss Working with the Data-Fig. 7.2 (TWE p. 211).

Read and discuss Sociology Today (TWE p. 213).

Discuss and assign Controversy and Debate (TWE p. 219).

Facilitate Cooperative Learning Activity (TWE p. 218).

Discuss and do Paired Learning Activity (TWE p. 220).

Close: Assign Interdisciplinary Activity-Creative Writing (TWE p. 217).

Ask students to read Sec. 5: Crime and Punishment (pp. 222-232).

Remind students that chapter presentations are due the following class session.

Notes and Comments: _____

_____

_____

_____

_____

_____

Chapter 7 DEVIANCE AND SOCIAL CONTROL

| **Day 17** | **Block Schedule** | **Week of** _____ |

Content: Ch. 7, Sec. 5: Crime and Punishment (pp. 222-232) and Chapter 7 Presentations

Objective: Students will identify the meaning of crime statistics, especially as related to juvenile delinquency, describe four approaches to crime control, and present projects and activities summarizing objective/s learned in the chapter.

Act. Type: Class Discussion, Class Activity, Independent Practice, Demonstration, Cooperative Learning, Role-playing, Presentations

Introduction: Read and discuss Focus on Research (TWE pp. 222-223).

Instruction: Do Demonstration (TWE pp. 224-225).

Facilitate Cooperative Learning Activity (TWE p. 226).

Read and discuss Making Connections to Other Cultures (TWE p. 227).

If possible, use Teaching Strategy (TWE p. 228) or Careers in Sociology (TWE p. 229) to invite a guest speaker to visit your class.

Have students do On-Demand Writing (TWE p. 227).

Ask students to Role Play (TWE p. 231).

Have students do presentations (See TWE Chapter Assessment: Sociology Projects and Technology Activities, p. 235.)

Close: Assign Chapter 7 Learning Goals Outline (see *Unit 2 Booklet*, TRB), due the day of the chapter evaluation.

Remind students to study for the chapter evaluation.

Notes and Comments: _____

_____

_____

_____

_____

_____

_____

Chapter 7 & 8

DEVIANCE AND SOCIAL CONTROL
AND
SOCIAL STRATIFICATION

Day 18 **Block Schedule** **Week of** _____

Content: Ch. 7, Assessment (pp. 233-235) and Evaluation; Unit 3, Chapter 8 Intro. (pp. 238-241) and Ch. 8, Sec. 1: Dimensions of Stratification (pp. 242-249).

Objective: Students will review for evaluation of the concepts learned in Chapter 7. Students will understand how the economic dimension of social stratification affects human motivation and will analyze the relationships among social class and other culture group membership and political power.

Act. Type: Class Discussion, Class Activity, Independent Practice, Demonstration, Cooperative Learning, Debate

Introduction: Review Chapter 7 Vocabulary Activity homework (see *Unit 2 Booklet*, TRB).

Do Chapter Assessment as needed (TWE pp. 233-235).

Evaluate: To evaluate the students' comprehension of the chapter, administer Chapter 7 Test A or B. You may want to use the Alternative Assessment found in the TRB. A test for Unit 2 is also available in the TRB.

Instruction: Use Lead-Off Activity (TWE p. 240-241).

Do activity found in Learning Styles-Bodily-Kinesthetic/Interpersonal (TWE p. 242).

Ask students to do On-Demand Writing (TWE p. 244).

Facilitate Cooperative Learning Activity (TWE pp. 246-247).

Close: Discuss Enrichment Reading (TWE pp. 236-237).

Ask students to read Sec. 2: Explanations of Stratification (pp. 250-253) and Sec. 3: Social Classes in America (pp. 254-257).

Assign Chapter 8 Vocabulary Activity (see *Unit 3 Booklet*, TRB), due the day of the chapter review.

Notes and Comments: _____

_____

_____

_____

Chapter 8

SOCIAL STRATIFICATION

Day 19   **Block Schedule**   Week of _____

Content: Ch. 8, Sec. 2: Explanations of Stratification (pp. 250-253) and Ch. 8, Sec. 3: Social Classes in America (pp. 254-257)

Objective: Students will state the differences between the functionalist, conflict, and symbolic interactionist approaches to social stratification and compare cultural values associated with socioeconomic stratification of the upper, middle, working, and underclasses.

Act. Type: Class Discussion, Class Activity, Independent Practice, Cooperative Learning, Demonstration, Debate, Role-playing

Introduction: Share Using the Section Preview (TWE p. 250).

Instruction: Share and discuss Controversy and Debate (TWE p. 251).

Review and discuss Working with the Data-Fig. 8.4 (TWE p. 252).

Do activity/demonstration described in Using the Section Preview (TWE p. 254).

Ask students to conduct a Survey (TWE p. 254).

Assign Increasing Your Reading Comprehension (see TRB) as needed.

Have students do Using Decision-Making Skills activity (TWE p. 258).

Close: Discuss Focus on Research and Using Problem-Solving Skills (TWE p. 253).

Assign On-Demand Writing (TWE p. 257).

Ask students to read Sec. 4: Poverty in America (pp. 258-264) and Sec. 5: Social Mobility (pp. 265-268).

Notes and Comments: _____

_____

_____

_____

_____

_____

Chapter 8

SOCIAL STRATIFICATION

Day 20   **Block Schedule**   **Week of** _____

Content: Ch. 8, Sec. 4: Poverty in America (pp. 258-264) and Sec. 5: Social Mobility (pp. 265-268)

Objective: Students will discuss the measurement and extent of poverty in the United States, evaluate commitment to poverty programs in the United States, and analyze the influence of motivation on socioeconomic consequences.

Act. Type: Class Discussion, Class Activity, Independent Practice, Cooperative Learning, Debate, Demonstration, and Presentations

Introduction: Use the Internet to do Using the Section Preview (TWE p. 259).

Instruction: Ask the students to do Paired Learning Activity (TWE p. 259).

Discuss and do Using Problem-Solving Skills activity (TWE pp. 260-261).

Lead discussion in Controversy and Debate (TWE p. 260).

Ask students to do Encouraging Citizenship Activity (TWE p. 263).

Read and discuss Tech Trends (TWE p. 264).

Close: Discuss and assign Sociology Today (TWE p. 258).

Assign Learning Styles-Intrapersonal/Spatial (TWE p. 265).

Assign Chapter 8 Learning Goals Outline (see *Unit 3 Booklet*, TRB), due the day of the chapter evaluation.

Assign Chapter 9, intro. (pp. 274-275) and Sec. 1: Minority, Race, and Ethnicity (pp. 276-279).

Remind students to study for the chapter evaluation.

Notes and Comments: _____

_____

_____

_____

_____

_____

_____

Chapter 8 & 9

SOCIAL STRATIFICATION
AND
INEQUALITIES OF RACE AND ETHNICITY

Day 21	Block Schedule	Week of _____

Content: Ch. 8, Assessment (pp. 269-271) and Evaluation; Ch. 9 Intro. (pp. 274-275) and Sec. 1: Minority, Race, and Ethnicity (pp. 276-279)

Objective: Students will review for evaluation of the concepts learned in Chapter 8. Students will compare various U.S. subculture groups such as ethnic and national origin and will describe what sociologists mean by minority, race, and ethnicity.

Act. Type: Class Discussion, Class Activity, Independent Practice, Demonstration, Cooperative Learning

Introduction: Review Chapter 8 Vocabulary Activity homework (see *Unit 3 Booklet*, TRB).

Do Chapter Assessment as needed (TWE pp. 269-271).

Evaluate: To evaluate the students' comprehension of the chapter, administer Chapter 8 Test A or B. You may want to use the Alternative Assessment found in the TRB.

Introduction: Use Lead-Off Activity (TWE p. 274-275).

Ask students to do Survey (TWE p. 276).

Review and discuss Working with the Data (TWE p. 278).

Close: Assign chapter project (see TWE pp. 305, Chapter Assessment: Sociology Projects and Technology Activities) to be presented to the class prior to final chapter evaluation.

Assign Chapter 9 Vocabulary Activity (see *Unit 3 Booklet*, TRB), due the day of the chapter review.

Ask students to read Sec. 2: Racial and Ethnic Relations (pp. 280-283) and Sec. 3: Theories of Prejudice and Discrimination (pp. 284-289).

Notes and Comments: _____

_____

_____

_____

_____

_____

| **Day 22** | **Block Schedule** | **Week of** _____ |

Content: Ch. 9, Sec. 2: Racial and Ethnic Relations and Sec. 3: Theories of Prejudice and Discrimination (pp. 284-289)

Objective: Students will discuss patterns of racial and ethnic relations and discuss the difference between prejudice and discrimination and will compare and contrast the perspectives of the three theories.

Act. Type: Class Discussion, Class Activity, Independent Practice, Cooperative Learning, Demonstration, Debate

Introduction: Read and discuss Another Place – The Travelling People (TWE p. 279) or Sociology Today – Bridging the Digital Divide (TWE p. 283).

Instruction: Ask students to do Using Problem-Solving Skills (TWE pp. 280-281).

Read and debate Using the Section Preview (TWE p. 284).

Have students do the Survey (TWE p. 284).

Do Learning Styles-Visual/Spatial activity (TWE pp. 286-287).

Ask students to interpret the map in Snapshot of America (TWE p. 287).

Review and discuss Working with the Data (TWE p. 288).

Close: Read and discuss Tech Trends-Spinning a Web of Hate (TWE p. 289).

Ask students to read Sec. 4: Minority Groups in the United States (pp. 290-301).

Remind students that chapter presentations are due the following class session.

Notes and Comments: _____

_____

_____

_____

_____

_____

_____

Chapter 9

INEQUALITIES OF RACE AND ETHNICITY

| **Day 23** | **Block Schedule** | **Week of** _____ |

Content: Sec. 4: Minority Groups in the United States (pp. 290-301); Chapter 9 Presentations (pp. 274-301)

Objective: Students will compare cultural socialization, norms, values, motivation, and communication between subculture groups and will present projects and activities summarizing objective/s learned in the chapter.

Act. Type: Class Discussion, Class Activity, Independent Practice, Cooperative Learning, Demonstration, Debate, Presentation

Introduction: Do demonstration activity in Using the Section Preview (TWE p. 290).

Instruction: Introduce and assign Learning Styles – Interpersonal (TWE pp. 292-293) and Learning Styles-Visual (TWE p. 295).

Have students research and debate Controversy and Debate-Casinos and Gambling (TWE p. 296).

Do Demonstration (TWE pp. 300-301).

Have students do presentations (See TWE, Chapter Assessment: Sociology Projects and Technology Activities, pp. 304-305).

Close: Read and discuss Focus on Research (TWE pp. 298-299).

Assign Chapter 9 Learning Goals Outline (see *Unit 3 Booklet*, TRB), due the day of the chapter evaluation.

Also remind students to study for the chapter evaluation.

Notes and Comments: _____

_____

_____

_____

_____

_____

_____

Day 24   Block Schedule   Week of _____

Content: Chapter Assessment (pp. 302-305) and Evaluation; Ch. 10 Intro. (pp. 308-309) and Ch. 10, Sec. 1: Sex and Gender Identity (pp. 310-315)

Objective: Students will review for evaluation of the concepts learned in Chapter 9. Students will compare various U.S. subculture groups such as gender and age, distinguish the concepts of sex, gender, and gender identity, and discuss research findings regarding gender and behavior.

Act. Type: Class Discussion, Class Activity, Independent Practice, Cooperative Learning, Demonstration, Experiment, Presentation

Introduction: Review Chapter 9 Vocabulary Activity homework (see *Unit 3 Booklet*, TRB).

Do Chapter Assessment as needed (TWE pp. 302-305).

Evaluate: To evaluate the students' comprehension of the chapter, administer Chapter 9 Test A or B. You may want to use the Alternative Assessment found in the TRB.

Instruction: Use Lead-Off Activity (TWE p. 308).

Do Demonstration (TWE p. 309).

Read and discuss Using Your Sociological Imagination (TWE p. 309).

Have students do Cooperative Learning Activity (TWE pp. 310-311).

Close: Assign Chapter 10 Vocabulary Activity (see *Unit 3 Booklet*, TRB), due the day of the chapter review.

Ask students to read Sec. 2: Theoretical Perspectives on Gender (pp. 316-320).

Notes and Comments: _____

_____

_____

_____

_____

Chapter 10 — INEQUALITIES OF GENDER AND AGE

Day 25	Block Schedule	Week of _____

Content: Ch. 10, Sec. 2: Theoretical Perspectives on Gender (pp. 316-320) and Sec. 3: Gender Inequality (pp. 320-329)

Objective: Students will outline the perspectives on gender taken by the three theories and describe the occupational, economic, legal, and political status of women in the United States.

Act. Type: Class Discussion, Class Activity, Independent Practice, Demonstration, Cooperative Learning, Debate, Role-playing

Introduction: Read and discuss Another Time-Manly Hearted Woman (TWE p. 315).

Do Demonstration-Gender Roles (TWE p. 318-319).

Instruction: Ask students to do On-Demand Writing (TWE p. 316).

Ask students to interpret the map in World View (TWE p. 318).

Review and discuss Working with the Data (TWE p. 319).

Read and discuss Sociology Today-Gender-Based Hierarchy (TWE p. 321).

Use activity in Controversy and Debate (TWE p. 324).

Have students do role-plays as in Teaching Strategy (TWE p. 327).

Ask students to do Paired-Learning Activity (TWE p. 328).

Close: Read and discuss Tech Trends-Men, Women, and the Internet (TWE p. 329).

Discuss and assign Learning Styles-Musical/Interpersonal (TWE p. 337).

Ask students to read Sec. 4: Ageism (pp. 330-332) and Sec. 5: Inequality in America's Elderly Population (pp. 333-338).

Notes and Comments: _____

_____

_____

_____

_____

Day 26   Block Schedule   Week of _____

Content: Ch. 10, Sec. 4: Ageism (pp. 330-332) and Sec. 5: Inequality in America's Elderly Population (pp. 333-338)

Objective: Students will distinguish between age stratification and ageism and will describe the economic, legal, and political status of the elderly in the United States.

Act. Type: Class Discussion, Class Activity, Independent Practice, Cooperative Learning, Demonstration, and Presentations

Introduction: Ask students to do Cooperative Learning Activity (TWE p. 329).

Instruction: Review and discuss Working with the Data (TWE p. 331).

Do Internet activity in Using the Section Preview (TWE p. 333).

Read and discuss Focus on Research (TWE pp. 334-335).

Discuss results from Learning Styles-Musical/Interpersonal activity (TWE p. 337).

Ask students to interpret the map in Snapshot of America (TWE p. 337).

Ask students to do On-Demand Writing (TWE p. 336).

Review and discuss Working with the Data (TWE p. 338).

Close: Assign Chapter 10 Learning Goals Outline (see *Unit 3 Booklet*, TRB), due the day of the chapter evaluation.

Remind students to study for the chapter evaluation.

Assign Unit 4 Intro., Chapter 11 intro. (pp. 344-347) and Sec. 1: Family and Marriage Across Cultures (pp. 348-355).

Notes and Comments: _____

_____

_____

_____

_____

INEQUALITIES OF GENDER AND AGE

AND

THE FAMILY

Day 27   **Block Schedule**   Week of _____

Content:	Ch. 10 Assessment (pp. 339-341) and Evaluation; Ch. 11 Intro. (pp. 344-347) and Ch. 11, Sec. 1: Family and Marriage Across Cultures (pp. 348-355)
Objective:	Students will review for evaluation of the concepts learned in Chapter 10. Students will understand how the social institution of family meets basic needs in society, summarize the functions of the social institution of the family, and will describe norms for marriage arrangements.
Act. Type:	Class Discussion, Class Activity, Independent Practice, Demonstration, Presentation
Introduction:	Review Chapter 10 Vocabulary Activity homework (see *Unit 3 Booklet*, TRB).
	Do Chapter Assessment as needed (TWE pp. 339-341).
Evaluate:	To evaluate the students' comprehension of the chapter, administer Chapter 10 Test A or B. You may want to use the Alternative Assessment found in the TRB.
Instruction:	Use Lead-Off Activity (TWE p. 346).
	Ask students to do Cooperative Learning Activity (TWE p. 348).
	Ask students to write in response to Open-Response Question (TWE p. 348).
	Ask students to interpret the map in World View (TWE p. 353).
Close:	Discuss Enrichment Reading (TWE pp. 342-343).
	Assign Chapter 11 Vocabulary Activity (see *Unit 4 Booklet*, TRB), due the day of the chapter review.
	Ask students to read Ch. 11, Sec. 2: Theoretical Perspectives and the Family (pp. 356-361) and Sec. 3: Family and Marriage in the United States (pp. 362-369)

Notes and Comments: _____

_____

_____

_____

_____

_____

Chapter 11

THE FAMILY

Day 28   **Block Schedule**   Week of _____

Content: Ch. 11, Sec. 2: Theoretical Perspectives and the Family (pp. 356-361) and Sec. 3: Family and Marriage in the United States (pp. 362-369)

Objective: Students and will compare and contrast views of the family proposed by the three major perspectives and will outline the extent and causes of divorce and family violence in the United States.

Act. Type: Class Discussion, Class Activity, Independent Practice, Cooperative Learning, Demonstration, Experiment, Debate

Introduction: Have students do Cooperative Learning Activity (TWE pp. 354-355).

Instruction: Do Demonstration (TWE pp. 358-359).

Do activity in Working with the Data (TWE p. 358).

Do Controversy and Debate (TWE p. 359).

Have students do Using Decision-Making Skills (TWE pp. 360-361).

Review and discuss Working with the Data (TWE p. 364) and (TWE p. 368).

Ask students to interpret the map in Snapshot of America (TWE p. 365).

Have students do Cooperative Learning Activity (TWE pp. 366-367).

Close: Read and discuss Another Time-Courtship and Marriage Among the Hopi (TWE p. 356).

Ask students to read Sec. 3: Family and Marriage in the United States (pp. 362-369) and Sec. 4: Changes in Marriage and Family – Blended Families; Single-Parent Families; Childless Marriages; Dual-Employed Marriages (pp. 370-375).

Notes and Comments: _____

_____

_____

_____

_____

_____

Chapter 11

THE FAMILY

| **Day 29** | **Block Schedule** | **Week of** _____ |

Content: Ch. 11, Sec. 4: Changes in Marriage and Family (pp. 370-380)

Objective: Students and will describe alternatives to the traditional nuclear family structure and will evaluate the importance of the social institution of the family in the United States.

Act. Type: Class Discussion, Class Activity, Independent Practice, Cooperative Learning, Demonstration, Debate, Role-playing

Introduction: Read and discuss Tech Trends-Technology and the Family (TWE p. 370).

Instruction: Introduce Teaching Strategy (TWE pp. 371-372).

Have students do Learning Styles activity (TWE p. 375).

Share More About...Lasting Marriages and More About...Happy Marriages (TWE p. 378).

Ask students to do On-Demand Writing (TWE pp. 378-379).

Read and discuss Focus on Research (TWE pp. 376-377).

Close: Do Cooperative Learning Activity (TWE p. 374).

Assign Chapter 11 Learning Goals Outline (see *Unit 4 Booklet*, TRB), due the day of the chapter evaluation.

Remind students to study for the chapter evaluation.

Assign Chapter 12, intro. (pp. 386-387) and Sec. 1: Development and Structure of Education.

Notes and Comments: _____

_____

_____

_____

_____

_____

_____

Day 30   **Block Schedule**   Week of _____

Content:	Ch. 11 Assessment (pp. 381-383) and Evaluation; Ch. 12 Intro. (pp. 386-387) and Sec. 1: Development and Structure of Education (pp. 388-395)
Objective:	Students will review for evaluation of the concepts learned in Chapter 11. Students will understand how the social institution of education meets basic needs in society, discuss schools as bureaucracies, and discuss alternative forms of education.
Act. Type:	Class Discussion, Class Activity, Independent Practice, Cooperative Learning, Demonstration, Debate, Presentation
Introduction:	Review Chapter 11 Vocabulary Activity homework (see *Unit 4 Booklet*, TRB).
	Do Chapter Assessment as needed (TWE pp. 381-383).
Evaluate:	To evaluate the students' comprehension of the chapter, administer Chapter 11 Test A or B. You may want to use the Alternative Assessment found in the TRB.
Instruction:	Use Lead-Off Activity (TWE pp. 386-387).
	Ask students to do the Survey (TWE p. 389).
	Do Controversy and Debate (TWE p. 390).
	Have students do the Cooperative Learning Activity (TWE p. 393).
Close:	Read and discuss Another Time-Understanding Freedom and Education in America (TWE p. 392) or Enrichment Reading (TWE pp. 384-385).
	Assign chapter project (see Chapter Assessment: Sociology Projects and Technology Activities) to be presented to the class prior to final chapter evaluation.
	Ask students to read Sec. 2: Functionalist Perspective Sec. 3: Conflict Perspective, and Sec. 4: Symbolic Interactionism (pp. 396-415)

Notes and Comments: _____

_____

_____

_____

_____

EDUCATION

Day 31   **Block Schedule**   Week of _____

Content:	Ch. 12, Sec. 2: Functionalist Perspective (pp. 396-399), Sec. 3: Conflict Perspective (pp. 400-407), and Sec. 4: Symbolic Interactionism (pp. 409-415)
Objective:	Students will summarize the functions of the social institution of education, evaluate the merit-based nature of public education and educational equality, and evaluate the importance of the social institution of education in the United States.
Act. Type:	Class Discussion, Class Activity, Independent Practice, Experiment, Role-playing, Debate, Presentation
Introduction:	Do the activity in Using the Section Preview (TWE p. 396).
Instruction:	Read and discuss Sociology Today (TWE p. 399).
	Show video as described in Using the Section Preview (TWE p. 400).
	Ask students to do Using Conflict Resolution Skills (TWE pp. 400-401).
	Conduct the debate in Learning Styles-Linguistic/Bodily-Kinesthetic (TWE pp. 402-403).
	Do Interdisciplinary Activity (TWE pp. 404-405).
	Introduce research project in Using the Section Preview (TWE p. 409).
	Do Controversy and Debate (TWE p. 410).
Close:	Assign On-Demand Writing (TWE pp. 398-399 or p. 412).
	Assign Chapter 12 Vocabulary Activity or Assign Learning Goals Outline (see *Unit 4 Booklet*, TRB), due the day of the chapter evaluation.
	Remind students that chapter presentations are due the following class session.
	Remind students to study for the chapter evaluation.

Notes and Comments: _____

_____

_____

_____

_____

Chapter 12

EDUCATION

Day 32   **Block Schedule**   Week of _____

Content: Ch. 12 Presentations (pp. 386-415), Assessment (pp. 416-419), and Evaluation

Objective: Students will present projects and activities summarizing objective/s learned in the chapter and will review for evaluation of the concepts learned in this chapter.

Act. Type: Class Discussion, Class Activity, and Presentations

Introduction: Have students do presentations (See TWE, Chapter Assessment: Sociology Projects and Technology Activities, pp. 418-419).

Instruction: Review Chapter 12 Vocabulary Activity homework (see *Unit 4 Booklet*, TRB).

Do Chapter Assessment as needed (TWE pp. 416-419).

Evaluate: To evaluate the students' comprehension of the chapter, administer Chapter 12 Test A or B. You may want to use the Alternative Assessment found in the TRB.

Close: Discuss Enrichment Reading (TWE pp. 420-421).

Assign Chapter 13, Intro. (pp. 422-423), Sec. 1: Power and Authority, Sec. 2: Political Power in American Society (pp. 433-439).

Assign Another Place-China's One-Child Policy (TWE p. 432).

Notes and Comments: _____

_____

_____

_____

_____

_____

_____

_____

_____

_____

| **Day 33** | **Block Schedule** | **Week of** _____ |

Content: Ch. 13 Intro. (pp. 422-423), Sec. 1: Power and Authority (pp. 424-431), and Sec. 2: Political Power in American Society (pp. 433-439)

Objective: Students will understand how political and economic social institutions meet basic needs in society, discuss differences among democracy, totalitarianism, and authoritarianism, explain how voting is an exercise of power, and evaluate the importance of political social institutions in the United States.

Act. Type: Class Discussion, Class Activity, Independent Practice, Cooperative Learning, Presentation

Introduction: Use Lead-Off Activity (TWE pp. 422-423).

Discuss assignment Another Place-China's One-Child Policy (TWE p. 432).

Instruction: Do activity in Using the Section Preview (TWE p. 424).

Do Demonstration (TWE pp. 424-425).

Ask students to interpret the map in World View (TWE p. 429).

Have students write and share On-Demand Writing (TWE p. 429).

Have students do Net Worthy activities (TWE p. 434).

Review and discuss Working with the Data (TWE pp. 437-438).

Close: Assign Chapter 13 Vocabulary Activity (see *Unit 4 Booklet*, TRB), due the day of the chapter review.

Ask students to read Sec. 3: Economic Systems (pp. 440-444), Sec. 4: The Modern Corporation (pp. 446-449), and Sec. 5: Work in the Modern Economy (pp. 450-456).

Assign Sociology Today-Employee Rights (TWE p. 448).

Notes and Comments: _____

_____

_____

_____

_____

_____

Chapter 13

POLITICAL AND ECONOMIC INSTITUTIONS

Day 34   Block Schedule   Week of _____

Content: Ch. 13, Sec. 3: Economic Systems (pp. 440-444), Sec. 4: The Modern Corporation (pp. 446-449), Sec. 5: Work in the Modern Economy (pp. 450-456)

Objective: Students will list characteristics of capitalism and socialism, analyze the influence of corporations on economic decisions, analyze the influence of cultural values on economic behavior, and evaluate the importance of economic social institutions in the United States.

Act. Type: Class Discussion, Class Activity, Independent Practice, Demonstration, Cooperative Learning, Presentation

Introduction: Discuss assignment Sociology Today-Employee Rights (TWE p. 448).

Instruction: Review and discuss Working with the Data (TWE p. 442).

Have students do Cooperative Learning Activity (TWE p. 446).

Compare results from above with Making Connections to Other Cultures (TWE p. 447).

Review and discuss Working with the Data (TWE p. 447).

Read and discuss Focus on Research (TWE pp. 452-453).

Have students do Observation (TWE pp. 452-453).

Close: Ask students to do Survey (TWE pp. 450-451).

Assign Chapter 13 Learning Goals Outline (see *Unit 4 Booklet*, TRB), due the day of the chapter evaluation.

Remind students to study for the chapter evaluation.

Assign Chapter 14 Intro. (pp. 462-463) and Sec. 1: Religion and Society.

Notes and Comments: _____

_____

_____

_____

_____

Chapter 13 & 14

POLITICAL AND ECONOMIC INSTITUTIONS
RELIGION

Day 35   **Block Schedule**   **Week of** _____

Content: Ch. 13 Assessment (pp. 457-459) and Evaluation; Ch. 14 Intro. (pp. 462-463) and Sec. 1: Religion and Society (pp. 464-466)

Objective: Students will review for evaluation of the concepts learned in Chapter 13. Students will understand how the social institution of religion meets basic needs in society and explain the sociological meaning of religion.

Act. Type: Class Discussion, Class Activity, Independent Practice, Cooperative Learning, Demonstration, Experiment, Debate, Role-playing, Presentation

Introduction: Discuss Enrichment Reading (TWE pp. 460-461).

Review Chapter 13 Vocabulary Activity homework (see *Unit 4 Booklet*, TRB).

Do Chapter Assessment as needed (TWE pp. 457-459).

Evaluate: To evaluate the students' comprehension of the chapter, administer Chapter 13 Test A or B. You may want to use the Alternative Assessment found in the TRB.

Introduction: Use Lead-Off Activity (TWE pp. 462-463).

Read and discuss Using Your Sociological Imagination (TWE p. 463).

Do Demonstration (TWE p. 464).

Discuss More About...Studying Religion (TWE p. 464).

Close: Read and discuss Another Place-Religion at War (TWE p. 466).

Assign Chapter 14 Vocabulary Activity (see *Unit 4 Booklet*, TRB), due the day of the chapter review.

Ask students to read Sec. 2: Theoretical Perspectives (pp. 467-473); Sec. 3: Religious Organization and Religiosity (pp. 475-480); and Sec. 4: Religion in the United States.

Notes and Comments: _____

_____

_____

_____

_____

Chapter 14

RELIGION

Day 36   **Block Schedule**   Week of _____

Content:	Ch. 14, Sec. 2: Theoretical Perspectives (pp. 467-473); Sec. 3: Religious Organization and Religiosity (pp. 475-480); Sec. 4: Religion in the United States (pp. 481-488)
Objective:	Students will describe the sociological functions of religion, analyze the relationship between cultural values and religion, discuss the meaning and nature of religiosity and analyze the relationship between secularization and religion in the United States.
Act. Type:	Class Discussion, Class Activity, Independent Practice, Cooperative Learning, Demonstration, Role-playing
Introduction:	Discuss Careers in Sociology (TWE pp. 466-467).
Instruction:	Discuss and compare Working with the Data (TWE p. 468) and World View (TWE p. 469).
	Have students do On-Demand Writing (TWE pp. 470-471).
	Discuss Tech Trends (TWE p. 474).
	Have students do Encouraging Citizenship Activity (TWE p. 476).
	Facilitate Cooperative Learning Activity (TWE pp. 478-479).
	Discuss Addressing Current Social Issues (TWE p. 485).
	Have students do Using Decision-Making Skills (TWE pp. 486-487).
Close:	Assign Tech Trends (TWE p. 474).
	Assign Chapter 14 Learning Goals Outline (see *Unit 4 Booklet*, TRB), due the day of the chapter evaluation.
	Remind students to study for the chapter evaluation.
	Assign Chapter 15, Intro. (pp. 494-495) and Ch. 15, Sec. 1: The Nature of Sport (pp. 496-501).

Notes and Comments: _____

_____

_____

Chapter 14 & 15

RELIGION & SPORT

Day 37   Block Schedule   Week of _____

Content: Ch. 14 Assessment (pp. 489-491) and Evaluation; Ch. 15 Intro. (pp. 494-495) and Sec. 1: The Nature of Sport (pp. 496-501)

Objective: Students will review for evaluation of the concepts learned in Chapter 14. Students will understand how social institutions of sport meet basic needs in society and will justify sport as an American institution.

Act. Type: Class Discussion, Class Activity, Independent Practice, Cooperative Learning, Experiment

Introduction: Review Chapter 14 Vocabulary Activity homework (see *Unit 4 Booklet*, TRB).

Do Chapter Assessment as needed (TWE pp. 489-491).

Evaluate: To evaluate the students' comprehension of the chapter, administer Chapter 14 Test A or B. You may want to use the Alternative Assessment found in the TRB.

Instruction: Use Lead-Off Activity (TWE pp. 494-495).

Read and discuss Using Your Sociological Imagination (TWE p. 495).

Discuss Using the Section Preview and Using the Illustration (TWE p. 496).

Discuss and graph Open-Response Questions (TWE p. 497-498).

Ask students to do Learning Styles (TWE p. 496).

Close: Discuss Enrichment Reading (TWE p. 492-493).

Assign Using Decision-Making Skills (TWE pp. 500-501).

Ask students to read Ch. 15, Sec. 2: Theoretical Perspectives and Sport (pp. 502-511) and Sec. 3: Social Issues in Sport (pp. 512-518).

Notes and Comments: _____

_____

_____

_____

_____

_____

Chapter
15

SPORT

Day 38   **Block Schedule**   Week of _____

Content:	Ch. 15, Sec. 2: Theoretical Perspectives and Sport (pp. 502-511) and Sec. 3: Social Issues in Sport (pp. 512-518).
Objective:	Students will compare and contrast sport in America from functionalist, conflict, and symbolic interactionist perspectives, define the relationship between American sport and social mobility, and cite evidence of sexism and racism in American sport.
Act. Type:	Class Discussion, Class Activity, Independent Practice, Cooperative Learning, Debate
Introduction:	Discuss assignment Using Decision-Making Skills (TWE pp. 500-501).
Instruction:	Have students do Controversy and Debate (TWE p. 504).
	Read and discuss Focus on Research (TWE pp. 510-511).
	Have students do Cooperative Learning Activity (TWE pp. 510-511).
	Show video from Using the Section Preview (TWE p. 512).
	Have students take the Survey (TWE pp. 512-513).
	Review and discuss Working with the Data (TWE p. 513-514).
	Ask students to interpret the map in Snapshot of America (TWE p. 516).
Close:	Read and discuss Sociology Today (TWE p. 519).
	Assign Chapter 15 Learning Goals Outline or Chapter 15 Vocabulary Activity (see *Unit 4 Booklet*, TRB), due the day of the chapter evaluation.
	Remind students to study for the chapter evaluation.

Notes and Comments: _____

_____

_____

_____

_____

_____

132

Chapter 15

SPORT

Day 39 **Block Schedule** Week of _____

SPECIAL PROJECT PLANNING DAY

Content:	Ch. 15 Presentations (pp. 494-519), Assessment (pp. 520-523), and Evaluation; *Doing Sociology: Focus on Research*
Objective:	Students will review for evaluation of the concepts learned in Chapter 15. Students will plan and carry out a complete research project, including presentation of results.
Act. Type:	Class Discussion, Class Activity, Independent Practice, Cooperative Learning, Demonstration, Experiment, Debate, Role-playing, Presentations
Introduction:	Review Chapter 15 homework (see *Unit 4 Booklet*, TRB).
	Read and discuss Tech Trends-Mass Media and Sports (TWE p. 502).
	Do Chapter Assessment as needed (TWE pp. 520-523).
Evaluate:	To evaluate the students' comprehension of the chapter, administer Chapter 15 Test A or B. You may want to use the Alternative Assessment found in the TRB.
Instruction:	Allow students to work with partners/groups to plan research projects.
Close:	Discuss timeline for research project presentation. Students will make presentations the last class session.
	Assign Unit 5, Chapter 16, Intro, (pp. 526-529), Sec. 1: The Dynamics of Demography (pp. 530-535), and Sec. 2: World Population (pp. 536-546).

Notes and Comments: _____

_____

_____

_____

_____

_____

_____

_____

Day 40   Block Schedule   Week of _____

Content: Ch. 16 Intro. (pp. 526-529), Sec. 1: The Dynamics of Demography (pp. 530-535), and Sec. 2: World Population (pp. 536-546)

Objective: Students will evaluate cause and effect on American institutions due to population and urbanization changes, evaluate cause and effect on global institutions due to population and urbanization changes, and predict world population trends.

Act. Type: Class Discussion, Class Activity, Independent Practice, Cooperative Learning, Demonstration

Introduction: Use Lead-Off Activity (TWE pp. 528-529).

Read and discuss Using Your Sociological Imagination (TWE p. 529).

Instruction: Discuss Using the Section Preview (TWE p. 530).

Ask students to interpret the map in Snapshot of America (TWE p. 532).

Conduct a Survey (TWE pp. 532-533).

Have students do Demonstration (TWE pp. 536-537).

Review and discuss Working with the Data (TWE p. 537) and (TWE p. 538).

Have students do Using Conflict-Resolution Skills (TWE pp. 540-541).

Ask students to do Cooperative Learning Activity (TWE pp. 542-543).

Close: Have students do On-Demand Writing (TWE pp. 544-545).

Assign Chapter 16 Vocabulary Activity (see *Unit 5 Booklet*, TRB), due the day of the chapter review.

Ask students to read Sec. 3: The Urban Transition (pp. 547-554) and Sec. 4: Urban Ecology (pp. 556-560).

Notes and Comments: _____

_____

_____

_____

_____

Chapter 16
POPULATION AND URBANIZATION

| **Day 41** | **Block Schedule** | **Week of** _____ |

Content: Ch. 16, Sec. 3: The Urban Transition (pp. 547-554) and Sec. 4: Urban Ecology (pp. 556-560)

Objective: Students will trace the development of preindustrial and modern cities and will compare and contrast four theories of city growth.

Act. Type: Class Discussion, Class Activity, Independent Practice, Demonstration, Role-playing, Presentation, Cooperative Learning

Introduction: Read and discuss Sociology Today (TWE p. 547).

Instruction: Do activity in Using the Section Preview (TWE p. 548).

Have students do Role Play (TWE pp. 548-549).

Ask students to interpret the map in World View (TWE p. 550).

Do transparency activity in Using the Section Preview (TWE pp. 556).

Have students do Learning Styles (TWE pp. 556-557).

Facilitate Cooperative Learning Activity (TWE pp. 558-559).

Close: Assign Tech Trends (TWE p. 555).

Assign Chapter 16 Learning Goals Outline (see *Unit 5 Booklet*, TRB), due the day of the chapter evaluation.

Remind students to study for the evaluation.

Assign Ch. 17 Intro. (pp. 566-567) and Ch. 17, Sec. 1: Social Change (pp. 568-575)

Notes and Comments: _____

_____

_____

_____

_____

_____

_____

Chapter 16 & 17

POPULATION AND URBANIZATION
AND
SOCIAL CHANGE AND COLLECTIVE BEHAVIOR

Day 42   **Block Schedule**   **Week of** _____

Content: Ch. 16 Assessment (pp. 561-563) and Evaluation; Ch. 17 Intro. (pp. 566-567) and Ch. 17, Sec. 1: Social Change (pp. 568-575)

Objective: Students will review for evaluation of the concepts learned in Chapter 16, and will understand basic sociological principles related to social change, and the impact of scientific and technological discoveries evidenced by social change.

Act. Type: Class Discussion, Class Activity, Independent Practice, Cooperative Learning, Demonstration, Experiment, Debate, Role-playing, Presentation

Introduction: Review Chapter 16 Vocabulary Activity homework (see *Unit 5 Booklet*, TRB).

Do Chapter Assessment as needed (TWE pp. 561-563).

Evaluate: To evaluate the students' comprehension of the chapter, administer Chapter 16 Test A or B. You may want to use the Alternative Assessment found in the TRB.

Instruction: Introduce and discuss Lead-Off Activity (TWE pp. 566-567).

Have the students do time lines in Using the Section Preview (TWE p. 568).

Introduce and have students do Learning Styles (TWE p. 568).

Ask students to interpret map in World View (TWE p. 574).

Close: Discuss Enrichment Reading (TWE pp. 564-565).

Assign Chapter 17 Intro. (pp. 566-567), Sec. 1: Social Change (pp. 568-575), Sec. 2: Theoretical Perspectives on Social Change (pp. 576-580), and Sec. 3: Collective Behavior (pp. 581-589).

Notes and Comments: _____

_____

_____

_____

_____

_____

Chapter 17

SOCIAL CHANGE AND COLLECTIVE BEHAVIOR

Day 43   Block Schedule   Week of _____

Content: Ch. 17, Sec. 2: Theoretical Perspectives on Social Change (pp. 576-580), Sec. 3: Collective Behavior (pp. 581-589)

Objective: Students will describe social change as viewed by the functionalist, conflict, and symbolic interactionist perspective, and analyze social problems within and across groups.

Act. Type: Class Discussion, Class Activity, Independent Practice, Cooperative Learning, Demonstration, Role-playing, Presentation

Introduction: Ask students to do Learning Styles activity (TWE pp. 572-573).

Instruction: Discuss Focus on Research (TWE pp. 576-577).

Have students do Role Play (TWE p. 581).

Discuss Using the Section Preview (TWE p. 581).

Use Teaching Strategy (TWE p. 583).

Have students do On-Demand Writing (TWE pp. 586-587).

Close: Assign students to prepare questions for guest speakers from Working with the Data (TWE p. 594).

Assign Chapter 17 Learning Goals Outline (see *Unit 5 Booklet*, TRB), due the day of the chapter evaluation.

Remind students to study for the chapter evaluation.

Notes and Comments: _____

_____

_____

_____

_____

_____

_____

Chapter 17

SOCIAL CHANGE AND COLLECTIVE BEHAVIOR

Day 44

Block Schedule   **Week of** _____

Content:	Ch. 17, Sec. 4: Social Movements (pp. 590-596); Ch. 17 Assessment (pp. 597-599) and Evaluation
Objective:	Students will identify types of social movements and will compare and contrast theories of social movements. Students will review for evaluation of the concepts learned in Chapter 17.
Act. Type:	Class Discussion, Class Activity, Independent Practice, Cooperative Learning, Presentation
Introduction:	Read and discuss Tech Trends (TWE p. 590).
Instruction:	Have students do Using Decision-Making Skills (TWE pp. 590-591).
	Review and discuss Working with the Data (TWE p. 592).
	Use Teaching Strategy (TWE p. 593).
	Discuss Working with the Data (TWE p. 594)
	Invite guest speakers from above to lead presentation/discussion.
	Review Chapter 17 Vocabulary Activity homework (see *Unit 5 Booklet*, TRB).
	Do Chapter Assessment as needed (TWE pp. 597-599).
Evaluate:	To evaluate the students' comprehension of the chapter, administer Chapter 17 Test A or B. You may want to use the Alternative Assessment found in the TRB. There is also a final exam for your use in the TRB.
Close:	Discuss Enrichment Reading (TWE pp. 600-601).
	Remind students that final presentations are due the following class session.

Notes and Comments: _____

_____

_____

_____

_____

_____

Chapter 17

SOCIAL CHANGE AND COLLECTIVE BEHAVIOR

Day 45 **Block Schedule** Week of _____

SPECIAL PROJECT PRESENTATION DAY

Content: *Doing Sociology: Focus on Research*

Objective: Students will present results of research projects.

Act. Type: Class Discussion, Class Activity, Independent Practice, Cooperative Learning, Demonstration, Experiment, Debate, Role-playing, Presentation

Introduction: Discuss reading from Culture Studies: The Sociological Perspective (see TRB).

Instruction: Allow time for students to present research projects.

Close: Give feedback on presentations.

Notes and Comments: _____

_____

_____

_____

_____

_____

_____

_____

_____

_____

_____

_____

_____

_____

_____

Planning Guide
Sociology and You

Year-long course – Traditional (36 weeks – 180 days)

Resource Key

TWE   Teacher's Wrap Edition
TRB   Teacher's Resource Box

Select the activities best suited to your students' needs and abilities.

Day 1

Week of _____

Day 1 of 8

Content:	Unit 1 Intro., Ch. 1 Intro., and Sec. 1: The Sociological Perspective – Acquiring the Sociological Imagination (pp. 2-5, 11)
Objective:	Students will understand the importance of the sociological imagination.
Act. Type:	Demonstration, Class Discussion, Class Activity, Independent Practice
Introduction:	Use one of the strategies described in the Ch. 1 Lead-Off Activity (TWE pp. 4-5).
Instruction:	Have students read and discuss Using Your Sociological Imagination (TWE p. 5).
	Discuss More About…C.Wright Mills (TWE p. 11).
	Do Demonstration-Sociological Imagination (TWE p. 12).
Close:	Assign chapter project (see Chapter Assessment: Sociology Projects and Technology Activities, pp. 33-34) to be presented to the class prior to final chapter evaluation.
	Ask students to read Sec. 1: The Sociological Perspective (pp. 6-13).

Notes and Comments: _____

_____

_____

_____

_____

_____

_____

_____

_____

_____

Day 2

Week of _____

Day 2 of 8

Content:	Ch. 1, Sec. 1: The Sociological Perspective – The Nature of Sociology, The Importance of Patterns (pp. 6-13).
Objective:	Students will describe uses of the sociological perspective.
Act. Type:	Class Discussion, Class Activity, Independent Practice, Demonstration
Introduction:	Using the Section Preview
Instruction:	Do Demonstration-Societal vs. Individual Responsibilities (TWE pp. 6-7).
	Have students do Demonstration-Perspectives (TWE p. 8).
	Read and discuss Reteaching – The Sociological Perspective (TWE p. 9).
	Ask students to answer the questions in Another Time – Native American's Speech (TWE p. 10).
Close:	Assign Chapter 1 Vocabulary Activity (see *Unit 1 Booklet*, TRB), due the day of the chapter review.
	Ask students to read Sec. 2: The Origins of Sociology – European Origins (pp. 14-18).

Notes and Comments: _____

_____

_____

_____

_____

_____

_____

_____

_____

144

Chapter 1 · AN INVITATION TO SOCIOLOGY

Day 3

Week of _____

Day 3 of 8

Content:	Ch. 1, Sec. 2: The Origins of Sociology – European Origins (pp. 14-18)
Objective:	Students will outline the contributions of the major European pioneers of sociology.
Act. Type:	Class Discussion, Class Activity, Independent Practice, Cooperative Learning
Introduction:	Do Using the Section Preview (TWE p. 14)
Instruction:	Discuss More About...August Comte (TWE p. 14).
	Ask students to do Interdisciplinary Activity – Current Events (TWE p. 14).
	Discuss More About...Emile Durkheim (TWE p. 16).
Close:	Ask students to read Sec. 2: The Origins of Sociology – Sociology in America (pp. 18-22).

Notes and Comments: _____

_____

_____

_____

_____

_____

_____

_____

_____

_____

_____

_____

Day 4

Week of _____

Day 4 of 8

Content:	Ch. 1, Sec. 2: The Origins of Sociology – Sociology in America (pp. 18-22)
Objective:	Students will summarize the development of sociology in the United States.
Act. Type:	Class Discussion, Class Activity, Independent Practice, Role-playing, Presentation
Introduction:	Discuss More About...Sociology in America (TWE p. 15)
Instruction:	Ask students to complete Ch. 1 Graphic Organizer (*Unit 1 Booklet*, TRB). Discuss More About...Jane Addams (TWE p. 19).
	Ask students to do activity described in Biography-W.E.B. DuBois (TWE p. 22).
	Read and discuss Focus on Research (pp. 20-21).
Close:	Ask students to read Sec. 3: Theoretical Perspectives (pp. 23-31).

Notes and Comments: _____

_____

_____

_____

_____

_____

_____

_____

_____

_____

_____

_____

146

Day 5

Week of _____

Day 5 of 8

Content:	Ch. 1, Sec. 3: Theoretical Perspectives (pp. 23-31)
Objective:	Students will understand the theoretical perspective of the historic interpretations of human social development.
Act. Type:	Class Discussion, Class Activity, Independent Practice, Cooperative Learning, Demonstration
Introduction:	Have students do Demonstration-The Chairs Game (TWE p. 24).
	Discuss Using the Section Preview (TWE p. 23).
	Introduce the terms *perception* and *perspective* as in Using the Illustration (TWE p. 23).
Instruction:	Ask students to interpret the map in World View (TWE p. 24).
	Have students answer questions about Working with the Data-Fig. 1.2: Focus on Theoretical Perspectives (TWE p. 27).
	Do Using Problem-Solving Skills-Conflict Perspective (TWE p. 27).
Close:	Discuss and have students answer questions in Tech Trends (TWE pp. 28-29).
	Remind students that chapter presentations are due the following class session.

Notes and Comments: _____

_____

_____

_____

_____

_____

_____

_____

Day 6

Week of _____

Day 6 of 8

Content: Chapter 1 (pp. 4-31)

Objective: Students will present projects and activities summarizing objective/s learned in the chapter.

Act. Type: Class Activity and Presentations

Introduction: Have students work in groups to do activity in Careers in Sociology (TWE pp. 28-29).

Instruction: Have student do presentations (See TWE, Chapter Assessment: Sociology Projects and Technology Activities, pp. 33-34).

Close: Assign Chapter 1 Learning Goals Outline (see *Unit 1 Booklet*, TRB), due the day of the chapter evaluation.

Notes and Comments: _____

_____

_____

_____

_____

_____

_____

_____

_____

_____

_____

_____

_____

_____

Chapter 1

AN INVITATION TO SOCIOLOGY

Day 7

Week of _____

Day 7 of 8

Content:	Ch. 1, Assessment (pp. 32-34)
Objective:	Students will review for evaluation of the concepts learned in this chapter.
Act. Type:	Class Discussion, Class Activity, Independent Practice, Cooperative Learning, Demonstration, Experiment, Debate, Role-playing, Presentation
Introduction:	Review Chapter 1 Vocabulary Activity homework (see *Unit 1 Booklet*, TRB).
Instruction:	Do Chapter Assessment as needed (TWE pp. 32-34).
Close:	Remind students to study for the chapter evaluation.

Notes and Comments: _____

_____

_____

_____

_____

_____

_____

_____

_____

_____

_____

_____

_____

_____

Day 8

Week of _____

Day 8 of 8

Evaluate: To evaluate the students' comprehension of the chapter, administer Chapter 1 Test A or B. You may want to use the Alternative Assessment found in the TRB.

Close: Discuss Enrichment Reading (pp. 35).

        Assign Chapter 2 Intro. (pp. 36-37).

Notes and Comments: _____

_____

_____

_____

_____

_____

_____

_____

_____

_____

_____

_____

_____

_____

_____

_____

_____

_____

Chapter 2

SOCIOLOGISTS DOING RESEARCH

Day 9

Week of _____

Day 1 of 8

Content:	Ch. 2 Intro. (pp. 36-37)
Objective:	Students will understand the importance of sociological research.
Act. Type:	Class Discussion, Class Activity
Introduction:	Have students do Lead-Off Activity (TWE pp. 36-37).
Instruction:	Read and discuss Using Your Sociological Imagination (TWE p. 37).
Close:	Assign chapter project (see Chapter Assessment: Sociology Projects and Technology Activities, TWE pp. 64-65) to be presented to the class prior to final chapter evaluation.
	Ask students to read Sec. 1: Research Methods (pp. 38-49).

Notes and Comments: _____

_____

_____

_____

_____

_____

_____

_____

_____

_____

_____

_____

_____

_____

Day 10

Week of _____

Day 2 of 8

Content:	Ch. 2, Sec. 1: Research Methods (pp. 38-49)
Objective:	Students will describe the major quantitative and qualitative research methods used by sociologists.
Act. Type:	Class Discussion, Class Activity, Independent Practice, Demonstration
Introduction:	Discuss Using the Section Preview
Instruction:	Do Demonstration-Quantitative Research (TWE p. 38).
	Have students learn mnemonic in Reinforcing Vocabulary (TWE p. 38).
	Do Demonstration-Qualitative Research (TWE p. 39).
	Review Fig.2.1 and 2.2 and then discuss Points to Stress (TWE p. 40).
	Do Demonstration-Surveys (TWE p. 40).
Close:	Ask students to do On-Demand Writing (TWE p. 44). Assign Chapter 2 Vocabulary Activity (see *Unit 1 Booklet*, TRB), due the day of the chapter review.

Notes and Comments: _____

_____

_____

_____

_____

_____

_____

_____

_____

_____

152

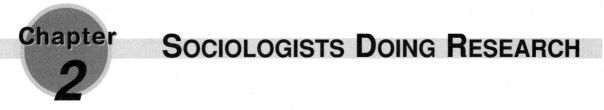

Day 11

Week of _____

Day 3 of 8

Content:	Ch. 2, Skills at a Glance (pp. 46-49)
Objective:	Students will use geographic and other tools to collect, analyze, and interpret sociological data.
Act. Type:	Class Discussion, Class Activity, Independent Practice, Cooperative Learning
Introduction:	Discuss More About the Census (TWE p. 46).
	Discuss Addressing Current Social Issues (TWE p. 42).
	Have students do Cooperative Learning Activity-School Census Survey (TWE pp. 42-43).
Instruction:	Introduce Working with the Data-Skills at a Glance (TWE p. 46).
	Have students do Cooperative Learning Activity-Statistics Review (pp. 46-47).
	Do Skills at a Glance, (pp. 46-49, answers in TWE pp. 47, 49).
Close:	Assign Doing Sociology: Focus on Research (see TRB). Ask students to read Sec. 2: Causation in Science (pp. 50-55).

Notes and Comments: _____

_____

_____

_____

_____

_____

_____

_____

Chapter 2

SOCIOLOGISTS DOING RESEARCH

Day 12

Week of _____

Day 4 of 8

Content:	Ch. 2, Sec. 2: Causation in Science (pp. 50-55)
Objective:	Students will discuss basic research concepts, including variables and correlations and the standards for proving a cause-and-effect relationship.
Act. Type:	Class Discussion, Class Activity, Independent Practice, Cooperative Learning, Demonstration
Introduction:	Introduce Using the Section Preview (TWE p. 50).
Instruction:	Ask students to interpret the map in World View (TWE p. 51).
	Do Demonstration-Variables (TWE p. 51).
	Ask students to do Paired Learning Activity (TWE p. 52) and Cooperative Learning Activity (TWE p. 53).
	Discuss Points to Stress (TWE p. 53).
	Have students do Paired Learning Activity (TWE p. 55).
Close:	Read and answer questions for Another Time – Reason and Science (TWE p. 54).
	Ask students to read Sec. 3: Procedures and Ethics in Research (pp. 56-61).

Notes and Comments: _____

_____

_____

_____

_____

_____

_____

_____

Day 13

Week of _____

Day 5 of 8

Content:	Ch. 2, Sec. 3: Procedures and Ethics in Research (pp. 56-61)
Objective:	Students will discuss ethics in sociological research.
Act. Type:	Class Discussion, Class Activity, Independent Practice, Cooperative Learning
Introduction:	Discuss Focus on Research (pp. 56-57, see TWE p. 56 for Teaching Strategy).
	*Optional - Invite a psychologist in to do Encouraging Citizenship Activity (TWE p. 57).
Instruction:	Discuss Using the Section Preview (TWE p. 58).
	Ask students to work in groups to do Encouraging Citizenship Activity (TWE pp. 58-59).
	Read and discuss Using Decision-Making Skills-Dr. Peter Publish (TWE pp. 60-61).
Close:	Discuss Tech Trends (p. 60).
	Remind students that chapter presentations are due the following class session.

Notes and Comments: _____

_____

_____

_____

_____

_____

_____

_____

_____

_____

Day 14

Week of _____

Day 6 of 8

Content:	Chapter 2 (pp. 36-62)
Objective:	Students will present projects and activities summarizing objective/s learned in the chapter.
Act. Type:	Class Activity and Presentations
Introduction:	Ask students to write using Ch. 2 Student Journal Prompts (*see Unit 1 Booklet, TRB*).
Instruction:	Have students do presentations (See TWE, Chapter Assessment: Sociology Projects and Technology Activities, pp. 64-65).
Close:	Assign Chapter 2 Learning Goals Outline (see *Unit 1 Booklet*, TRB), due the day of the chapter evaluation.

Notes and Comments: _____

_____

_____

_____

_____

_____

_____

_____

_____

_____

_____

_____

Day 15

Week of _____

Day 7 of 8

Content:	Ch. 2, Assessment (pp. 63-65)
Objective:	Students will review for evaluation of the concepts learned in this chapter.
Act. Type:	Class Discussion, Class Activity, Independent Practice, Cooperative Learning
Introduction:	Review Chapter 2 Vocabulary Activity homework (see *Unit 1 Booklet,* TRB).
Instruction:	Do Chapter Assessment as needed (TWE pp. 63-65).
Close:	Discuss Sociology Today (TWE p. 62).
	Remind students to study for the chapter evaluation.

Notes and Comments: _____

_____

_____

_____

_____

_____

_____

_____

_____

_____

_____

_____

_____

_____

_____

Day 16   Week of _____

Day 8 of 8

Evaluate: To evaluate the students' comprehension of the chapter, administer Chapter 2 Test A or B. You may want to use the Alternative Assessment found in the TRB. A test for Unit 1 is also available in the TRB.

Close: Read and discuss Enrichment Reading (TWE pp. 66-67).

Assign Unit 2, Chapter 3 Intro. (pp. 68-71).

Notes and Comments: _____

_____

_____

_____

_____

_____

_____

_____

_____

_____

_____

_____

_____

_____

_____

_____

Chapter 3

CULTURE

Day 17

Week of _____

Day 1 of 12

Content: Unit 2 Intro, Ch. 3 Intro. (pp. 68-71)

Objective: Students will understand the importance of culture in society.

Act. Type: Class Discussion, Class Activity, Independent Practice, Cooperative Learning

Introduction: Ask students to do Lead-Off Activity (TWE pp. 70-71).

Instruction: Discuss Using the Illustration (TWE p. 71).

Read and discuss Using Your Sociological Imagination (TWE p. 71).

Close: Assign chapter project (see Chapter Assessment: Sociology Projects and Technology Activities, pp. 104-105) to be presented to the class prior to final chapter evaluation.

Ask students to read Sec. 1: The Basis of Culture (pp. 72-75).

Notes and Comments: _____

_____

_____

_____

_____

_____

_____

_____

_____

_____

_____

_____

Day 18

Week of _____

Day 2 of 12

Content: Ch. 3, Sec. 1: The Basis of Culture (pp. 72-75)

Objective: Students will name the essential components of culture.

Act. Type: Class Discussion, Class Activity, Independent Practice, Cooperative Learning, Debate, Role-playing

Introduction: Introduce Using the Section Preview (TWE p. 72).

Instruction: Do activity in Using Conflict Resolution Skills (TWE p. 72).

Lead students in informal debate in Using Problem-Solving Skills (TWE p. 73).

Have students do Role Play (TWE p. 75).

Close: Ask students to read Sec. 2: Language and Culture – Symbols, Language, and Culture (pp. 76-77).

Assign Chapter 3 Vocabulary Activity (see *Unit 2 Booklet*, TRB), due the day of the chapter review.

Notes and Comments: _____

_____

_____

_____

_____

_____

_____

_____

_____

Chapter 3

CULTURE

Day 19

Week of _____

Day 3 of 12

Content:	Ch. 3, Sec. 2: Language and Culture – Symbols, Language, and Culture (pp. 76-77)
Objective:	Students will describe how language and culture are related.
Act. Type:	Class Discussion, Class Activity, Independent Practice, Demonstration
Introduction:	Discuss Another Time (TWE p. 76).
	Ask students to do On-Demand Writing (TWE p. 76).
Instruction:	Introduce Using the Section Preview (TWE p. 77).
	Do Demonstration-Knowing Your Culture (TWE p. 77).
	Review and discuss Working with the Data, Fig. 3.1 (TWE p. 78).
Close:	Ask students to read Sec. 2: Language and Culture – The Sapir-Whorf Hypothesis (pp. 78-80).

Notes and Comments: _____

_____

_____

_____

_____

_____

_____

_____

_____

_____

_____

_____

Chapter 3

CULTURE

Day 20 Week of _____

Day 4 of 12

Content:	Ch. 3, Sec. 2: Language and Culture – The Sapir-Whorf Hypothesis (pp. 78-80)
Objective:	Students will explain the hypothesis of linguistic relativity.
Act. Type:	Class Discussion, Class Activity, Demonstration
Introduction:	Discuss Working with the Quote (TWE p. 78).
Instruction:	Do Demonstration-Keeping the Time (TWE p. 78).
	Ask students to do Demonstration-The Importance of Language (TWE p. 79).
	Discuss Teaching Strategy (TWE p. 79).
	Read and discuss Sociology Today-Cultural Relativism (TWE p. 80).
Close:	Discuss Making Connections to Other Cultures (TWE p. 80).
	Ask students to read Sec. 3: Norms and Values – Norms: The Rules We Live By; Folkways, Mores, and Laws; Enforcing the Rules (pp. 81-88).

Notes and Comments: _____

_____

_____

_____

_____

_____

_____

_____

_____

_____

_____

Chapter 3

CULTURE

Day 21   Week of _____

Day 5 of 12

Content:	Ch. 3, Sec. 3: Norms and Values – Norms: The Rules We Live By; Folkways, Mores, and Laws; Enforcing the Rules (pp. 81-88)
Objective:	Students will identify various types of norms and how conformity to those norms is encouraged.
Act. Type:	Class Discussion, Class Activity, Independent Practice, Cooperative Learning, Demonstration, Role-playing
Introduction:	Do Using the Section Preview (TWE p. 81).
Instruction:	Discuss Working with the Data-Fig. 3.2 (TWE p. 82).
	*Optional - Use Teaching Strategy-*The Gods Must Be Crazy* (TWE p. 82).
	Discuss Using the Illustration (TWE p. 83).
	Ask students to enact scenarios in Learning Styles-Bodily-Kinesthetic (TWE p. 84).
	Ask students to interpret the map in World View (TWE p. 85).
	Discuss Working with the Data-Fig. 3.3 (TWE p. 86).
Close:	Ask students to do Learning Styles-Interpersonal/Linguistic (TWE p. 85, due in two class sessions).
	Ask students to read Sec. 3: Norms and Values – Values-The Basis for Norms; Basic Values in the United States (pp. 89-91).

Notes and Comments: _____

_____

_____

_____

_____

_____

Day 22   Week of _____

Day 6 of 12

Content: Ch. 3, Sec. 3: Norms and Values – Values-The Basis for Norms; Basic Values in the United States (pp. 89-91)

Objective: Students will understand that cultural values vary in different locations.

Act. Type: Class Discussion, Class Activity, Independent Practice, Cooperative Learning, Experiment, Debate

Introduction: Ask students to do Cooperative Learning Activity (TWE pp. 86-87).

Instruction: Use Teaching Strategy (TWE p. 89).

Have students do Cooperative Learning Activity(TWE p. 90).

Explain and discuss Working with the Quote (TWE p. 90).

Close: Ask students to do the writing described in Pulling It All Together (TWE p. 91).

Ask students to read Sec. 4: Beliefs and Material Culture (pp. 92-94).

Notes and Comments: _____

_____

_____

_____

_____

_____

_____

_____

_____

_____

PLANNING GUIDE   **164**

Chapter 3

CULTURE

Day 23

Week of _____

Day 7 of 12

Content:	Ch. 3, Sec. 4: Beliefs and Material Culture (pp. 92-94)
Objective:	Students will distinguish between nonmaterial, material, ideal, and real culture.
Act. Type:	Class Discussion, Class Activity, Independent Practice, Cooperative Learning
Introduction:	Discuss student-designed projects from Learning Styles, Day 5 of 12.
Instruction:	Have students do Paired-Learning Activity (TWE p. 92).
	Brainstorm with Using the Section Preview (TWE p. 92).
	Use Teaching Strategy (TWE p. 93).
	Discuss Observation – Ideal and Real Culture (TWE p. 94).
Close:	As needed, have students do the Ch. 3 Increasing Your Reading Comprehension worksheet in the *Unit 2 Booklet*, TRB.
	Ask students to read Sec. 5: Cultural Diversity and Similarity – Cultural Change; Cultural Diversity (pp. 95-98).

Notes and Comments: _____

_____

_____

_____

_____

_____

_____

_____

_____

Chapter 3

CULTURE

Day 24

Week of _____

Day 8 of 12

Content:	Ch. 3, Sec. 5: Cultural Diversity and Similarity – Cultural Change; Cultural Diversity (pp. 95-98)
Objective:	Students will discuss how cultural diversity is promoted within a society.
Act. Type:	Class Discussion, Class Activity, Independent Practice, Cooperative Learning, Experiment
Introduction:	Explain Using the Section Preview (TWE p. 95).
Instruction:	Present and discuss Using Problem-Solving Skills (TWE p. 95).
	Discuss and do activities in Survey (TWE pp. 96-97) and/or Survey (TWE p. 98).
Close:	Read and discuss Focus on Research-How Do Schools and Parents Fail Teens? (TWE pp. 96-97).
	Ask students to read Sec. 5: Cultural Diversity and Similarity – Ethnocentrism; Cultural Universals (pp. 98-102).

Notes and Comments: _____

_____

_____

_____

_____

_____

_____

_____

_____

Chapter 3

CULTURE

Day 25

Week of _____

Content:	Ch. 3, Sec. 5: Cultural Diversity and Similarity – Ethnocentrism; Cultural Universals (pp. 98-102)
Objective:	Students will compare and contrast cultural norms among subculture groups.
Act. Type:	Class Discussion, Class Activity, Independent Practice, Cooperative Learning, Debate
Introduction:	Discuss Reinforcing Vocabulary-Ethnocentrism (TWE p. 100).
Instruction:	Ask student to do Cooperative Learning Activity (TWE p. 100).
	Have students interpret the map in Snapshot of America (TWE p. 101).
	Discuss and have students analyze the graph in Working with the Data-Fig. 3.5 (TWE p. 102).
Close:	Remind students that chapter presentations are due the following class session.

Notes and Comments: _____

_____

_____

_____

_____

_____

_____

_____

_____

_____

_____

Chapter 3

CULTURE

Day 26

Week of _____

Day 10 of 12

Content:	Chapter 3 (pp. 70-102)
Objective:	Students will present projects and activities summarizing objective/s learned in the chapter.
Act. Type:	Class Activity and Presentation
Introduction:	Read and discuss Tech Trends-Star Wars and the Internet (TWE p. 99).
Instruction:	Have students do presentations (See TWE, Chapter Assessment: Sociology Projects and Technology Activities, pp. 104-105).
Close:	Assign Chapter 3 Learning Goals Outline (see *Unit 2 Booklet*, TRB), due the day of the chapter evaluation.

Notes and Comments: _____

_____

_____

_____

_____

_____

_____

_____

_____

_____

_____

_____

_____

Day 27   Week of _____

Day 11 of 12

Content: Ch. 3, Assessment (pp. 103-105)

Objective: Students will review for evaluation of the concepts learned in this chapter.

Act. Type: Class Discussion, Class Activity, Independent Practice, Cooperative Learning, Demonstration, Experiment, Debate, Role-playing, Presentation

Introduction: Review Chapter 3 Vocabulary Activity homework (see *Unit 2 Booklet*, TRB).

Instruction: Do Chapter Assessment as needed (TWE pp. 103-105).

Close: Remind students to study for the chapter evaluation.

Notes and Comments: _____

_____

_____

_____

_____

_____

_____

_____

_____

_____

_____

_____

_____

_____

_____

_____

Day 28

Week of _____

Day 12 of 12

Evaluate: To evaluate the students' comprehension of the chapter, administer Chapter 3 Test A or B. You may want to use the Alternative Assessment found in the TRB.

Close: Discuss Enrichment Reading (TWE pp. 106-107). Assign Chapter 4 intro. (pp. 108-109).

Notes and Comments: _____

_____

_____

_____

_____

_____

_____

_____

_____

_____

_____

_____

_____

_____

_____

_____

_____

170

Chapter 4

SOCIALIZATION

Day 29

Week of _____

Day 1 of 10

Content:	Ch. 4 Intro. (pp. 108-109)
Objective:	Students will understand the importance of socialization.
Act. Type:	Class Discussion, Class Activity
Introduction:	Ask students to do Lead-Off Activity (TWE p. 108-109).
Instruction:	Discuss Key Terms (TWE p. 109).
	Read and discuss Using Your Sociological Imagination (TWE p. 109).
Close:	Assign chapter project (see TWE pp. 134-135, Chapter Assessment: Sociology Projects and Technology Activities) to be presented to the class prior to final chapter evaluation.
	Ask students to read Sec. 1: The Importance of Socialization (pp. 110-114).

Notes and Comments: _____

_____

_____

_____

_____

_____

_____

_____

_____

_____

_____

Day 30

Week of _____

Day 2 of 10

Content:	Ch. 4, Sec. 1: The Importance of Socialization (pp. 110-114)
Objective:	Students will discuss the role socialization plays in human development.
Act. Type:	Class Discussion, Class Activity, Independent Practice, Cooperative Learning, Demonstration, Debate, Presentation
Introduction:	Do demonstration in Using the Section Preview (TWE p. 110).
Instruction:	Use Teaching Strategy (TWE p. 110).
	Ask students to do Interdisciplinary Activity-Animal Research Debate (TWE p. 111).
	Read and discuss Tech Trends (TWE p. 112).
	Ask students to do Learning Styles-Logical-Mathematical (TWE p. 112).
Close:	Ask students to read Sec. 2: Socialization and the Self – The Functionalist and Conflict Perspectives on Socialization (pp. 115-116).
	Assign Chapter 4 Vocabulary Activity (see *Unit 2 booklet,* TRB), due the day of the chapter review.

Notes and Comments: _____

_____

_____

_____

_____

_____

_____

_____

172

Day 31

Week of _____

Day 3 of 10

Content:	Ch. 4, Sec. 2: Socialization and the Self – The Functionalist and Conflict Perspectives on Socialization (pp. 115-116)
Objective:	Students will compare and contrast the functionalist and conflict perspectives on socialization.
Act. Type:	Class Discussion, Class Activity, Independent Practice
Introduction:	Do Using the Section Preview (TWE p. 115).
Instruction:	Discuss Points to Stress (TWE p. 116).
	As students to do On-Demand Writing-Self-Concept (TWE p. 116).
	Ask students to do Working with the Table -Fig. 4.1 (TWE p. 117).
Close:	Ask students to read Sec. 2: Socialization and the Self – Symbolic Interactionism and Socialization (pp. 116-119).

Notes and Comments: _____

_____

_____

_____

_____

_____

_____

_____

_____

_____

_____

Chapter 4

SOCIALIZATION

Day 32

Week of _____

Day 4 of 10

Content: Ch. 4, Sec. 2: Socialization and the Self – Symbolic Interactionism and Socialization (pp. 116-119)

Objective: Students will explain key concepts of socialization from the symbolic interactionist perspective.

Act. Type: Class Discussion, Class Activity, Cooperative Learning, Experiment

Introduction: Do Learning Styles-Musical/Interpersonal (TWE p. 118).

Instruction: Discuss Points to Stress (TWE p. 118).

Use Reteaching (TWE p. 118) for emphasis.

Close: Discuss Pulling It All Together (TWE p. 119).

Ask students to read Sec. 3: Agents of Socialization – The Family and Socialization; Socialization in Schools (pp. 120-123).

Notes and Comments: _____

_____

_____

_____

_____

_____

_____

_____

_____

_____

_____

Chapter 4   SOCIALIZATION

Day 33

Week of _____

Day 5 of 10

Content:	Ch. 4, Sec. 3: Agents of Socialization – The Family and Socialization; Socialization in Schools (pp. 120-123)
Objective:	Students will analyze the roles of the family and school in socializing young people.
Act. Type:	Class Discussion, Class Activity, Demonstration
Introduction:	Read and discuss Another Time (TWE p. 120).
Instruction:	Introduce socialization in the family as in Using the Section Preview (TWE p. 121).
	Discuss Using the Illustration (TWE p. 122).
	Share More About...School Socialization (TWE p. 122).
Close:	Introduce "Writing on the Wall" described in Learning Styles-Visual (TWE pp. 122-123).
	Ask students to read Sec. 3: Agents of Socialization – Peer Group Socialization; The Mass Media and Socialization (pp. 123-127).

Notes and Comments: _____

_____

_____

_____

_____

_____

_____

_____

_____

_____

Day 34

Week of _____

Day 6 of 10

Content:	Ch. 4, Sec. 3: Agents of Socialization – Peer Group Socialization; The Mass Media and Socialization (pp. 123-127)
Objective:	Students will evaluate mass media techniques used to influence perceptions, attitudes, and behaviors of individuals and groups.
Act. Type:	Class Discussion, Class Activity, Cooperative Learning, Presentation
Introduction:	Discuss Points to Stress (TWE p. 123).
Instruction:	Share Making Connections to Other Cultures (TWE p. 123).
	Ask students to do Cooperative Learning Activity (TWE p. 121).
	Ask students to interpret the map in World View (TWE p. 125).
	Do Interdisciplinary Activity-Culture Studies (TWE pp. 124-125).
Close:	Ask students to read Sec. 4: Processes of Socialization (pp. 128-132).

Notes and Comments: _____

_____

_____

_____

_____

_____

_____

_____

_____

_____

_____

_____

176

Chapter 4

SOCIALIZATION

Day 35

Week of _____

Content:	Ch. 4, Sec. 4: Processes of Socialization (pp. 128-132)
Objective:	Students will discuss processes for socialization in adulthood.
Act. Type:	Class Discussion, Class Activity, Independent Practice, Presentation
Introduction:	Follow-up on Interdisciplinary Activity-Culture Studies (TWE pp. 124-125) from previous session.
Instruction:	Read and discuss Sociology Today-Struggling Through the Teen Years (TWE pp. 126-127).
	Share More About...Total Institutions (TWE p. 128).
	Ask students to interpret the map in Snapshot of America (TWE p. 129).
Close:	Assign On-Demand Writing (TWE p. 130).
	Remind students that chapter presentations are due the following class session.

Notes and Comments: _____

_____

_____

_____

_____

_____

_____

_____

_____

_____

_____

         PLANNING GUIDE

Day 36

Week of _____

Day 8 of 10

Content:	Chapter 4 (pp. 108-132)
Objective:	Students will present projects and activities summarizing objective/s learned in the chapter.
Act. Type:	Class Activity, Role Play, and Presentation
Introduction:	Read and do Focus on Research (TWE p. 130-131).
	Ask students to do Role Play (TWE p. 131).
Instruction:	Have student do presentations (See TWE, Chapter Assessment: Sociology Projects and Technology Activities, pp. 134-135).
Close:	Assign Chapter 4 Learning Goals Outline (see *Unit 2 booklet,* TRB), due the day of the chapter evaluation.

Notes and Comments: _____

_____

_____

_____

_____

_____

_____

_____

_____

_____

_____

Day 37

Week of _____

Day 9 of 10

Content:	Ch. 4, Assessment (pp. 133-135)
Objective:	Students will review for evaluation of the concepts learned in this chapter.
Act. Type:	Class Discussion, Class Activity, Independent Practice, Cooperative Learning, Demonstration, Experiment, Debate, Role-playing, Presentation
Introduction:	Review Chapter 4 Vocabulary Activity homework (see *Unit 2 booklet,* TRB).
Instruction:	Do Chapter Assessment as needed (TWE pp. 133-135).
Close:	Remind students to study for the chapter evaluation.

Notes and Comments: _____

_____

_____

_____

_____

_____

_____

_____

_____

_____

_____

_____

_____

_____

Day 38

Week of _____

Day 10 of 10

Evaluate: To evaluate the students' comprehension of the chapter, administer Chapter 4 Test A or B. You may want to use the Alternative Assessment found in the TRB.

Close: Discuss Enrichment Reading (TWE pp. 136-137).

Assign Chapter 5, intro. (pp. 138-139).

Notes and Comments: _____

_____

_____

_____

_____

_____

_____

_____

_____

_____

_____

_____

_____

_____

_____

_____

_____

SOCIAL STRUCTURE AND SOCIETY

Day 39

Week of _____

Day 1 of 12

Content:	Ch. 5 Intro. (pp. 138-139)
Objective:	Students will understand the effects of social structure.
Act. Type:	Class Discussion, Class Activity, Independent Practice, Cooperative Learning, Presentation
Introduction:	Direct students in Lead-Off Activity (TWE p. 138).
Instruction:	Discuss Key Terms (TWE p. 140).
	Read and discuss Using Your Sociological Imagination (TWE p. 139).
Close:	Assign chapter project (see TWE pp. 166-167, Chapter Assessment: Sociology Projects and Technology Activities) to be presented to the class prior to final chapter evaluation. Ask students to read Sec. 1: Social Structure and Status (pp. 140-143).

Notes and Comments: _____

_____

_____

_____

_____

_____

_____

_____

_____

_____

_____

_____

_____

Chapter 5
SOCIAL STRUCTURE AND SOCIETY

Day 40

Week of _____

Day 2 of 12

Content: Ch. 5, Sec. 1: Social Structure and Status (pp. 140-143)

Objective: Students will explain what sociologists mean by social structure and how statuses are related to that social structure.

Act. Type: Class Discussion, Class Activity, Independent Practice, Cooperative Learning, Demonstration, Role-playing

Introduction: Discuss Using the Section Preview (TWE p. 140).

Instruction: Do Demonstration (TWE p. 140).

                      Have students do Role Play activity (TWE p. 141).

                      Use Reteaching (TWE p. 142) suggestion as needed.

Close: Introduce and assign Teaching Strategy-Act.#5 from Ch. Assessment (TWE p. 167).

                      Ask students to read Sec. 2: Social Structure and Roles – Rights and Obligations; Role Performance and Social Interaction (pp. 144-148).

                      Assign Chapter 5 Vocabulary Activity (see *Unit 2 booklet*, TRB), due the day of the chapter review.

Notes and Comments: _____

_____

_____

_____

_____

_____

_____

_____

_____

Day 41

Week of _____

Day 3 of 12

Content:	Ch. 5, Sec. 2: Social Structure and Roles – Rights and Obligations; Role Performance and Social Interaction (pp. 144-148)
Objective:	Students will discuss how roles are related to social structure.
Act. Type:	Class Discussion, Class Activity, Independent Practice, Presentation
Introduction:	Follow up on Teaching Strategy-Act.#5 from Ch. Assessment.
Instruction:	Read and discuss Focus on Research (TWE pp. 144-145).
	As students to do On-Demand Writing (TWE p. 145).
	Ask students to do Demonstration (TWE p. 146).
Close:	Ask students to read Sec. 2: Social Structure and Roles – Role Conflict and Role Strain (pp. 149-151).

Notes and Comments: _____

_____

_____

_____

_____

_____

_____

_____

_____

_____

_____

_____

Chapter 5

SOCIAL STRUCTURE AND SOCIETY

Day 42

Day 4 of 12

Content:	Ch. 5, Sec. 2: Social Structure and Roles – Role Conflict and Role Strain (pp. 149-151)
Objective:	Students will define and explain how to manage role conflict and role strain.
Act. Type:	Class Discussion, Class Activity, Independent Practice, Cooperative Learning, Demonstration, Role-playing
Introduction:	Discuss Using the Section Preview (TWE p. 146).
Instruction:	Ask students to do Role Play (TWE p. 149).
	Ask students to interpret the map in Snapshot of America (TWE p. 149).
	Conduct Survey (TWE p. 150).
	Read and discuss Sociology Today (TWE p. 152).
Close:	Assign Learning Styles-Linguistic/Spatial (TWE p. 147).
	Ask students to read Sec. 3: Preindustrial Societies – Types of Society; Hunting and Gathering Societies; The Hunting and Gathering Society; Horticultural Societies (pp. 153-155).

Notes and Comments: _____

_____

_____

_____

_____

_____

_____

_____

_____

_____

184

Chapter 5 — SOCIAL STRUCTURE AND SOCIETY

Day 43   Week of _____

Day 5 of 12

Content:	Ch. 5, Sec. 3: Preindustrial Societies – Types of Society; Hunting and Gathering Societies; The Hunting and Gathering Society; Horticultural Societies (pp. 153-155)
Objective:	Students will describe the means of subsistence in the following preindustrial societies – hunting and gathering, horticultural.
Act. Type:	Class Discussion, Class Activity, Demonstration, Presentation, Independent Practice
Introduction:	Show video as described in Using the Section Preview (TWE p. 153).
Instruction:	Do Demonstration (TWE p. 153).
	*Optional - Do Interdisciplinary Activity (TWE p. 154).
Close:	Assign Learning Styles-Artistic (TWE p. 155) as appropriate.
	Ask students to read Sec. 3: Preindustrial Societies – Pastoral Societies; Agricultural Societies (pp. 156-157).

Notes and Comments: _____

_____

_____

_____

_____

_____

_____

_____

_____

_____

_____

Day 44   Week of _____

Day 6 of 12

Content:	Ch. 5, Sec. 3: Preindustrial Societies – Pastoral Societies; Agricultural Societies (pp. 156-157)
Objective:	Students will describe the means of subsistence in the following preindustrial societies – pastoral, agricultural.
Act. Type:	Class Discussion, Class Activity, Independent Practice, Cooperative Learning
Introduction:	Discuss Using the Illustration-Timeline (TWE p. 155).
Instruction:	Ask students to do Paired Learning Activity (TWE p. 156).
	Discuss Pulling It All Together (TWE p. 156).
Close:	Ask students to read Sec. 4: Industrial and Postindustrial Societies – Basic Features of Industrial Societies (pp. 158-160).

Notes and Comments: _____

_____

_____

_____

_____

_____

_____

_____

_____

_____

_____

_____

Chapter 5 SOCIAL STRUCTURE AND SOCIETY

Day 45

Week of _____

Day 7 of 12

Content: Ch. 5, Sec. 4: Industrial and Postindustrial Societies – Basic Features of Industrial Societies (pp. 158-160)

Objective: Students will describe changes that take place when agricultural societies become industrial societies.

Act. Type: Class Discussion, Class Activity, Cooperative Learning, Role-playing, Presentation

Introduction: Read and discuss Another Place (TWE p. 158).

Instruction: Share information in Using the Section Preview (TWE p. 159).

Ask students to do Role Play (TWE p. 160).

Close: Discuss World View (TWE p. 161).

Ask students to read Sec. 4: Industrial and Postindustrial Societies – A Conversation with Two Sociologists (pp. 160-162).

Notes and Comments: _____

_____

_____

_____

_____

_____

_____

_____

_____

_____

Chapter 5

SOCIAL STRUCTURE AND SOCIETY

Day 46

Week of _____

Content:	Ch. 5, Sec. 4: Industrial and Postindustrial Societies – A Conversation with Two Sociologists (pp. 160-162)
Objective:	Students will explain the contributions of early sociologists who wrote about preindustrial and industrial societies.
Act. Type:	Class Discussion, Class Activity, Cooperative Learning, Role-playing, Presentation
Introduction:	Discuss and do activity in Using Decision-Making Skills (TWE p. 162).
Instruction:	Discuss and ask students to do Learning Styles-Bodily/Kinesthetic (TWE p. 159).
Close:	Ask students to read Sec. 4: Industrial and Postindustrial Societies – Major Features of Postindustrial Society; Social Instability in Postindustrial Society (pp. 162-163).

Notes and Comments: _____

_____

_____

_____

_____

_____

_____

_____

_____

_____

_____

_____

_____

Chapter 5 SOCIAL STRUCTURE AND SOCIETY

Day 47

Week of _____

Day 9 of 12

Content:	Ch. 5, Sec. 4: Industrial and Postindustrial Societies – Major Features of Postindustrial Society; Social Instability in Postindustrial Society (pp. 162-163)
Objective:	Students will analyze changes resulting from industrialization.
Act. Type:	Class Discussion, Class Activity
Introduction:	Discuss Pulling It All Together (TWE p. 163).
Instruction:	Share information in Points to Stress (TWE p. 162).
	Use Reteaching suggestion (TWE p. 162) as needed.
	*Optional - Do Encouraging Citizenship activity (TWE p. 163).
Close:	Remind students that chapter presentations are due the following class session.

Notes and Comments: _____

_____

_____

_____

_____

_____

_____

_____

_____

_____

_____

_____

Chapter 5

SOCIAL STRUCTURE AND SOCIETY

Day 48   Week of _____

Day 10 of 12

Content:	Chapter 5 (pp. 138-164)
Objective:	Students will present projects and activities summarizing objective/s learned in the chapter.
Act. Type:	Class Activity, Cooperative Learning, and Presentation
Introduction:	Read and discuss Tech Trends (TWE p. 164).
	Have students do Cooperative Learning Activity (TWE p. 164).
Instruction:	Have students do presentations (See TWE Chapter Assessment: Sociology Projects and Technology Activities, pp. 166-167).
Close:	Assign Chapter 5 Learning Goals Outline (see *Unit 2 booklet*, TRB), due the day of the chapter evaluation.

Notes and Comments: _____

_____

_____

_____

_____

_____

_____

_____

_____

_____

_____

_____

_____

Day 49

Week of _____

Day 11 of 12

Content:	Ch. 5, Assessment (pp. 165)
Objective:	Students will review for evaluation of the concepts learned in this chapter.
Act. Type:	Class Discussion, Class Activity, Independent Practice, Cooperative Learning, Demonstration, Experiment, Debate, Role-playing, Presentation
Introduction:	Review Chapter 5 Vocabulary Activity homework (see *Unit 2 booklet,* TRB).
Instruction:	Do Chapter Assessment as needed (TWE pp. 165-167)
Close:	Remind students to study for the chapter evaluation.

Notes and Comments: _____

_____

_____

_____

_____

_____

_____

_____

_____

_____

_____

_____

_____

_____

_____

SOCIAL STRUCTURE AND SOCIETY

Day 50

Week of _____

Day 12 of 12

Evaluate: To evaluate the students' comprehension of the chapter, administer Chapter 5 Test A or B. You may want to use the Alternative Assessment found in the TRB.

Close: Discuss Enrichment Reading (TWE pp. 168-169). Assign Chapter 6, intro. (pp. 170-171).

Notes and Comments: _____

_____

_____

_____

_____

_____

_____

_____

_____

_____

_____

_____

_____

_____

_____

_____

_____

_____

GROUPS AND FORMAL ORGANIZATIONS

Day 51

Week of _____

Day 1 of 10

Content:	Ch. 6 Intro. (pp. 170-171)
Objective:	Students will understand the effects of group membership.
Act. Type:	Class Discussion, Class Activity, Independent Practice
Introduction:	Introduce Lead-Off Activity (TWE p. 170).
Instruction:	Discuss Key Terms (p. 172).
	Read and discuss Using Your Sociological Imagination (TWE p. 171).
Close:	Assign chapter project (see TWE pp. 198-199, Chapter Assessment: Sociology Projects and Technology Activities) to be presented to the class prior to final chapter evaluation. Ask students to read Sec. 1: Primary and Secondary Groups – Groups, Categories, and Aggregates; Primary Groups (pp. 172-174).

Notes and Comments: _____

_____

_____

_____

_____

_____

_____

_____

_____

_____

_____

_____

_____

Day 52

Week of _____

Day 2 of 10

Content:	Ch. 6, Sec. 1: Primary and Secondary Groups – Groups, Categories, and Aggregates; Primary Groups (pp. 172-174)
Objective:	Students will compare the roles of group membership in primary groups.
Act. Type:	Class Discussion, Class Activity, Independent Practice
Introduction:	Introduce Using the Section Preview (TWE p. 172).
Instruction:	Ask students to do On-Demand Writing (TWE p. 172).
	Discuss Using the Illustration (TWE p. 172).
	Share and discuss More About...Gender Interaction (TWE p. 173).
Close:	Ask students to read Sec. 1: Primary and Secondary Groups – Secondary Groups (pp. 174-175). Assign Chapter 6 Vocabulary Activity (see *Unit 2 Booklet*, TRB), due the day of the chapter review.

Notes and Comments: _____

_____

_____

_____

_____

_____

_____

_____

_____

_____

_____

_____

194

Chapter 6

GROUPS AND FORMAL ORGANIZATIONS

Day 53

Day 3 of 10

Content: Ch. 6, Sec. 1: Primary and Secondary Groups – Secondary Groups (pp. 174-175)

Objective: Students will compare the roles of group membership in secondary groups.

Act. Type: Class Discussion, Class Activity, Independent Practice, Cooperative Learning, Demonstration

Introduction: Do activity as described in Making Connections to Other Cultures (TWE p. 174).

Instruction: Ask students to do Observation (TWE p. 174).

Conduct Survey-Primary and Secondary Groups (TWE p. 175).

Close: Ask students to read Sec. 2: Other Groups and Networks (pp. 177-179).

Notes and Comments: _____

_____

_____

_____

_____

_____

_____

_____

_____

_____

_____

_____

Day 54

Week of _____

Day 4 of 10

Content:	Ch. 6, Sec. 2: Other Groups and Networks (pp. 177-179)
Objective:	Students will explain the purposes of reference groups and social networks.
Act. Type:	Class Discussion, Class Activity, Independent Practice, Cooperative Learning, Presentation
Introduction:	Brainstorm as in Using the Section Preview (TWE p. 177).
	Discuss Using the Illustration (TWE p. 178).
Instruction:	Facilitate students in doing Cooperative Learning Activity (TWE p. 177).
	Do Observation (TWE p. 178).
Close:	Ask students to read Sec. 3: Types of Social Interaction – Five Types of Group Social Interaction; Cooperation; Conflict; Social Exchange (pp. 180-183).

Notes and Comments: _____

_____

_____

_____

_____

_____

_____

_____

_____

_____

_____

_____

_____

Day 55

Week of _____

Day 5 of 10

Content:	Ch. 6, Sec. 3: Types of Social Interaction – Five Types of Group Social Interaction; Cooperation; Conflict; Social Exchange (pp. 180-183)
Objective:	Students will discuss how these interactions affect the members of groups.
Act. Type:	Class Discussion, Class Activity, Independent Practice, Cooperative Learning, Debate
Introduction:	Do Using Problem-Solving Skills (TWE p. 179).
Instruction:	Use Using the Section Preview (TWE p. 181).
	As students to do Cooperative Learning Activity (TWE p. 181).
	Discuss Controversy and Debate (TWE p. 182).
	Discuss Looking Ahead (TWE p. 184).
Close:	Discuss and assign Sociology Today (TWE p. 180).
	Ask students to read Sec. 3: Types of Social Interaction – Coercion; Conformity (pp. 184-186).

Notes and Comments: _____

_____

_____

_____

_____

_____

_____

_____

_____

Day 56

Week of _____

Day 6 of 10

Content: Ch. 6, Sec. 3: Types of Social Interaction – Coercion; Conformity (pp. 184-186)

Objective: Students will compare and contrast coercion and conformity.

Act. Type: Class Discussion, Class Activity, Independent Practice, Cooperative Learning, Demonstration, Experiment

Introduction: Lead students in doing the Encouraging Citizenship Activity (TWE p. 183).

Instruction: Have students do Demonstration (TWE p. 184).

Discuss Using the Illustration (TWE p. 185).

Share and discuss information in Working with the Data-Fig. 6.2 (TWE p. 186).

Close: Assign Learning Styles-Intrapersonal/Linguistic (TWE p. 186). Ask students to read Sec. 4: Formal Organizations (pp. 190-196).

Notes and Comments: _____

_____

_____

_____

_____

_____

_____

_____

_____

_____

Day 57

Week of _____

Day 7 of 10

Content:	Ch. 6, Sec. 4: Formal Organizations (pp. 190-196)
Objective:	Students will discuss the use of power and its effect on the roles of group membership in formal organizations.
Act. Type:	Class Discussion, Class Activity, Independent Practice, Demonstration
Introduction:	Read and discuss Tech Trends (TWE p. 187).
Instruction:	Have students do Using the Section Preview (TWE p. 190).
	Lead Observation (TWE pp. 190-191).
	Review and discuss Working with the Data-Fig. 6.3 (TWE p. 191).
	With students, do Demonstration (TWE p. 193).
Close:	Discuss Snapshot of America (TWE p. 193).
	Remind students that chapter presentations are due the following class session.

Notes and Comments: _____

_____

_____

_____

_____

_____

_____

_____

_____

_____

_____

Day 58

Week of _____

Day 8 of 10

Content:	Chapter 6 (pp. 170-196)
Objective:	Students will present projects and activities summarizing objective/s learned in the chapter.
Act. Type:	Class Activity, Demonstration, and Presentation
Introduction:	Read and discuss Focus on Research (TWE pp. 188-189).
	If possible, do Demonstration (TWE p. 188).
Instruction:	Have students do presentations (See TWE, Chapter Assessment: Sociology Projects and Technology Activities, pp. 198-199)
Close:	Assign Chapter 6 Learning Goals Outline (see *Unit 2 booklet*, TRB), due the day of the chapter evaluation.

Notes and Comments: _____

_____

_____

_____

_____

_____

_____

_____

_____

_____

_____

_____

Day 59

Week of _____

Day 9 of 10

Content:	Ch. 6, Assessment (pp. 197-199)
Objective:	Students will review for evaluation of the concepts learned in this chapter.
Act. Type:	Class Discussion, Class Activity, Independent Practice, Cooperative Learning, Demonstration, Experiment, Debate, Role-playing, Presentation
Introduction:	Review Chapter 6 Vocabulary Activity homework (see *Unit 2 Booklet*, TRB).
Instruction:	Do Chapter Assessment as needed (TWE pp. 197-199).
Close:	Remind students to study for the chapter evaluation.

Notes and Comments: _____

_____

_____

_____

_____

_____

_____

_____

_____

_____

_____

_____

_____

_____

_____

Day 60

Week of _____

Day 10 of 10

Evaluate: To evaluate the students' comprehension of the chapter, administer Chapter 6 Test A or B. You may want to use the Alternative Assessment found in the TRB.

Close: Discuss Enrichment Reading (TWE pp. 200-201).

Assign Chapter 7, intro. (pp. 202-203).

Notes and Comments: _____

_____

_____

_____

_____

_____

_____

_____

_____

_____

_____

_____

_____

_____

_____

_____

_____

Chapter 7

DEVIANCE AND SOCIAL CONTROL

Day 61

Week of _____

Day 1 of 12

Content:	Ch. 7 Intro. (pp. 202-203)
Objective:	Students will understand the effect of social control on deviance.
Act. Type:	Class Discussion, Class Activity, Independent Practice, Demonstration
Introduction:	Have students do Lead-Off Activity (TWE pp. 202-203).
Instruction:	Discuss Key Terms (p. 204).
	Read and discuss Using Your Sociological Imagination (TWE p. 203).
Close:	Assign chapter project (see TWE p. 235, Chapter Assessment: Sociology Projects and Technology Activities) to be presented to the class prior to final chapter evaluation.
	Ask students to read Sec. 1: Deviance and Social Control (pp. 204-208).

Notes and Comments: _____

_____

_____

_____

_____

_____

_____

_____

_____

_____

_____

_____

_____

Day 62

Week of _____

Day 2 of 12

Content:	Ch. 7, Sec. 1: Deviance and Social Control (pp. 204-208)
Objective:	Students will identify the major types of social control.
Act. Type:	Class Discussion, Class Activity, Independent Practice, Debate
Introduction:	Share and discuss Using the Section Preview (TWE p. 204).
Instruction:	Review and discuss Working with the Data-Fig. 7.1 (TWE p. 204).
	Discuss Open-Response Question (TWE p. 204).
	Discuss and do activity/ies in Using Conflict-Resolution Skills (TWE pp. 204-205) or Observation (TWE p. 207).
	Ask students to interpret the map in Snapshot of America (TWE p. 206).
Close:	Discuss Another Time (TWE p. 208).
	Ask students to read Sec. 2: Functionalism and Deviance – Costs and Benefits of Deviance (pp. 209-210).
	Assign Chapter 7 Vocabulary Activity (see *Unit 2 Booklet*, TRB), due the day of the chapter review.

Notes and Comments: _____

_____

_____

_____

_____

_____

_____

_____

_____

_____

Chapter 7 DEVIANCE AND SOCIAL CONTROL

Day 63

Week of _____

Day 3 of 12

Content:	Ch. 7, Sec. 2: Functionalism and Deviance – Costs and Benefits of Deviance (pp. 209-210)
Objective:	Students will explain the positive and negative consequences of deviance.
Act. Type:	Class Discussion, Class Activity, Cooperative Learning, Role-playing
Introduction:	Introduce Using the Section Preview (TWE p. 209).
Instruction:	Ask students to do Role Play (TWE p. 209).
Close:	Ask students to read Sec. 2: Functionalism and Deviance – Strain Theory; Control Theory (pp. 210-212).

Notes and Comments: _____

_____

_____

_____

_____

_____

_____

_____

_____

_____

_____

_____

Chapter 7 DEVIANCE AND SOCIAL CONTROL

Day 64

Week of _____

Day 4 of 12

Content:	Ch. 7, Sec. 2: Functionalism and Deviance – Strain Theory; Control Theory (pp. 210-212)
Objective:	Students will differentiate the major functional theories of deviance.
Act. Type:	Class Discussion, Independent Practice, Debate
Introduction:	Share More About Strain Theory (TWE p. 210).
Instruction:	Share and discuss Controversy and Debate (TWE p. 210).
	Review and discuss Working with the Data-Fig. 7.2 (TWE p. 211).
	Ask students to do On-Demand Writing (TWE p. 210).
Close:	Ask students to read Sec. 3: Symbolic Interactionism and Deviance (pp. 213-217).

Notes and Comments: _____

_____

_____

_____

_____

_____

_____

_____

_____

_____

_____

_____

Chapter 7   DEVIANCE AND SOCIAL CONTROL

Day 65

Week of _____

Day 5 of 12

Content:	Ch. 7, Sec. 3: Symbolic Interactionism and Deviance (pp. 213-217)
Objective:	Students will compare and contrast cultural transmission theory and labeling theory.
Act. Type:	Class Discussion, Class Activity, Independent Practice, Demonstration, Experiment
Introduction:	Read and discuss Sociology Today (TWE p. 213).
Instruction:	Discuss Using the Section Preview (TWE p. 214).
	Share More About...Deviance and Labeling Theory (TWE p. 215).
	Use Teaching Strategy-the Labeling Game (TWE p. 216).
Close:	Assign Interdisciplinary Activity-Creative Writing (TWE p. 217).
	Ask students to read Sec. 4: Conflict Theory and Deviance – Deviance in Industrial Society (p. 218).

Notes and Comments: _____

_____

_____

_____

_____

_____

_____

_____

_____

_____

Chapter 7 DEVIANCE AND SOCIAL CONTROL

Day 66

Week of _____

Day 6 of 12

Content:	Ch. 7, Sec. 4: Conflict Theory and Deviance – Deviance in Industrial Society Society (p. 218)
Objective:	Students will discuss the conflict theory view of deviance.
Act. Type:	Class Discussion, Class Activity, Cooperative Learning, Debate
Introduction:	Share Using the Section Preview (TWE p. 218).
	Discuss and assign Controversy and Debate (TWE p. 219).
Instruction:	Facilitate Cooperative Learning Activity (TWE p. 218).
Close:	Ask students to read Sec. 4: Conflict Theory and Deviance – Race, Ethnicity, and Crime; White Collar Crime (pp. 218-221).

Notes and Comments: _____

_____

_____

_____

_____

_____

_____

_____

_____

_____

_____

_____

_____

Day 67

Week of _____

Day 7 of 12

Content:	Ch. 7, Sec. 4: Conflict Theory and Deviance – Race, Ethnicity, and Crime; White Collar Crime (pp. 218-221)
Objective:	Students will discuss the relationship between minorities, white-collar crime, and the judicial system.
Act. Type:	Class Discussion, Class Activity, Cooperative Learning
Introduction:	Lead students in Cooperative Learning Activity (TWE p. 219).
Instruction:	Ask students to do Reinforcing Vocabulary (TWE p. 220).
	Discuss and do Paired Learning Activity (TWE p. 220).
Close:	Discuss Pulling It All Together (TWE p. 221).
	Ask students to read Sec. 5: Crime and Punishment – Measurement of Crime; Juvenile Crime (pp. 222-227).

Notes and Comments: _____

_____

_____

_____

_____

_____

_____

_____

_____

_____

_____

Chapter 7
DEVIANCE AND SOCIAL CONTROL

Day 68

Week of _____

Day 8 of 12

Content:	Ch. 7, Sec. 5: Crime and Punishment – Measurement of Crime; Juvenile Crime (pp. 222-227)
Objective:	Students will identify the meaning of crime statistics, especially as related to juvenile delinquency.
Act. Type:	Class Discussion, Class Activity, Independent Practice, Demonstration
Introduction:	Read and discuss Focus on Research (TWE pp. 222-223).
Instruction:	Introduce Using the Section Preview (TWE p. 224).
	Do Demonstration (TWE pp. 224-225).
	Review and discuss Working with the Data-Fig.7.6 (TWE p. 225).
Close:	Assign On-Demand Writing (TWE p. 227).
	Ask students to read Sec. 5: Crime and Punishment – Approaches to Crime Control (pp. 227-232).

Notes and Comments: _____

_____

_____

_____

_____

_____

_____

_____

_____

_____

Chapter 7 DEVIANCE AND SOCIAL CONTROL

Day 69   Week of _____

Content:	Ch. 7, Sec. 5: Crime and Punishment – Approaches to Crime Control (pp. 227-232)
Objective:	Students will describe four approaches to crime control.
Act. Type:	Class Discussion, Class Activity, Independent Practice, Cooperative Learning, Presentation
Introduction:	Facilitate Cooperative Learning Activity (TWE p. 226).
Instruction:	Read and discuss Making Connections to Other Cultures (TWE p. 227).
	If possible, use Teaching Strategy (TWE p. 228) or Careers in Sociology (TWE p. 229) to invite a guest speaker to visit your class.
	Read and discuss Tech Trends (TWE p. 228).
Close:	Remind students that chapter presentations are due the following class session.

Notes and Comments: _____

_____

_____

_____

_____

_____

_____

_____

_____

_____

_____

_____

Day 70

Week of _____

Day 10 of 12

Content: Chapter 7 (pp. 202-232).

Objective: Students will present projects and activities summarizing objective/s learned in the chapter.

Act. Type: Class Activity, Role-playing, and Presentation

Introduction: Ask students to Role Play (TWE p. 231).

Instruction: Have students do presentations (See TWE Chapter Assessment: Sociology Projects and Technology Activities, p. 235.)

Close: Assign Chapter 7 Learning Goals Outline (see *Unit 2 booklet*), due the day of the chapter evaluation.

Notes and Comments: _____

_____

_____

_____

_____

_____

_____

_____

_____

_____

_____

_____

_____

_____

212

Chapter 7 DEVIANCE AND SOCIAL CONTROL

Day 71

Day 11 of 12

Content:	Ch. 7, Assessment (pp. 233-235)
Objective:	Students will review for evaluation of the concepts learned in this chapter.
Act. Type:	Class Discussion, Class Activity, Independent Practice, Cooperative Learning, Demonstration, Experiment, Debate, Role-playing, Presentation
Introduction:	Review Chapter 7 Vocabulary Activity homework (see *Unit 2 Booklet*, TRB).
Instruction:	Do Chapter Assessment as needed (TWE pp. 233-235).
Close:	Remind students to study for the chapter evaluation.

Notes and Comments: _____

_____

_____

_____

_____

_____

_____

_____

_____

_____

_____

_____

_____

_____

_____

Day 72

Week of _____

Day 12 of 12

Evaluate: To evaluate the students' comprehension of the chapter, administer Chapter 7 Test A or B. You may want to use the Alternative Assessment found in the TRB. A test for Unit 2 is also available in the TRB.

Close: Discuss Enrichment Reading (TWE pp. 236-237).

Assign Unit 3, Chapter 8 Intro. (pp. 238-241).

Notes and Comments: _____

_____

_____

_____

_____

_____

_____

_____

_____

_____

_____

_____

_____

_____

_____

_____

Chapter 8

SOCIAL STRATIFICATION

Day 73

Week of _____

Day 1 of 12

Content: Unit 3 Intro., and Ch. 8 Intro. (pp. 238-241)

Objective: Students will understand the effects of group membership.

Act. Type: Class Discussion, Class Activity, Independent Practice, Demonstration

Introduction: Use Lead-Off Activity (TWE p. 240-241).

Instruction: Discuss Key Terms (p. 242).

Read and discuss Using Your Sociological Imagination (TWE p. 241).

Close: Assign chapter project (see TWE p. 271, Chapter Assessment: Sociology Projects and Technology Activities) to be presented to the class prior to final chapter evaluation.

Ask students to read Sec. 1: Dimensions of Stratification – Social Stratification and Social Class; The Economic Dimension (pp. 242-245).

Notes and Comments: _____

_____

_____

_____

_____

_____

_____

_____

_____

_____

_____

_____

Chapter 8 — SOCIAL STRATIFICATION

Day 74 Week of _____

Day 2 of 12

Content:	Ch. 8, Sec. 1: Dimensions of Stratification – Social Stratification and Social Class; The Economic Dimension (pp. 242-245)
Objective:	Students will understand how the economic dimension of social stratification affects human motivation.
Act. Type:	Class Discussion, Class Activity, Independent Practice, Cooperative Learning, Debate
Introduction:	Discuss Using the Section Preview (TWE p. 242)
Instruction:	Do activity found in Learning Styles-Bodily-Kinesthetic/Interpersonal (TWE p. 242).
	Ask students to interpret the map in World View (TWE p. 243).
	Share Points to Stress (TWE p. 244).
	Ask students to do On-Demand Writing (TWE p. 244).
Close:	Ask students to read Sec. 1: Dimensions of Stratification – The Power Dimension; The Prestige Dimension (pp. 245-249).
	Assign Chapter 8 Vocabulary Activity (see *Unit 3 Booklet*, TRB), due the day of the chapter review.

Notes and Comments: _____

_____

_____

_____

_____

_____

_____

_____

_____

Day 75

Week of _____

Day 3 of 12

Content:	Ch. 8, Sec. 1: Dimensions of Stratification – The Power Dimension; The Prestige Dimension (pp. 245-249)
Objective:	Students will analyze the relationships among social class and other culture group membership and political power.
Act. Type:	Class Discussion, Class Activity, Independent Practice, Cooperative Learning
Introduction:	Discuss Using the Illustration (TWE p. 246).
	Discuss Reinforcing Vocabulary (TWE p. 246).
Instruction:	Facilitate Cooperative Learning Activity (TWE pp. 246-247).
	Review and discuss Working with the Data-Fig.8.3 (TWE p. 247).
	Share and discuss Careers in Sociology (TWE pp. 248-249).
Close:	Discuss and assign Another Time (TWE p. 249).
	Ask students to read Sec. 2: Explanations of Stratification (pp. 250-253).

Notes and Comments: _____

_____

_____

_____

_____

_____

_____

_____

_____

_____

Day 76

Week of _____

Day 4 of 12

Content:	Ch. 8, Sec. 2: Explanations of Stratification (pp. 250-253)
Objective:	Students will state the differences between the functionalist, conflict, and symbolic interactionist approaches to social stratification.
Act. Type:	Class Discussion, Class Activity, Debate, Role-playing
Introduction:	Share Using the Section Preview (TWE p. 250).
Instruction:	Ask students to Role Play (TWE p. 250).
	Share and discuss Controversy and Debate (TWE p. 251).
	Review and discuss Working with the Data-Fig. 8.4 (TWE p. 252).
Close:	Discuss Focus on Research and Using Problem-Solving Skills (TWE p. 253).
	Ask students to read Sec. 3: Social Classes in America – Class Consciousness; The Upper Class; The Middle Classes (pp. 254-256).

Notes and Comments: _____

_____

_____

_____

_____

_____

_____

_____

_____

_____

Chapter 8

SOCIAL STRATIFICATION

Day 77

Week of _____

Day 5 of 12

Content:	Ch. 8, Sec. 3: Social Classes in America – Class Consciousness; The Upper Class; The Middle Classes (pp. 254-256)
Objective:	Students will compare cultural values associated with socioeconomic stratification of the upper and middle classes.
Act. Type:	Class Discussion, Class Activity, Independent Practice, Cooperative Learning, Demonstration
Introduction:	Do activity/demonstration described in Using the Section Preview (TWE p. 254).
Instruction:	Ask students to conduct a Survey (TWE p. 254).
	Share More About...Social Mobility (TWE p. 255).
	Assign Increasing Your Reading Comprehension (see TRB) as needed.
Close:	Ask students to read Sec. 3: Social Classes in America – The Working Class; The Working Poor; The Underclass (pp. 256-258).

Notes and Comments: _____

_____

_____

_____

_____

_____

_____

_____

_____

_____

Day 78

Week of _____

Day 6 of 12

Content:	Ch. 8, Sec. 3: Social Classes in America – The Working Class; The Working Poor; The Underclass (pp. 256-257)
Objective:	Students will compare cultural values associated with socioeconomic stratification of the working and underclasses.
Act. Type:	Class Discussion, Class Activity, Independent Practice, Cooperative Learning
Introduction:	Share Points to Stress (TWE p. 256).
Instruction:	If possible, use Teaching Strategy (TWE p. 256).
	Have students do Using Decision-Making Skills activity (TWE p. 258).
Close:	Assign On-Demand Writing (TWE p. 257).
	Ask students to read Sec. 4: Poverty in America – Measuring Poverty; Identifying the Poor (pp. 258-261).

Notes and Comments: _____

_____

_____

_____

_____

_____

_____

_____

_____

_____

_____

_____

SOCIAL STRATIFICATION

Day 79

Week of _____

Content:	Ch. 8, Sec. 4: Poverty in America – Measuring Poverty; Identifying the Poor (pp. 258-261)
Objective:	Students will discuss the measurement and extent of poverty in the United States.
Act. Type:	Class Discussion, Class Activity, Independent Practice, Cooperative Learning
Introduction:	Use the Internet to do Using the Section Preview (TWE p. 259).
Instruction:	Ask the students to do Paired Learning Activity (TWE p. 259).
	Discuss Points to Stress (TWE p. 259).
Close:	Discuss and assign Sociology Today – Parenting Across Class Lines (TWE p. 258).
	Ask students to read Sec. 4: Poverty in America – Responses to the Problem of Poverty; Welfare Reform (pp. 262-264).

Notes and Comments: _____

_____

_____

_____

_____

_____

_____

_____

_____

_____

_____

_____

Day 80

Week of _____

Day 8 of 12

Content:	Ch. 8, Sec. 4: Poverty in America – Responses to the Problem of Poverty; Welfare Reform (pp. 262-264).
Objective:	Students will evaluate commitment to poverty programs in the United States.
Act. Type:	Class Discussion, Class Activity, Cooperative Learning, Debate
Introduction:	Discuss and do Using Problem-Solving Skills activity (TWE pp. 260-261).
Instruction:	Lead discussion in Controversy and Debate (TWE p. 260).
	Ask students to do Encouraging Citizenship Activity (TWE p. 263).
Close:	Ask students to read Sec. 5: Social Mobility (pp. 265-268).

Notes and Comments: _____

_____

_____

_____

_____

_____

_____

_____

_____

_____

_____

_____

_____

_____

222

Day 81   Week of _____

Day 9 of 12

Content:	Ch. 8, Sec. 5: Social Mobility (pp. 265-268)
Objective:	Students will analyze the influence of motivation on socioeconomic consequences.
Act. Type:	Class Discussion, Class Activity, Independent Practice, Cooperative Learning, Demonstration
Introduction:	Do demonstration in Using the Section Preview (TWE p. 265).
Instruction:	Facilitate Cooperative Learning Activity (TWE p. 268).
Close:	Assign Learning Styles-Intrapersonal/Spatial (TWE p. 265).
	Remind students that chapter presentations are due the following class session.

Notes and Comments: _____

_____

_____

_____

_____

_____

_____

_____

_____

_____

_____

_____

                                       PLANNING GUIDE

Day 82

Week of _____

Day 10 of 12

Content:	Chapter 8 (pp. 242-268)
Objective:	Students will present projects and activities summarizing objective/s learned in the chapter.
Act. Type:	Class Activity and Presentation
Introduction:	Read and discuss Tech Trends (TWE p. 264).
Instruction:	Have students do presentations (See TWE, Chapter Assessment: Sociology Projects and Technology Activities, p. 271).
Close:	Assign Chapter 8 Learning Goals Outline (see *Unit 3 Booklet*, TRB), due the day of the chapter evaluation.

Notes and Comments: _____

_____

_____

_____

_____

_____

_____

_____

_____

_____

_____

_____

_____

Chapter 8

SOCIAL STRATIFICATION

Day 83

Week of _____

Day 11 of 12

Content: Ch. 8, Assessment (pp. 269-271)

Objective: Students will review for evaluation of the concepts learned in this chapter.

Act. Type: Class Discussion, Class Activity, Independent Practice, Cooperative Learning, Demonstration, Experiment, Debate, Role-playing, Presentation

Introduction: Review Chapter 8 Vocabulary Activity homework (see *Unit 3 Booklet*, TRB).

Instruction: Do Chapter Assessment as needed (TWE pp. 269-271).

Close: Remind students to study for the chapter evaluation.

Notes and Comments: _____

_____

_____

_____

_____

_____

_____

_____

_____

_____

_____

_____

_____

_____

_____

_____

Day 84

Week of _____

Day 12 of 12

Evaluate: To evaluate the students' comprehension of the chapter, administer Chapter 8 Test A or B. You may want to use the Alternative Assessment found in the TRB.

Close: Discuss Enrichment Reading (TWE pp. 272-273).

Assign Chapter 9, intro. (pp. 274-275).

Notes and Comments: _____

_____

_____

_____

_____

_____

_____

_____

_____

_____

_____

_____

_____

_____

_____

_____

_____

_____

_____

_____

226

Chapter 9

INEQUALITIES OF RACE AND ETHNICITY

Day 85

Week of _____

Day 1 of 10

Content:	Ch. 9 Intro. (pp. 274-275)
Objective:	Students will compare various U.S. subculture groups such as ethnic and national origin.
Act. Type:	Class Discussion, Class Activity, Independent Practice, Demonstration
Introduction:	Use Lead-Off Activity (TWE p. 274-275).
Instruction:	Discuss Key Terms (p. 276).
	Read and discuss Using Your Sociological Imagination (TWE p. 275).
Close:	Assign chapter project (see TWE p. 305, Chapter Assessment: Sociology Projects and Technology Activities) to be presented to the class prior to final chapter evaluation.
	Ask students to read Sec. 1: Minority, Race, and Ethnicity (pp. 276-279).

Notes and Comments: _____

_____

_____

_____

_____

_____

_____

_____

_____

_____

_____

_____

Chapter 9 — INEQUALITIES OF RACE AND ETHNICITY

Day 86

Week of _____

Day 2 of 10

Content:	Ch. 9, Sec. 1: Minority, Race, and Ethnicity (pp. 276-279)
Objective:	Students will describe what sociologists mean by minority, race, and ethnicity.
Act. Type:	Class Discussion, Class Activity, Independent Practice, Cooperative Learning
Introduction:	Do Using the Section Preview (TWE p. 276).
Instruction:	Use Teaching Strategy (TWE p. 276).
	Ask students to do Survey (TWE p. 276).
	Ask Open-Response Question (TWE p. 277).
	Review and discuss Working with the Data (TWE p. 278).
Close:	Do Making Connections to Other Cultures (TWE p. 278).
	Ask students to read Sec. 2: Racial and Ethnic Relations (pp. 280-283).
	Assign Chapter 9 Vocabulary Activity (see *Unit 3 Booklet*, TRB), due the day of the chapter review.

Notes and Comments: _____

_____

_____

_____

_____

_____

_____

_____

_____

Day 87

Week of _____

Day 3 of 10

Content:	Ch. 9, Sec. 2: Racial and Ethnic Relations
Objective:	Students will discuss patterns of racial and ethnic relations.
Act. Type:	Class Discussion, Class Activity, Independent Practice, Cooperative Learning, Demonstration
Introduction:	Read and discuss Another Place – The Travelling People (TWE p. 279).
Instruction:	Discuss Using the Section Preview (TWE p. 280).
	Ask students to do Using Problem-Solving Skills (TWE pp. 280-281).
	Do Pulling It All Together activity (TWE p. 282).
Close:	Read and discuss Sociology Today – Bridging the Digital Divide (TWE p. 283).
	Ask students to read Sec. 3: Theories of Prejudice and Discrimination – Prejudice, Racism, and Discrimination; Hate Crimes; Stereotypes (pp. 284-286).

Notes and Comments: _____

_____

_____

_____

_____

_____

_____

_____

_____

_____

_____

Day 88

Week of _____

Day 4 of 10

Content:	Ch. 9, Sec. 3: Theories of Prejudice and Discrimination – Prejudice, Racism, and Discrimination; Hate Crimes; Stereotypes (pp. 284-286)
Objective:	Students will discuss the difference between prejudice and discrimination.
Act. Type:	Class Discussion, Class Activity, Independent Practice, Cooperative Learning, Debate
Introduction:	Read and debate Using the Section Preview (TWE p. 284).
Instruction:	Discuss Open-Response Question (TWE p. 284).
	Have students do the Survey (TWE p. 284).
	Use the first Teaching Strategy (TWE p. 286).
	Do Learning Styles-Visual/Spatial activity (TWE pp. 286-287).
Close:	Ask students to read Sec. 3: Theories of Prejudice and Discrimination – The Functionalist Perspective; The Conflict Perspective; The Symbolic Interactionist Perspective (pp. 286-289).

Notes and Comments: _____

_____

_____

_____

_____

_____

_____

_____

_____

_____

_____

Day 89   Week of _____

Day 5 of 10

Content:	Ch. 9, Sec. 3: Theories of Prejudice and Discrimination – The Functionalist Perspective; The Conflict Perspective; The Symbolic Interactionist Perspective (pp. 286-289)
Objective:	Students will compare and contrast the perspectives of the three theories.
Act. Type:	Class Discussion, Class Activity, Independent Practice
Introduction:	Use the second Teaching Strategy (TWE p. 286).
Instruction:	Ask students to interpret the map in Snapshot of America (TWE p. 287).
	Share information in Teaching Strategy (TWE p. 287).
	Review and discuss Working with the Data (TWE p. 288).
Close:	Read and discuss Tech Trends-Spinning a Web of Hate (TWE p. 289).
	Ask students to read Sec. 4: Minority Groups in the United States – Institutionalized Discrimination; African Americans; Latinos (pp. 290-295).

Notes and Comments: _____

_____

_____

_____

_____

_____

_____

_____

_____

_____

_____

INEQUALITIES OF RACE AND ETHNICITY

Day 90

Week of _____

Day 6 of 10

Content:	Ch. 9, Sec. 4: Minority Groups in the United States – Institutionalized Discrimination; African Americans; Latinos (pp. 290-295)
Objective:	Students will compare cultural socialization, norms, values, motivation, and communication between subculture groups.
Act. Type:	Class Discussion, Class Activity, Independent Practice, Cooperative Learning, Demonstration, Experiment, Debate, Role-playing, Presentation
Introduction:	Do demonstration activity in Using the Section Preview (TWE p. 290).
Instruction:	Ask students to do Demonstration (TWE p. 290).
	If possible, use Teaching Strategy (TWE p. 291).
	Review and discuss Working with the Data (TWE p. 292 and p. 294).
	Introduce and assign Learning Styles – Interpersonal (TWE pp. 292-293).
Close:	Assign Cooperative Learning Activity (TWE p. 291).
	Ask students to read Sec. 4: Minority Groups in the United States – Native Americans; Asian Americans; White Ethnics (pp. 295-301).

Notes and Comments: _____

_____

_____

_____

_____

_____

_____

_____

_____

Chapter 9

INEQUALITIES OF RACE AND ETHNICITY

Day 91   Week of _____

Day 7 of 10

Content:	Ch. 9, Sec. 4: Minority Groups in the United States – Native Americans; Asian Americans; White Ethnics (pp. 295-301)
Objective:	Students will compare cultural socialization, norms, values, motivation, and communication between subculture groups.
Act. Type:	Class Discussion, Class Activity, Independent Practice, Demonstration, Debate
Introduction:	Discuss and assign Learning Styles-Visual (TWE p. 295).
Instruction:	Use Teaching Strategy (TWE p. 296).
	Have students research and debate Controversy and Debate-Casinos and Gambling (TWE p. 296).
	Discuss information in the first Teaching Strategy (TWE p. 297).
	Share Points to Stress (TWE p. 297).
	Review and discuss Working with the Data (TWE p. 300).
	Do Demonstration (TWE pp. 300-301).
Close:	Read and discuss Focus on Research (TWE pp. 298-299).
	Remind students that chapter presentations are due the following class session.

Notes and Comments: _____

_____

_____

_____

_____

_____

_____

Chapter 9

INEQUALITIES OF RACE AND ETHNICITY

Day 92

Week of _____

Day 8 of 10

Content: Chapter 9 (pp. 274-301)

Objective: Students will present projects and activities summarizing objective/s learned in the chapter.

Act. Type: Class Activity and Presentation

Introduction: Discuss Pulling It All Together (TWE p. 301).

Instruction: Have students do presentations (See TWE, Chapter Assessment: Sociology Projects and Technology Activities, p. 305).

Close: Assign Chapter 9 Learning Goals Outline (see *Unit 3 Booklet*, TRB), due the day of the chapter evaluation.

Notes and Comments: _____

_____

_____

_____

_____

_____

_____

_____

_____

_____

_____

_____

_____

Day 93

Week of _____

Day 9 of 10

Content:	Ch. 9, Assessment (pp. 302-305)
Objective:	Students will review for evaluation of the concepts learned in this chapter.
Act. Type:	Class Discussion, Class Activity, Independent Practice, Cooperative Learning, Demonstration, Experiment, Debate, Role-playing, Presentation
Introduction:	Review Chapter 9 Vocabulary Activity homework (see *Unit 3 Booklet*, TRB).
Instruction:	Do Chapter Assessment as needed (TWE pp. 302-305)
Close:	Remind students to study for the chapter evaluation.

Notes and Comments: _____

_____

_____

_____

_____

_____

_____

_____

_____

_____

_____

_____

_____

_____

_____

_____

Chapter 9

INEQUALITIES OF RACE AND ETHNICITY

Day 94

Week of _____

Day 10 of 10

Evaluate: To evaluate the students' comprehension of the chapter, administer Chapter 9 Test A or B. You may want to use the Alternative Assessment found in the TRB.

Close: Discuss Enrichment Reading (TWE pp. 306-307).

Assign Chapter 10 intro. (pp. 308-309).

Notes and Comments: _____

_____

_____

_____

_____

_____

_____

_____

_____

_____

_____

_____

_____

_____

_____

_____

_____

_____

_____

Day 95

Week of _____

Day 1 of 12

Content:	Ch. 10 Intro. (pp. 308-309)
Objective:	Students will compare various U.S. subculture groups such as gender and age.
Act. Type:	Class Discussion, Class Activity, Independent Practice, Demonstration
Introduction:	Use Lead-Off Activity (TWE p. 308).
Instruction:	Do Demonstration (TWE p. 309).
	Discuss Using the Illustration (TWE p. 309).
	Read and discuss Using Your Sociological Imagination (TWE p. 309).
Close:	Assign chapter project (see TWE pp. 340-341, Chapter Assessment: Sociology Projects and Technology Activities) to be presented to the class prior to final chapter evaluation.
	Ask students to read Sec. 1: Sex and Gender Identity – Defining Male and Female.

Notes and Comments: _____

_____

_____

_____

_____

_____

_____

_____

_____

_____

_____

_____

Chapter 10 INEQUALITIES OF GENDER AND AGE

Day 96

Week of ______________________________

Day 2 of 12

Content: Ch. 10, Sec. 1: Sex and Gender Identity – Defining Male and Female

Objective: Students will distinguish the concepts of sex, gender, and gender identity.

Act. Type: Class Discussion, Class Activity, Independent Practice, Cooperative Learning, Demonstration, Presentation

Introduction: Introduce Using the Section Preview (TWE p. 310).

Instruction: Use Teaching Strategy to make assignment (TWE p. 310).

Have students do Cooperative Learning Activity (TWE pp. 310-311).

Close: Assign Chapter 10 Vocabulary Activity (see *Unit 3 Booklet*, TRB), due the day of the chapter review.

Ask students to read Sec. 1: Sex and Gender Identity – Biology, Culture, and Behavior (pp. 312-315).

Notes and Comments: ______________________________

Day 97   Week of _____

Day 3 of 12

Content: Ch. 10, Sec. 1: Sex and Gender Identity – Biology, Culture, and Behavior (pp. 312-315)

Objective: Students will discuss the research findings regarding gender and behavior.

Act. Type: Class Discussion, Class Activity, Independent Practice, Demonstration, Experiment

Introduction: Emphasize definitions using Points to Stress (TWE p. 312).

Instruction: Discuss and ask students to do Demonstration (TWE pp. 314-315).

Discuss Points to Stress (TWE p. 313).

Close: Read and discuss Another Time-Manly Hearted Woman (TWE p. 315).

Ask students to read Sec. 2: Theoretical Perspectives on Gender (pp. 316-320).

Notes and Comments: _____

_____

_____

_____

_____

_____

_____

_____

_____

_____

_____

INEQUALITIES OF GENDER AND AGE

Day 98

Week of ______________________________

Day 4 of 12

Content: Ch. 10, Sec. 2: Theoretical Perspectives on Gender (pp. 316-320)

Objective: Students will outline the perspectives on gender taken by the three theories.

Act. Type: Class Discussion, Class Activity, Independent Practice, Demonstration

Introduction: Do Demonstration-Gender Roles (TWE p. 318-319).

Discuss Using the Section Preview (TWE p. 316).

Instruction: Ask students to do On-Demand Writing (TWE p. 316).

If possible, ask students to do Demonstration (TWE p. 317).

Ask students to interpret the map in World View (TWE p. 318).

Review and discuss Working with the Data (TWE p. 319).

Close: Ask students to read Sec. 3: Gender Inequality – Women as a Minority Group; Occupational and Economic Inequality (pp. 320-325).

Notes and Comments: ______________________________

Day 99   Week of _____

Day 5 of 12

Content:	Ch. 10, Sec. 3: Gender Inequality – Women as a Minority Group; Occupational and Economic Inequality (pp. 320-325)
Objective:	Students will describe the occupational and economic status of women in the United States.
Act. Type:	Class Discussion, Class Activity, Independent Practice, Cooperative Learning, Debate
Introduction:	Read and discuss Sociology Today-Gender-Based Hierarchy (TWE p. 321).
Instruction:	Share Using the Section Preview (TWE p. 322).
	Review and discuss Working with the Data (TWE p. 323), (TWE p. 324), and (TWE p. 325).
	Use activity in Controversy and Debate (TWE p. 324).
Close:	Assign Observation (TWE p. 322).
	Ask students to read Sec. 3: Gender Inequality – Legal and Political Inequality (pp. 325-329).

Notes and Comments: _____

_____

_____

_____

_____

_____

_____

_____

_____

_____

Day 100   Week of _____

Day 6 of 12

Content:	Ch. 10, Sec. 3: Gender Inequality – Legal and Political Inequality (pp. 325-329)
Objective:	Students will describe the legal and political status of women in the United States.
Act. Type:	Class Discussion, Class Activity, Independent Practice, Cooperative Learning, Role-playing
Introduction:	Discuss results from Observation assignment (TWE p. 322).
Instruction:	Review and discuss Working with the Data (TWE p. 326 and p. 327).
	Have students do role-plays as in Teaching Strategy (TWE p. 327).
	Ask students to do Paired-Learning Activity (TWE p. 328).
Close:	Read and discuss Tech Trends-Men, Women, and the Internet (TWE p. 329).
	Ask students to read Sec. 4: Ageism (pp. 330-332).

Notes and Comments: _____

_____

_____

_____

_____

_____

_____

_____

_____

_____

_____

Chapter 10 INEQUALITIES OF GENDER AND AGE

Day 101

Week of _____

Day 7 of 12

Content:	Ch. 10, Sec. 4: Ageism (pp. 330-332)
Objective:	Students will distinguish between age stratification and ageism.
Act. Type:	Class Discussion, Class Activity, Independent Practice, Cooperative Learning
Introduction:	Ask students to do Cooperative Learning Activity (TWE p. 329).
Instruction:	Do the activity in Using the Section Preview (TWE p. 330).
	Discuss Points to Stress (TWE p. 331).
	Review and discuss Working with the Data (TWE p. 331).
Close:	Discuss and assign Using Problem-Solving Skills (TWE p. 332).
	Ask students to read Sec. 5: Inequality in America's Elderly Population – Elderly People as a Minority Group; Economics of the Elderly (pp. 333-336).

Notes and Comments: _____

_____

_____

_____

_____

_____

_____

_____

_____

_____

_____

Day 102

Week of _____

Day 8 of 12

Content:	Ch. 10, Sec. 5: Inequality in America's Elderly Population – Elderly People as a Minority Group; Economics of the Elderly (pp. 333-336)
Objective:	Students will describe the economic status of the elderly in the United States.
Act. Type:	Class Discussion, Class Activity, Independent Practice
Introduction:	Do Internet activity in Using the Section Preview (TWE p. 333).
Instruction:	Read and discuss Focus on Research (TWE pp. 334-335).
	Discuss and ask students to do On-Demand Writing (TWE pp. 334-335).
Close:	Assign Encouraging Citizenship Activity (TWE p. 333).
	Ask students to read Sec. 5: Inequality in America's Elderly Population – Political Power and the Elderly (pp. 337-

Notes and Comments: _____

_____

_____

_____

_____

_____

_____

_____

_____

_____

_____

_____

_____

Chapter 10 INEQUALITIES OF GENDER AND AGE

Day 103   Week of _____

Day 9 of 12

Content:	Ch. 10, Sec. 5: Inequality in America's Elderly Population – Political Power and the Elderly
Objective:	Students will describe the legal and political status of the elderly in the United States.
Act. Type:	Class Discussion, Class Activity, Independent Practice, Demonstration
Introduction:	Discuss Open-Response Question (TWE p. 336).
Instruction:	Ask students to interpret the map in Snapshot of America (TWE p. 337).
	Ask students to do On-Demand Writing (TWE p. 336).
	Review and discuss Working with the Data (TWE p. 338).
Close:	Discuss and assign Learning Styles-Musical/Interpersonal (TWE p. 337).
	Remind students that chapter presentations are due the following class session.

Notes and Comments: _____

_____

_____

_____

_____

_____

_____

_____

_____

_____

_____

                                       PLANNING GUIDE

Chapter 10 INEQUALITIES OF GENDER AND AGE

Day 104

Week of ______________________

Day 10 of 12

Content: Chapter 10 (pp. 308-338)

Objective: Students will present projects and activities summarizing objective/s learned in the chapter.

Act. Type: Class Activity and Presentation

Introduction: Discuss results from Learning Styles-Musical/Interpersonal activity (TWE p. 337).

Instruction: Have students do presentations (See TWE, Chapter Assessment: Sociology Projects and Technology Activities, pp. 340-341).

Close: Assign Chapter 10 Learning Goals Outline (see *Unit 3 Booklet*, TRB), due the day of the chapter evaluation.

Notes and Comments: ______________________

Chapter 10 — INEQUALITIES OF GENDER AND AGE

Day 105

Week of _____

Day 11 of 12

Content:	Ch. 10, Assessment (pp. 339-341)
Objective:	Students will review for evaluation of the concepts learned in this chapter.
Act. Type:	Class Discussion, Class Activity, Independent Practice, Cooperative Learning, Demonstration, Experiment, Debate, Role-playing, Presentation
Introduction:	Review Chapter 10 Vocabulary Activity homework (see *Unit 3 Booklet*, TRB).
Instruction:	Do Chapter Assessment as needed (TWE pp. 339-341).
Close:	Remind students to study for the chapter evaluation.

Notes and Comments: _____

_____

_____

_____

_____

_____

_____

_____

_____

_____

_____

_____

_____

_____

Day 106

Week of _____

Day 12 of 12

Evaluate: To evaluate the students' comprehension of the chapter, administer Chapter 10 Test A or B. You may want to use the Alternative Assessment found in the TRB.

Close: Discuss Enrichment Reading (TWE pp. 342-343).

Ask students to do On-Demand Writing (TWE p. 313).

Assign Unit 4 Intro., Chapter 11 intro. (pp. 344-347).

Notes and Comments: _____

_____

_____

_____

_____

_____

_____

_____

_____

_____

_____

_____

_____

_____

_____

_____

_____

248

Chapter 11

THE FAMILY

Day 107

Week of _____

Day 1 of 10

Content:	Unit 4 Intro., Chapter 11 intro. (pp. 344-347)
Objective:	Students will understand how the social institution of family meets basic needs in society.
Act. Type:	Class Discussion, Class Activity, Independent Practice
Introduction:	Use Lead-Off Activity (TWE p. 346).
Instruction:	Discuss Key Terms (p. 348).
	Read and discuss Using Your Sociological Imagination (TWE p. 347).
Close:	Assign chapter project (see Chapter Assessment: Sociology Projects and Technology Activities) to be presented to the class prior to final chapter evaluation.
	Ask students to read Sec. 1: Family and Marriage Across Cultures – Defining the Family; Two Basic Types of Families; Patterns of Family Structure (pp. 348-351).

Notes and Comments: _____

_____

_____

_____

_____

_____

_____

_____

_____

_____

_____

_____

Chapter 11

THE FAMILY

Day 108   Week of _____

Day 2 of 10

Content: Ch. 11, Sec. 1: Family and Marriage Across Cultures – Defining the Family; Two Basic Types of Families; Patterns of Family Structure (pp. 348-351)

Objective: Students will summarize the functions of the social institution of the family.

Act. Type: Class Discussion, Class Activity, Independent Practice, Demonstration, Presentation

Introduction: Ask students to do Cooperative Learning Activity (TWE p. 348).

Instruction: Ask students to write in response to Open-Response Question (TWE p. 348).

Share and discuss Using the Section Preview (TWE p. 348).

Ask students to do research project/bulletin board in Making Connections to Other Cultures (TWE p. 349 and TWE p. 350.)

Close: Do Learning Styles-Visual(TWE p. 350).

Ask students to read Sec. 1: Family and Marriage Across Cultures – Marriage Arrangements; Choosing a Mate (pp. 351-355).

Notes and Comments: _____

_____

_____

_____

_____

_____

_____

_____

_____

_____

_____

Chapter 11

THE FAMILY

Day 109

Day 3 of 10

Content:	Ch. 11, Sec. 1: Family and Marriage Across Cultures – Marriage Arrangements; Choosing a Mate (pp. 351-355)
Objective:	Students will describe norms for marriage arrangements.
Act. Type:	Class Discussion, Class Activity, Independent Practice, Cooperative Learning, Demonstration
Introduction:	Use Teaching Strategy (TWE p. 351).
Instruction:	Discuss Points to Stress (TWE p. 352).
	Ask students to interpret the map in World View (TWE p. 353).
	Review and discuss Working with the Data (TWE p. 354).
	Have students do Cooperative Learning Activity (TWE pp. 354-355).
Close:	Assign On-Demand Writing (TWE p. 353).
	Ask students to read Sec. 2: Theoretical Perspectives and the Family (pp. 356-361).

Notes and Comments: _____

_____

_____

_____

_____

_____

_____

_____

_____

_____

Chapter 11   THE FAMILY

Day 110

Week of _____

Day 4 of 10

Content:	Ch. 11, Sec. 2: Theoretical Perspectives and the Family (pp. 356-361)
Objective:	Students will compare and contrast views of the family proposed by the three major perspectives.
Act. Type:	Class Discussion, Class Activity, Independent Practice, Demonstration, Experiment, Debate
Introduction:	Do Demonstration (TWE pp. 358-359).
Instruction:	Discuss Using the Section Preview (TWE p. 357).
	Do activity in Working with the Data (TWE p. 358).
	Do Controversy and Debate (TWE p. 359).
Close:	Read and discuss Another Time-Courtship and Marriage Among the Hopi (TWE p. 356).
	Ask students to read Sec. 3: Family and Marriage in the United States (pp. 362-369).

Notes and Comments: _____

_____

_____

_____

_____

_____

_____

_____

_____

_____

Chapter 11   THE FAMILY

Day 111

Week of _____

Day 5 of 10

Content:	Ch. 11, Sec. 3: Family and Marriage in the United States (pp. 362-369)
Objective:	Students will outline the extent and cause of divorce and family violence in the United States.
Act. Type:	Class Discussion, Class Activity, Independent Practice, Cooperative Learning, Demonstration, Role-playing
Introduction:	Have students do Using Decision-Making Skills (TWE pp. 360-361).
Instruction:	Read and discuss Sociology Today (TWE p. 362).
	Discuss More About...Age and Marriage (TWE p. 363).
	Do Demonstration (TWE p. 369).
	Review and discuss Working with the Data (TWE p. 364 and p. 368).
	Ask students to interpret the map in Snapshot of America (TWE p. 365).
	Have students do Cooperative Learning Activity (TWE pp. 366-367).
Close:	Ask students to read Sec. 4: Changes in Marriage and Family – Blended Families; Single-Parent Families; Childless Marriages; Dual-Employed Marriages (pp. 370-375).

Notes and Comments: _____

_____

_____

_____

_____

_____

_____

_____

Chapter 11

THE FAMILY

Day 112   Week of _____

Content: Ch. 11, Sec. 4: Changes in Marriage and Family – Blended Families; Single-Parent Families; Childless Marriages; Dual-Employed Marriages (pp. 370-375)

Objective: Students will describe alternatives to the traditional nuclear family structure.

Act. Type: Class Discussion, Class Activity, Independent Practice, Cooperative Learning, Debate

Introduction: Read and discuss Tech Trends-Technology and the Family (TWE p. 370).

Instruction: Introduce Teaching Strategy (TWE p. 371 and p. 372).

Review and discuss Working with the Data (TWE p. 373).

Close: Do Cooperative Learning Activity (TWE p. 374).

Ask students to read Sec. 4: Changes in Marriage and Family – Cohabitation; Same Sex Domestic Partners; Single Life; Boomerang Kids; Looking Forward (pp. 375-380).

Notes and Comments: _____

_____

_____

_____

_____

_____

_____

_____

_____

_____

Chapter 11

THE FAMILY

Day 113

Week of _____

Content: Ch. 11, Sec. 4: Changes in Marriage and Family – Cohabitation; Same Sex Domestic Partners; Single Life; Boomerang Kids; Looking Forward (pp. 375-380)

Objective: Students will evaluate the importance of the social institution of the family in the United States.

Act. Type: Class Discussion, Class Activity, Independent Practice, Cooperative Learning, Debate

Introduction: Have students do Learning Styles activity (TWE p. 375).

Instruction: Share More About...Lasting Marriages and More About...Happy Marriages (TWE p. 378)

Ask students to do On-Demand Writing (TWE pp. 378-379).

Close: Remind students that chapter presentations are due the following class session.

Notes and Comments: _____

_____

_____

_____

_____

_____

_____

_____

_____

_____

_____

_____

Day 114

Week of _____

Day 8 of 10

Content:	Chapter 11 (pp. 346-380)
Objective:	Students will present projects and activities summarizing objective/s learned in the chapter.
Act. Type:	Class Activity and Presentation
Introduction:	Read and discuss Focus on Research (TWE pp. 376-377).
Instruction:	Have students do presentations (See TWE, Chapter Assessment: Sociology Projects and Technology Activities, pp. 382-383).
Close:	Assign Chapter 11 Learning Goals Outline (see *Unit 4 Booklet*, TRB), due the day of the chapter evaluation.

Notes and Comments: _____

_____

_____

_____

_____

_____

_____

_____

_____

_____

_____

_____

_____

Chapter 11

THE FAMILY

Day 115   Week of _____

Day 9 of 10

Content: Ch. 11, Assessment (pp. 381-383)

Objective: Students will review for evaluation of the concepts learned in this chapter.

Act. Type: Class Discussion, Class Activity, Independent Practice, Cooperative Learning, Demonstration, Experiment, Debate, Role-playing, Presentation

Introduction: Review Chapter 11 Vocabulary Activity homework (see *Unit 4 Booklet*, TRB).

Instruction: Do Chapter Assessment as needed (TWE pp. 381-383).

Close: Remind students to study for the chapter evaluation.

Notes and Comments: _____

_____

_____

_____

_____

_____

_____

_____

_____

_____

_____

_____

_____

Day 116   Week of _____

Day 10 of 10

Evaluate: To evaluate the students' comprehension of the chapter, administer Chapter 11 Test A or B. You may want to use the Alternative Assessment found in the TRB.

Close: Discuss Enrichment Reading (TWE pp. 384-385). Assign Chapter 12, intro. (pp. 386-387).

Notes and Comments: _____

_____

_____

_____

_____

_____

_____

_____

_____

_____

_____

_____

_____

_____

_____

_____

PLANNING GUIDE   **258**

Chapter
12

EDUCATION

Day 117

Week of _____

Day 1 of 10

Content:	Ch. 12 Intro. (pp. 386-387)
Objective:	Students will understand how the social institution of education meets basic needs in society.
Act. Type:	Class Discussion, Class Activity, Independent Practice, Presentation
Introduction:	Use Lead-Off Activity (TWE pp. 386-387).
Instruction:	Discuss Key Terms (p. 388).
	Read and discuss Using Your Sociological Imagination (TWE p. 387) with guest speaker, if possible.
Close:	Assign chapter project (see Chapter Assessment: Sociology Projects and Technology Activities) to be presented to the class prior to final chapter evaluation. Ask students to read Sec. 1: Development and Structure of Education – Bureaucracy in Education; Democratic Reforms in the Classroom (pp. 388-391).

Notes and Comments: _____

_____

_____

_____

_____

_____

_____

_____

_____

_____

_____

_____

Day 118

Week of _____

Day 2 of 10

Content: Ch. 12, Sec. 1: Development and Structure of Education – Bureaucracy in Education; Democratic Reforms in the Classroom (pp. 388-391)

Objective: Students will discuss schools as bureaucracies.

Act. Type: Class Discussion, Class Activity, Independent Practice, Cooperative Learning, Presentation

Introduction: Use the activity in Using the Section Preview (TWE p. 388).

Instruction: Discuss Using the Illustration (TWE p. 388).

Ask students to do the Survey (TWE p. 389).

Do Controversy and Debate (TWE p. 390).

Share More About...Cooperative Learning (TWE p. 391).

Close: Assign students to do the Paired-Learning Activity (TWE p. 392).

Ask students to read Sec. 1: Development and Structure of Education – Back-to-Basics Movement; Competitors to the Public School (pp. 392-395).

Notes and Comments: _____

_____

_____

_____

_____

_____

_____

_____

_____

_____

260

EDUCATION

Day 119

Week of _____

Day 3 of 10

Content:	Ch. 12, Sec. 1: Development and Structure of Education – Back-to-Basics Movement; Competitors to the Public School (pp. 392-395)
Objective:	Students will discuss alternative forms of education.
Act. Type:	Class Discussion, Class Activity, Independent Practice, Cooperative Learning, Demonstration, Debate
Introduction:	Read and discuss Another Time-Understanding Freedom and Education in America (TWE p. 392).
Instruction:	Share More About...American Education (TWE p. 393)
	Discuss Points to Stress (TWE p. 392).
	Have students do the Cooperative Learning Activity (TWE p. 393).
Close:	Assign the Critical Thinking questions from the Section Assessment (p. 395).
	Ask students to read Sec. 2: Functionalist Perspective (pp. 396-399).

Notes and Comments: _____

_____

_____

_____

_____

_____

_____

_____

_____

_____

_____

_____

Day 120

Week of _____

Day 4 of 10

Content:	Ch. 12, Sec. 2: Functionalist Perspective (pp. 396-399)
Objective:	Students will summarize the functions of the social institution of education.
Act. Type:	Class Discussion, Class Activity, Independent Practice
Introduction:	Do the activity in Using the Section Preview (TWE p. 396).
Instruction:	Discuss Careers in Sociology (TWE pp. 396-397).
	Ask students to interpret the map in World View (TWE p. 397).
	Read and discuss Sociology Today-Educating Yourself for the Future (TWE p. 399).
Close:	Assign On-Demand Writing (TWE pp. 398-399).
	Ask students to read Sec. 3: Conflict Perspective – Meritocracy (pp. 400-403).

Notes and Comments: _____

_____

_____

_____

_____

_____

_____

_____

_____

_____

_____

Chapter 12

EDUCATION

Day 121   Week of _____

Day 5 of 10

Content:	Ch. 12, Sec. 3: Conflict Perspective – Meritocracy (pp. 400-403)
Objective:	Students will evaluate the merit-based nature of public education.
Act. Type:	Class Discussion, Class Activity, Independent Practice, Debate, Presentation
Introduction:	Show video as described in Using the Section Preview (TWE p. 400).
Instruction:	Review and discuss Working with the Data (TWE p. 401 and p. 402).
	Ask students to do Using Conflict Resolution Skills (TWE pp. 400-401).
	Share and discuss More About...College Entrance Exams (TWE p. 401).
	Conduct the debate in Learning Styles-Linguistic/Bodily-Kinesthetic (TWE pp. 402-403).
Close:	Ask students to read Sec. 3: Conflict Perspective – Equality and Inequality in Education; Cognitive Ability; Promoting Educational Equality (pp. 403-407).

Notes and Comments: _____

_____

_____

_____

_____

_____

_____

_____

_____

_____

_____

Day 122

Week of _____

Day 6 of 10

Content:	Ch. 12, Sec. 3: Conflict Perspective – Equality and Inequality in Education; Cognitive Ability; Promoting Educational Equality (pp. 403-407)
Objective:	Students will evaluate educational equality.
Act. Type:	Class Discussion, Class Activity, Independent Practice, Experiment, Role-playing
Introduction:	Ask students to interpret the map in Snapshot of America-School Expenditures (TWE p. 404).
Instruction:	Do Interdisciplinary Activity (TWE pp. 404-405).
	Share Points to Stress (TWE p. 404).
	Use Reteaching suggestion (TWE p. 405).
	Ask students to discuss Open-Response Questions (TWE p. 406).
	Do Role Play activity (TWE p. 407).
Close:	Ask students to read Sec. 4: Symbolic Interactionism (pp. 409-415).

Notes and Comments: _____

_____

_____

_____

_____

_____

_____

_____

_____

_____

_____

Chapter 12

EDUCATION

Day 123   Week of _____

Day 7 of 10

Content:	Ch. 12, Sec. 4: Symbolic Interactionism (pp. 409-415)
Objective:	Students will evaluate the importance of the social institution of education in the United States.
Act. Type:	Class Discussion, Class Activity, Independent Practice, Demonstration, Experiment, Debate
Introduction:	Introduce research project in Using the Section Preview (TWE p. 409).
Instruction:	Do Demonstration (TWE pp. 410-411).
	Do Controversy and Debate (TWE p. 410).
	Review and discuss Working with the Data (TWE p. 411).
	Read and discuss Focus on Research (TWE pp. 414-415).
Close:	Assign On-Demand Writing (TWE p. 412).
	Remind students that chapter presentations are due the following class session.

Notes and Comments: _____

_____

_____

_____

_____

_____

_____

_____

_____

_____

               PLANNING GUIDE

Chapter 12

EDUCATION

Day 124

Day 8 of 10

Content:	Chapter 12 (pp. 386-415)
Objective:	Students will present projects and activities summarizing objective/s learned in the chapter.
Act. Type:	Class Activity and Presentation
Introduction:	Read and discuss Tech Trends (TWE p. 408).
Instruction:	Have students do presentations (See TWE, Chapter Assessment: Sociology Projects and Technology Activities, pp. 418-419)
Close:	Assign Chapter 12 Learning Goals Outline (see *Unit 4 Booklet*, TRB), due the day of the chapter evaluation.

Notes and Comments: _____

_____

_____

_____

_____

_____

_____

_____

_____

_____

_____

_____

_____

_____

266

Day 125

Week of _____

Day 9 of 10

Content:	Ch. 12, Assessment (pp. 416-419)
Objective:	Students will review for evaluation of the concepts learned in this chapter.
Act. Type:	Class Discussion, Class Activity, Independent Practice, Cooperative Learning, Demonstration, Experiment, Debate, Role-playing, Presentation
Introduction:	Review Chapter 12 Vocabulary Activity homework (see *Unit 4 Booklet, TRB)*.
Instruction:	Do Chapter Assessment as needed (TWE pp. 416-419).
Close:	Remind students to study for the chapter evaluation.

Notes and Comments: _____

_____

_____

_____

_____

_____

_____

_____

_____

_____

_____

_____

_____

_____

Day 126   Week of _____

Day 10 of 10

Evaluate: To evaluate the students' comprehension of the chapter, administer Chapter 12 Test A or B. You may want to use the Alternative Assessment found in the TRB.

Close: Discuss Enrichment Reading (TWE pp. 420-421). Assign Chapter 13 Intro. (pp. 422-423).

Notes and Comments: _____

_____

_____

_____

_____

_____

_____

_____

_____

_____

_____

_____

_____

_____

_____

_____

_____

_____

Chapter 13

POLITICAL AND ECONOMIC INSTITUTIONS

Day 127

Week of _____

Day 1 of 12

Content: Ch. 13 Intro. (pp. 422-423)

Objective: Students will understand how the political and economic social institutions meet basic needs in society.

Act. Type: Class Discussion, Class Activity, Independent Practice, Debate, Presentation

Introduction: Use Lead-Off Activity (TWE pp. 422-423).

Instruction: Discuss Key Terms (p. 423).

Read and discuss Using Your Sociological Imagination (TWE p. 423).

Close: Assign chapter project (see Chapter Assessment: Sociology Projects and Technology Activities) to be presented to the class prior to final chapter evaluation.

Ask students to read Sec. 1: Power and Authority – Definitions of Power and Authority; Forms of Authority (pp. 424-427).

Notes and Comments: _____

_____

_____

_____

_____

_____

_____

_____

_____

_____

_____

_____

Day 128   Week of _____

Day 2 of 12

Content: Ch. 13, Sec. 1: Power and Authority – Definitions of Power and Authority;
                    Forms of Authority (pp. 424-427)

Objective: Students will identify three forms of authority.

Act. Type: Class Discussion, Class Activity, Simulation, Cooperative Learning,
                    Demonstration

Introduction: Do activity in Using the Section Preview (TWE p. 424).

Instruction: Do Demonstration (TWE pp. 424-425).

                    Use Teaching Strategy (TWE p. 426).

Close: Assign Chapter 13 Vocabulary Activity (see *Unit 4 Booklet*, TRB), due the day
                    of the chapter review.

                    Ask students to read Sec. 1: Power and Authority – Types of Political Systems;
                    Democracy; Totalitarianism; Authoritarianism (pp. 427-431).

Notes and Comments: _____

_____

_____

_____

_____

_____

_____

_____

_____

_____

_____

Day 129   Week of _____

Day 3 of 12

Content:	Ch. 13, Sec. 1: Power and Authority – Types of Political Systems; Democracy; Totalitarianism; Authoritarianism (pp. 427-431)
Objective:	Students will discuss differences among democracy, totalitarianism, and authoritarianism.
Act. Type:	Class Discussion, Class Activity, Independent Practice, Role-playing, Presentation
Introduction:	Do Learning Styles activity (TWE pp. 426-427).
Instruction:	Discuss Points to Stress (TWE p. 428).
	Ask students to interpret the map in World View (TWE p. 429).
	Have students write and share On-Demand Writing (TWE p. 429).
	Discuss Working with the Quote (TWE p. 430).
Close:	Review and discuss Working with the Data (TWE p. 430).
	Assign Another Place-China's One-Child Policy (TWE p. 432).
	Ask students to read Sec. 2: Political Power in American Society – Influence of the Vote (pp. 433-435).

Notes and Comments: _____

_____

_____

_____

_____

_____

_____

_____

_____

Chapter 13

POLITICAL AND ECONOMIC INSTITUTIONS

Day 130

Week of _____

Day 4 of 12

Content:	Ch. 13, Sec. 2: Political Power in American Society – Influence of the Vote (pp. 433-435)
Objective:	Students will explain how voting is an exercise of power.
Act. Type:	Class Discussion, Class Activity, Independent Practice
Introduction:	Discuss assignment Another Place-China's One-Child Policy (TWE p. 432).
Instruction:	Discuss Using the Section Preview (TWE p. 433).
	Use Using the Illustration (TWE p. 433).
	Review and discuss Working with the Data (TWE p. 435).
	Share Points to Stress (TWE p. 435).
	Have students do Net Worthy activities (TWE p. 434).
Close:	Ask students to interpret the map in Snapshot of America (TWE p. 436).
	Ask students to read Sec. 2: Political Power in American Society – Two Models of Political Power; Functionalist Perspective: Pluralism; Conflict Perspective: The Power Elite (pp. 435-439).

Notes and Comments: _____

_____

_____

_____

_____

_____

_____

_____

_____

_____

Chapter 13

POLITICAL AND ECONOMIC
INSTITUTIONS

Day 131   Week of _____

Day 5 of 12

Content: Ch. 13, Sec. 2: Political Power in American Society – Two Models of Political
                      Power; Functionalist Perspective: Pluralism; Conflict Perspective: The Power
                      Elite (pp. 435-439)

Objective: Students will evaluate the importance of political social institutions in the
                      United States.

Act. Type: Class Discussion, Class Activity, Independent Practice, Cooperative Learning,
                      Presentation

Introduction: Review and discuss Working with the Data (TWE p. 437).

Instruction: Use Teaching Strategy (TWE p. 437).

                      Review and discuss Working with the Data (TWE p. 438).

                      Do Interdisciplinary Activity (TWE pp. 436-437).

Close: Ask students to read Sec. 3: Economic Systems (pp. 440-444).

Notes and Comments: _____

_____

_____

_____

_____

_____

_____

_____

_____

_____

_____

Chapter 13

POLITICAL AND ECONOMIC INSTITUTIONS

Day 132

Day 6 of 12

Content:	Ch. 13, Sec. 3: Economic Systems (pp. 440-444)
Objective:	Students will list characteristics of capitalism and socialism.
Act. Type:	Class Discussion, Class Activity, Independent Practice, Cooperative Learning
Introduction:	Pre-assess by Using the Section Preview (TWE p. 440).
Instruction:	Review and discuss Working with the Data (TWE p. 442).
	Share More About...Socialism (TWE p. 442).
Close:	Assign Paired Learning Activity (TWE p. 440).
	Ask students to read Sec. 4: The Modern Corporation (pp. 446-449).

Notes and Comments: _____

_____

_____

_____

_____

_____

_____

_____

_____

_____

_____

274

POLITICAL AND ECONOMIC INSTITUTIONS

Day 133

Week of _____

Day 7 of 12

Content:	Ch. 13, Sec. 4: The Modern Corporation (pp. 446-449)
Objective:	Students will analyze the influence of corporations on economic decisions.
Act. Type:	Class Discussion, Class Activity, Independent Practice, Cooperative Learning
Introduction:	Introduce Using the Section Preview (TWE p. 446).
Instruction:	Have students do Cooperative Learning Activity (TWE p. 446).
	Compare results from above with Making Connections to Other Cultures (TWE p. 447).
	Review and discuss Working with the Data (TWE p. 447).
Close:	Assign Sociology Today-Employee Rights (TWE p. 448).
	Ask students to read Sec. 5: Work in the Modern Economy – The Changing Nature of Work (pp. 450-453).

Notes and Comments: _____

_____

_____

_____

_____

_____

_____

_____

_____

_____

_____

_____

Chapter 13

POLITICAL AND ECONOMIC INSTITUTIONS

Day 134

Week of _____

Day 8 of 12

Content:	Ch. 13, Sec. 5: Work in the Modern Economy – The Changing Nature of Work (pp. 450-453)
Objective:	Students will analyze the influence of cultural values on economic behavior.
Act. Type:	Class Discussion, Class Activity, Independent Practice, Cooperative Learning, Presentation
Introduction:	Discuss assignment Sociology Today-Employee Rights (TWE p. 448).
Instruction:	Discuss Using the Section Preview (TWE p. 450).
	Get student participation using Teaching Strategy (TWE p. 450).
	Read and discuss Focus on Research (TWE pp. 452-453).
Close:	Review and discuss Working with the Data (TWE p. 451).
	Ask students to do Survey (TWE pp. 450-451).
	Ask students to read Sec. 5: Work in the Modern Economy – Occupational Structure; Downsizing and Contingent Employment (pp. 454-456).

Notes and Comments: _____

_____

_____

_____

_____

_____

_____

_____

_____

_____

_____

POLITICAL AND ECONOMIC INSTITUTIONS

Day 135

Week of _____

Day 9 of 12

Content:	Ch. 13, Sec. 5: Work in the Modern Economy – Occupational Structure; Downsizing and Contingent Employment (pp. 454-456)
Objective:	Students will evaluate the importance of economic social institutions in the United States.
Act. Type:	Class Discussion, Class Activity, Independent Practice, Demonstration, Presentation
Introduction:	Discuss Reteaching (TWE p. 455).
Instruction:	Do Demonstration (TWE p. 456).
	Have students do Observation (TWE pp. 452-453).
	Discuss Pulling It All Together (TWE p. 456).
Close:	Remind students that chapter presentations are due the following class session.

Notes and Comments: _____

_____

_____

_____

_____

_____

_____

_____

_____

_____

_____

POLITICAL AND ECONOMIC
INSTITUTIONS

Day 136

Week of _____

Day 10 of 12

Content:	Chapter 13 (pp. 422-455)
Objective:	Students will present projects and activities summarizing objective/s learned in the chapter.
Act. Type:	Class Activity and Presentation
Introduction:	Read and discuss Tech Trends (TWE p. 445).
Instruction:	Have students do presentations (See TWE, Chapter Assessment: Sociology Projects and Technology Activities, p. 459.)
Close:	Assign Chapter 13 Learning Goals Outline (see *Unit 4 Booklet, TRB)*, due the day of the chapter evaluation.

Notes and Comments: _____

_____

_____

_____

_____

_____

_____

_____

_____

_____

_____

_____

_____

_____

_____

Chapter 13

POLITICAL AND ECONOMIC INSTITUTIONS

Day 137

Week of _____

Day 11 of 12

Content:	Ch. 13, Assessment (pp. 457-459)
Objective:	Students will review for evaluation of the concepts learned in this chapter.
Act. Type:	Class Discussion, Class Activity, Independent Practice, Cooperative Learning, Demonstration, Experiment, Debate, Role-playing, Presentation
Introduction:	Review Chapter 13 Vocabulary Activity homework (see *Unit 4 Booklet, TRB*).
Instruction:	Do Chapter Assessment as needed (TWE pp. 457-459).
Close:	Remind students to study for the chapter evaluation.

Notes and Comments: _____

_____

_____

_____

_____

_____

_____

_____

_____

_____

_____

_____

_____

_____

PLANNING GUIDE

Chapter 13

POLITICAL AND ECONOMIC INSTITUTIONS

Day 138   Week of _____

Day 12 of 12

Evaluate: To evaluate the students' comprehension of the chapter, administer Chapter 13 Test A or B. You may want to use the Alternative Assessment found in the TRB.

Close: Discuss Enrichment Reading (TWE pp. 460-461).

                  Assign Chapter 14 Intro. (pp. 462-463).

Notes and Comments: _____

_____

_____

_____

_____

_____

_____

_____

_____

_____

_____

_____

_____

_____

_____

_____

_____

_____

Chapter 14   RELIGION

Day 139   Week of _____

Day 1 of 10

Content:	Ch. 14 Intro. (pp. 462-463)
Objective:	Students will understand how the social institution of religion meets basic needs in society.
Act. Type:	Class Discussion, Class Activity, Independent Practice
Introduction:	Use Lead-Off Activity (pp. 462-463).
Instruction:	Discuss Key Terms (p. 464).
	Read and discuss Using Your Sociological Imagination (TWE p. 463).
Close:	Assign chapter project (see Chapter Assessment: Sociology Projects and Technology Activities) to be presented to the class prior to final chapter evaluation.
	Ask students to read Sec. 1: Religion and Sociology (pp. 464-466).

Notes and Comments: _____

_____

_____

_____

_____

_____

_____

_____

_____

_____

_____

_____

_____

Chapter 14

RELIGION

Day 140

Week of _____

Day 2 of 10

Content:	Ch. 14, Sec. 1: Religion and Sociology (pp. 464-466)
Objective:	Students will explain the sociological meaning of religion.
Act. Type:	Class Discussion, Class Activity, Demonstration, Debate
Introduction:	Share Using the Section Preview (TWE p. 464).
Instruction:	Do Demonstration (TWE p. 464).
	Discuss More About...Studying Religion (TWE p. 464).
	Have students do Demonstration (TWE p. 465).
Close:	Read and discuss Another Place-Religion at War (TWE p. 466).
	Assign Chapter 14 Vocabulary Activity (see *Unit 4 Booklet*, TRB), due the day of the chapter review.
	Ask students to read Sec. 2: Theoretical Perspectives – Functionalism and Religion (pp. 467-470).

Notes and Comments: _____

_____

_____

_____

_____

_____

_____

_____

_____

_____

_____

_____

Day 141   Week of _____

Day 3 of 10

Content:	Ch. 14, Sec. 2: Theoretical Perspectives – Functionalism and Religion (pp. 467-470)
Objective:	Students will describe the sociological functions of religion.
Act. Type:	Class Discussion, Class Activity, Independent Practice
Introduction:	Discuss Careers in Sociology (TWE pp. 466-467).
Instruction:	Discuss Teaching Strategy (TWE p. 467).
	Discuss Using the Section Preview (TWE p. 467).
	Ask students to do On-Demand Writing (TWE pp. 468-469).
	Discuss and compare Working with the Data (TWE p. 468) and World View (TWE p. 469).
Close:	Ask students to read Sec. 2: Theoretical Perspectives – Conflict Theory and Religion; Symbolic Interactionism and Religion (pp. 470-473).

Notes and Comments: _____

_____

_____

_____

_____

_____

_____

_____

_____

_____

_____

Day 142
Week of _____

Day 4 of 10

Content:	Ch. 14, Sec. 2: Theoretical Perspectives – Conflict Theory and Religion; Symbolic Interactionism and Religion (pp. 470-473)
Objective:	Students will analyze the relationship between cultural values and religion.
Act. Type:	Class Discussion, Class Activity, Independent Practice, Cooperative Learning, Demonstration
Introduction:	Introduce Demonstration (TWE p. 472).
	Share and discuss More About...Marx (TWE p. 470).
Instruction:	Have students do On-Demand Writing (TWE pp. 470-471).
	Discuss both Open-Response Questions (TWE p. 472).
	Have students do Cooperative Learning Activity (TWE p. 473).
Close:	Assign Tech Trends (TWE p. 474).
	Ask students to read Sec. 3: Religious Organization and Religiosity (pp. 475-480).

Notes and Comments: _____

_____

_____

_____

_____

_____

_____

_____

_____

_____

_____

Chapter 14

RELIGION

Day 143

Week of _____

Day 5 of 10

Content:	Ch. 14, Sec. 3: Religious Organization and Religiosity (pp. 475-480)
Objective:	Students will discuss the meaning and nature of religiosity.
Act. Type:	Class Discussion, Class Activity, Independent Practice, Cooperative Learning
Introduction:	Discuss Tech Trends (TWE p. 474).
Instruction:	Ask students to do On-Demand Writing (TWE pp. 474-475).
	Have students do Encouraging Citizenship Activity (TWE p. 476).
	Facilitate Cooperative Learning Activity (TWE pp. 478-479).
	Read and discuss Sociology Today (TWE pp. 476-477).
Close:	Assign On-Demand Writing (TWE p. 477).
	Ask students to read Sec. 4: Religion in the United States – The Development of Religion in America; Secularization in the United States (pp. 481-485).

Notes and Comments: _____

_____

_____

_____

_____

_____

_____

_____

_____

_____

_____

RELIGION

Chapter 14

Day 144

Week of _____

Day 6 of 10

Content:	Ch. 14, Sec. 4: Religion in the United States – The Development of Religion in America; Secularization in the United States (pp. 481-485)
Objective:	Students will analyze the relationship between secularization and religion in the United States.
Act. Type:	Class Discussion, Class Activity, Independent Practice, Demonstration
Introduction:	Have students do Demonstration (TWE p. 481).
Instruction:	Introduce and have students do the Survey (TWE p. 482).
	Review and discuss Working with the Data (TWE p. 482 and p. 483).
	Share More About...Church Attendance (TWE p. 483).
Close:	Ask students to read Sec. 4: Religion in the United States – Religious Preferences; Fundamentalism in America; Religion, Class, and Politics; Religion, Science, and Society (pp. 485-488).

Notes and Comments: _____

_____

_____

_____

_____

_____

_____

_____

_____

_____

286

Chapter 14

RELIGION

Day 145

Week of _____

Day 7 of 10

Content: Ch. 14, Sec. 4: Religion in the United States – Religious Preferences; Fundamentalism in America; Religion, Class, and Politics; Religion, Science, and Society (pp. 485-488)

Objective: Students will discuss how the social institution of religion meets basic needs of society.

Act. Type: Class Discussion, Class Activity, Cooperative Learning, Role-playing

Introduction: Discuss results of the Survey (TWE p. 482).

Instruction: Review and discuss Working with the Data (TWE p. 485 and p. 486).

Discuss Addressing Current Social Issues (TWE p. 485).

Have students do Using Decision-Making Skills (TWE pp. 486-487).

Close: Discuss Learning Styles (TWE p. 488).

Remind students that chapter presentations are due the following class session.

Notes and Comments: _____

_____

_____

_____

_____

_____

_____

_____

_____

_____

_____

Day 146

Week of _____

Day 8 of 10

Content:	Chapter 14 (pp. 462-488)
Objective:	Students will present projects and activities summarizing objective/s learned in the chapter.
Act. Type:	Class Activity and Presentation
Introduction:	Read and discuss Focus on Research (TWE p. 484).
Instruction:	Have students do presentations (See TWE, Chapter Assessment: Sociology Projects and Technology Activities, p. 491).
Close:	Assign Chapter 14 Learning Goals Outline (see *Unit 4 Booklet, TRB)*, due the day of the chapter evaluation.

Notes and Comments: _____

_____

_____

_____

_____

_____

_____

_____

_____

_____

_____

_____

_____

_____

_____

Day 147

Week of _____

Day 9 of 10

Content:	Ch. 14, Assessment (pp. 489-491)
Objective:	Students will review for evaluation of the concepts learned in this chapter.
Act. Type:	Class Discussion, Class Activity, Independent Practice, Cooperative Learning, Demonstration, Experiment, Debate, Role-playing, Presentation
Introduction:	Review Chapter 14 Vocabulary Activity homework (see *Unit 4 Booklet, TRB)*.
Instruction:	Do Chapter Assessment as needed (TWE pp. 489-491).
Close:	Remind students to study for the chapter evaluation.

Notes and Comments: _____

_____

_____

_____

_____

_____

_____

_____

_____

_____

_____

_____

_____

Day 148

Week of _____

Day 10 of 10

Evaluate: To evaluate the students' comprehension of the chapter, administer Chapter 14 Test A or B. You may want to use the Alternative Assessment found in the TRB.

Close: Discuss Enrichment Reading (TWE p. 492-493).

Assign Chapter 15 Intro. (pp. 494-495).

Notes and Comments: _____

_____

_____

_____

_____

_____

_____

_____

_____

_____

_____

_____

_____

_____

_____

_____

_____

Day 149

Week of _____

Day 1 of 8

Content:	Ch. 15 Intro. (pp. 494-495)
Objective:	Students will understand how the social institution of sport meets basic needs in society.
Act. Type:	Class Discussion, Class Activity, Independent Practice
Introduction:	Use Lead-Off Activity (TWE pp. 494-495).
Instruction:	Discuss Using the Illustration (TWE p. 495).
	Read and discuss Using Your Sociological Imagination (TWE p. 495).
Close:	Assign chapter project (see Chapter Assessment: Sociology Projects and Technology Activities) to be presented to the class prior to final chapter evaluation.
	Ask students to read Sec. 1: The Nature of Sport (pp. 496-501).

Notes and Comments: _____

_____

_____

_____

_____

_____

_____

_____

_____

_____

_____

_____

Chapter 15 — SPORT

Day 150

Week of _____

Content: Ch. 15, Sec. 1: The Nature of Sport (pp. 496-501)

Objective: Students will justify sport as an American institution.

Act. Type: Class Discussion, Class Activity, Independent Practice, Cooperative Learning, Experiment

Introduction: Discuss Using the Section Preview and Using the Illustration (TWE p. 496).

Instruction: Discuss and graph Open-Response Questions (TWE p. 497) and (TWE p. 498).

Discuss Addressing Current Social Issues (TWE p. 500).

Ask students to do Learning Styles (TWE p. 496).

Close: Assign Using Decision-Making Skills (TWE pp. 500-501).

Ask students to read Sec. 2: Theoretical Perspectives and Sport – Culture and Sport; Functionalism (pp. 503-506).

Notes and Comments: _____

_____

_____

_____

_____

_____

_____

_____

_____

_____

_____

Chapter 15 — SPORT

Day 151

Week of _____

Day 3 of 8

Content:	Ch. 15, Sec. 2: Theoretical Perspectives and Sport – Culture and Sport; Functionalism (pp. 503-506)
Objective:	Students will identify the institution of sport from a functionalist perspective.
Act. Type:	Class Discussion, Class Activity, Independent Practice, Debate
Introduction:	Discuss assignment Using Decision-Making Skills (TWE pp. 500-501).
Instruction:	Discuss Using the Section Preview (TWE p. 503).
	Review and discuss Working with the Data (TWE p. 504).
	Have students do Controversy and Debate (TWE p. 504).
	Ask students to interpret World View (TWE p. 506).
Close:	Assign Observation (TWE p. 507).
	Ask students to read Sec. 2: Theoretical Perspectives and Sport – Conflict Theory; Symbolic Interactionism (pp. 507-511).

Notes and Comments: _____

_____

_____

_____

_____

_____

_____

_____

_____

_____

_____

Day 152   Week of _____

Day 4 of 8

Content:	Ch. 15, Sec. 2: Theoretical Perspectives and Sport – Conflict Theory; Symbolic Interactionism (pp. 507-511)
Objective:	Students will compare and contrast sport in America from a conflict and symbolic interactionist perspective.
Act. Type:	Class Discussion, Class Activity, Independent Practice
Introduction:	Discuss findings from Observation (TWE p. 507).
Instruction:	Discuss Reinforcing Vocabulary (TWE p. 507).
	Review and discuss Working with the Data (TWE p. 508).
	Read and discuss Focus on Research (TWE pp. 510-511).
Close:	Ask students to do On-Demand Writing (TWE p. 509).
	Ask students to read Sec. 3: Social Issues in Sport (pp. 512-518).

Notes and Comments: _____

_____

_____

_____

_____

_____

_____

_____

_____

_____

_____

Chapter 15

SPORT

Day 153

Day 5 of 8

Content:	Ch. 15, Sec. 3: Social Issues in Sport (pp. 512-518)
Objective:	Students will define the relationship between American sport and social mobility and will cite evidence of sexism and racism in American sport.
Act. Type:	Class Discussion, Class Activity, Cooperative Learning
Introduction:	Have students do Cooperative Learning Activity (TWE pp. 510-511).
Instruction:	Show video from Using the Section Preview (TWE p. 512).
	Have students take the Survey (TWE pp. 512-513).
	Review and discuss Working with the Data (TWE p. 513 and p. 514).
	Ask students to interpret the map in Snapshot of America (TWE p. 516).
	Discuss Points to Stress (TWE p. 516).
	Share Making Connections to Other Cultures (TWE p. 517).
Close:	Read and discuss Sociology Today (TWE p. 519).
	Assign Chapter 15 Vocabulary Activity (see *Unit 4 Booklet*, TRB), due the day of the chapter review.
	Remind students that chapter presentations are due the following class session.

Notes and Comments: _____

_____

_____

_____

_____

_____

_____

_____

Day 154

Week of _____

Day 6 of 8

Content:	Chapter 15 (pp. 494-519)
Objective:	Students will present projects and activities summarizing objective/s learned in the chapter.
Act. Type:	Class Activity and Presentation
Introduction:	Read and discuss Tech Trends-Mass Media and Sports (TWE p. 502).
Instruction:	Have students do presentations (See TWE, Chapter Assessment: Sociology Projects and Technology Activities, pp. 522-523).
Close:	Assign Chapter 15 Learning Goals Outline (see *Unit 4 Booklet, TRB)*, due the day of the chapter evaluation.

Notes and Comments: _____

_____

_____

_____

_____

_____

_____

_____

_____

_____

_____

_____

Day 155

Week of _____

Day 7 of 8

Content:	Ch. 15, Assessment (pp. 520-523)
Objective:	Students will review for evaluation of the concepts learned in this chapter.
Act. Type:	Class Discussion, Class Activity, Independent Practice, Cooperative Learning, Demonstration, Experiment, Debate, Role-playing, Presentation
Introduction:	Review Chapter 15 Vocabulary Activity homework (see *Unit 4 Booklet,* TRB*)*.
Instruction:	Do Chapter Assessment as needed (TWE pp. 520-523).
Close:	Remind students to study for the chapter evaluation.

Notes and Comments: _____

_____

_____

_____

_____

_____

_____

_____

_____

_____

_____

_____

_____

_____

Chapter 15

SPORT

Day 156

Week of _____

Day 8 of 8

Evaluate: To evaluate the students' comprehension of the chapter, administer Chapter 15 Test A or B. You may want to use the Alternative Assessment found in the TRB.

Close: Read and discuss Careers in Sociology (TWE pp. 518-519).

Notes and Comments: _____

_____

_____

_____

_____

_____

_____

_____

_____

_____

_____

_____

_____

_____

_____

_____

_____

_____

_____

298

Day 157

Week of _____

SPECIAL PROJECT PLANNING DAY

Content: *Doing Sociology: Focus on Research*

Objective: Students will plan and carry out a complete research project, including presentation of results.

Act. Type: Class Discussion, Class Activity, Independent Practice, Cooperative Learning, Demonstration, Experiment, Debate, Role-playing, Presentation

Introduction: Assign student research projects. (See TRB, *Doing Sociology: Focus on Research),* Research Projects 10-15.

Instruction: Allow students to work with partners/groups to plan research projects.

Close: Discuss timeline for research project presentation-students will make presentations the last two class sessions.

Notes and Comments: _____

_____

_____

_____

_____

_____

_____

_____

_____

_____

_____

_____

_____

Chapter 15

SPORT

Day 158

Week of _____

SPECIAL PROJECT PLANNING DAY

Content: *Doing Sociology: Focus on Research*

Objective: Students will plan and carry out a complete research project, including presentation of results.

Act. Type: Class Discussion, Class Activity, Independent Practice, Cooperative Learning, Demonstration, Experiment, Debate, Role-playing, Presentation

Introduction: Discuss reading from Culture Studies: The Sociological Perspective (see TRB).

Instruction: Allow students to work with partners/groups to plan research projects.

Close: Assign Unit 5, Chapter 16, Intro. (pp. 526-529).

Notes and Comments: _____

_____

_____

_____

_____

_____

_____

_____

_____

_____

_____

_____

_____

Chapter 16 POPULATION AND URBANIZATION

Day 159

Week of _____

Day 1 of 10

Content:	Ch. 16 Intro. (pp. 526-529)
Objective:	Students will understand the importance of urbanization resulting in changes in American institutions.
Act. Type:	Class Discussion, Class Activity, Independent Practice
Introduction:	Use Lead-Off Activity (TWE pp. 528-529).
Instruction:	Discuss Key Terms (p. 530).
	Read and discuss Using Your Sociological Imagination (TWE p. 529).
Close:	Assign chapter project (see Chapter Assessment: Sociology Projects and Technology Activities) to be presented to the class prior to final chapter evaluation.
	Ask students to read Sec. 1: The Dynamics of Demography (pp. 530-535).

Notes and Comments: _____

_____

_____

_____

_____

_____

_____

_____

_____

_____

_____

_____

_____

Day 160

Week of _____

Day 2 of 10

Content:	Ch. 16, Sec. 1: The Dynamics of Demography (pp. 530-535)
Objective:	Students will evaluate cause and effect on American institutions due to population and urbanization changes.
Act. Type:	Class Discussion, Class Activity, Independent Practice, Cooperative Learning, Demonstration
Introduction:	Discuss Using the Section Preview (TWE p. 530).
Instruction:	Share and have students draw graphic representations of information in Teaching Strategy (TWE p. 530).
	Ask students to do Demonstration (TWE pp. 530-531).
	Ask students to interpret the map in Snapshot of America (TWE p. 532).
	Conduct a Survey (TWE pp. 532-533).
	Read and discuss Another Place (TWE p. 535).
Close:	Assign Chapter 16 Vocabulary Activity (see *Unit 5 Booklet*, TRB), due the day of the chapter review.
	Ask students to read Sec. 2: World Population – The Problem of Population Growth; Malthus and Population Growth; The Demographic Transition (pp. 536-540).

Notes and Comments: _____

_____

_____

_____

_____

_____

_____

Chapter 16

POPULATION AND URBANIZATION

Day 161

Week of _____

Day 3 of 10

Content:	Ch. 16, Sec. 2: World Population – The Problem of Population Growth; Malthus and Population Growth; The Demographic Transition (pp. 536-540)
Objective:	Students will evaluate cause and effect on global institutions due to population and urbanization changes.
Act. Type:	Class Discussion, Class Activity, Demonstration
Introduction:	Do activity in Using the Section Preview (TWE p. 536).
Instruction:	Have students do Demonstration (TWE pp. 536-537).
	Review and discuss Working with the Data (TWE p. 537) and (TWE p. 538).
	Do Demonstration (TWE pp. 538-539).
Close:	Ask students to read Sec. 2: World Population – Future World Population Growth; Population Control; Population Pyramids (pp. 540-546).

Notes and Comments: _____

_____

_____

_____

_____

_____

_____

_____

_____

_____

_____

_____

Chapter 16

POPULATION AND URBANIZATION

Day 162

Week of _____

Day 4 of 10

Content:	Ch. 16, Sec. 2: World Population – Future World Population Growth; Population Control; Population Pyramids (pp. 540-546)
Objective:	Students will predict world population trends.
Act. Type:	Class Discussion, Class Activity, Independent Practice, Cooperative Learning, Demonstration
Introduction:	Use demonstration in Teaching Strategy (TWE p. 541).
Instruction:	Have students do Using Conflict-Resolution Skills (TWE pp. 540-541).
	Ask students to do Cooperative Learning Activity (TWE pp. 542-543).
	Share More About...Population Control (TWE p. 543).
Close:	Have students do On-Demand Writing (TWE pp. 544-545).
	Ask students to read Sec. 3: The Urban Transition – Defining a City; Urbanization: Preindustrial Cities (pp. 547-549).

Notes and Comments: _____

_____

_____

_____

_____

_____

_____

_____

_____

_____

_____

_____

Chapter
16

POPULATION AND URBANIZATION

Day 163

Week of _____

Day 5 of 10

Content:	Ch. 16, Sec. 3: The Urban Transition – Defining a City; Urbanization: Preindustrial Cities (pp. 547-549)
Objective:	Students will trace the development of preindustrial cities.
Act. Type:	Class Discussion, Class Activity, Independent Practice, Demonstration, Role-playing
Introduction:	Read and discuss Sociology Today (TWE p. 547).
Instruction:	Do activity in Using the Section Preview (TWE p. 548).
	Have students do Role Play (TWE pp. 548-549).
	Do Reteaching (TWE p. 549).
Close:	Ask students to read Sec. 3: The Urban Transition – The Rise of the Modern City; World Urbanization; Suburbanization in the United States (pp. 550-554).

Notes and Comments: _____

_____

_____

_____

_____

_____

_____

_____

_____

_____

_____

_____

Chapter 16 POPULATION AND URBANIZATION

Day 164

Week of ______________________________

Day 6 of 10

Content: Ch. 16, Sec. 3: The Urban Transition – The Rise of the Modern City; World Urbanization; Suburbanization in the United States (pp. 550-554)

Objective: Students will trace the development of modern cities.

Act. Type: Class Discussion, Class Activity, Independent Practice, Presentation

Introduction: Ask students to interpret the map in World View (TWE p. 550).

Instruction: Discuss Reinforcing Vocabulary (TWE p. 552).

Review and discuss Working with the Data (TWE p. 551 and p. 553).

Ask students to do On-Demand Writing (TWE pp. 554-555).

Close: Discuss Careers in Sociology (TWE pp. 552-553).

Assign Tech Trends (TWE p. 555).

Ask students to read Sec. 4: Urban Ecology (pp. 556-560).

Notes and Comments: ______________________________

Chapter 16   POPULATION AND URBANIZATION

Day 165

Week of _____

Day 7 of 10

Content:	Ch. 16, Sec. 4: Urban Ecology (pp. 556-560)
Objective:	Students will compare and contrast four theories of city growth.
Act. Type:	Class Discussion, Class Activity, Independent Practice, Cooperative Learning, Demonstration
Introduction:	Do transparency activity in Using the Section Preview (TWE pp. 556).
Instruction:	Discuss Open-Response Question (TWE p. 556).
	Have students do Learning Styles (TWE pp. 556-557).
	Facilitate Cooperative Learning Activity (TWE pp. 558-559).
	Use Teaching Strategy (TWE p. 559).
Close:	Ask students to do On-Demand Writing (TWE pp. 560-561).
	Remind students that chapter presentations are due the following class session.

Notes and Comments: _____

_____

_____

_____

_____

_____

_____

_____

_____

_____

_____

Day 166

Day 8 of 10

Content:	Chapter 16 (pp. 528-560)
Objective:	Students will present projects and activities summarizing objective/s learned in the chapter.
Act. Type:	Class Activity and Presentation
Introduction:	Read and discuss Focus on Research (TWE p. 558).
Instruction:	Have students do presentations (See TWE, Chapter Assessment: Sociology Projects and Technology Activities, pp. 562-563).
Close:	Assign Chapter 16 Learning Goals Outline (see *Unit 5 Booklet,* TRB*)*, due the day of the chapter evaluation.

Notes and Comments: _____

_____

_____

_____

_____

_____

_____

_____

_____

_____

_____

_____

_____

_____

Day 167   Week of _____

Day 9 of 10

Content:	Ch. 16, Assessment (pp. 561-563)
Objective:	Students will review for evaluation of the concepts learned in this chapter.
Act. Type:	Class Discussion, Class Activity, Independent Practice, Cooperative Learning, Demonstration, Experiment, Debate, Role-playing, Presentation
Introduction:	Review Chapter 16 Vocabulary Activity homework (see *Unit 5 Booklet,* TRB).
Instruction:	Do Chapter Assessment as needed (TWE pp. 561-563).
Close:	Remind students to study for the chapter evaluation.

Notes and Comments: _____

_____

_____

_____

_____

_____

_____

_____

_____

_____

_____

_____

_____

_____

_____

Day 168

Week of _____

Day 10 of 10

Evaluate: To evaluate the students' comprehension of the chapter, administer Chapter 16 Test A or B. You may want to use the Alternative Assessment found in the TRB.

Close: Discuss Enrichment Reading (TWE pp. 564-565).

Assign Chapter 17 Intro. (pp. 566-567).

Notes and Comments: _____

_____

_____

_____

_____

_____

_____

_____

_____

_____

_____

_____

_____

_____

_____

_____

_____

_____

310

Chapter 17

SOCIAL CHANGE AND COLLECTIVE BEHAVIOR

Day 169

Week of _____

Day 1 of 10

Content: Ch. 17 Intro. (pp. 566-567)

Objective: Students will understand the relevance and importance of social change.

Act. Type: Class Discussion, Class Activity, Independent Practice

Introduction: Introduce Lead-Off Activity (TWE pp. 566-567).

Instruction: Discuss Key Terms (p. 568).

Read and discuss Using Your Sociological Imagination (TWE p. 567).

Close: Assign chapter project (see Chapter Assessment: Sociology Projects and Technology Activities) to be presented to the class prior to final chapter evaluation.

Ask students to read Sec. 1: Social Change – Defining Social Change; Social Processes (pp. 568-571).

Notes and Comments: _____

_____

_____

_____

_____

_____

_____

_____

_____

_____

_____

_____

_____

Chapter 17

SOCIAL CHANGE AND COLLECTIVE BEHAVIOR

Day 170

Week of _____

Day 2 of 10

Content:	Ch. 17, Sec. 1: Social Change – Defining Social Change; Social Processes (pp. 568-571)
Objective:	Students will understand basic sociological principles related to social change.
Act. Type:	Class Discussion, Class Activity, Independent Practice, Cooperative Learning
Introduction:	Discuss results of Lead-Off Activity (TWE pp. 566-567).
Instruction:	Have the students do time lines in Using the Section Preview (TWE p. 568).
	Review and discuss Working with the Data (TWE p. 569).
	Share Points to Stress (TWE p. 568).
	Introduce and have students do Learning Styles (TWE p. 568).
Close:	Assign Chapter 17 Vocabulary Activity (see *Unit 5 Booklet*, TRB), due the day of the chapter review.
	Ask students to read Sec. 1: Social Change – Technology; Population; The Natural Environment; Revolution and War (pp. 571-575).

Notes and Comments: _____

_____

_____

_____

_____

_____

_____

_____

_____

_____

Chapter 17

SOCIAL CHANGE AND COLLECTIVE BEHAVIOR

Day 171 .

Week of _____

Day 3 of 10

Content:	Ch. 17, Sec. 1: Social Change – Technology; Population; The Natural Environment; Revolution and War (pp. 571-575)
Objective:	Students will understand the impact of scientific and technological discoveries evidenced by social change.
Act. Type:	Class Discussion, Class Activity, Independent Practice, Cooperative Learning, Role-playing
Introduction:	Share More About...the Internet and discuss Using the Illustration (both on TWE p. 570).
Instruction:	Ask students to interpret map in World View (TWE p. 574).
	Ask students to do Learning Styles activity (TWE pp. 572-573).
	Read and discuss Another Time (TWE p. 573).
Close:	Introduce and assign Paired Learning Activity (TWE pp. 574-575).
	Ask students to read Sec. 2: Theoretical Perspectives on Social Change (pp. 576-580).

Notes and Comments: _____

_____

_____

_____

_____

_____

_____

_____

Chapter 17

SOCIAL CHANGE AND COLLECTIVE BEHAVIOR

Day 172

Week of _____

Day 4 of 10

Content:	Ch. 17, Sec. 2: Theoretical Perspectives on Social Change (pp. 576-580)
Objective:	Students will describe social change as viewed by the functionalist, conflict, and symbolic interactionist perspective.
Act. Type:	Class Discussion, Class Activity, Independent Practice, Demonstration
Introduction:	Discuss results from Paired Learning Activity (TWE pp. 574-575).
Instruction:	Discuss Focus on Research (TWE pp. 576-577).
	Ask students to do On-Demand Writing (TWE pp. 576-577).
	Review and discuss Working with the Data (TWE p. 579).
Close:	Do Demonstration (TWE p. 580).
	Ask students to read Sec. 3: Collective Behavior (pp. 581-589).

Notes and Comments: _____

_____

_____

_____

_____

_____

_____

_____

_____

_____

_____

_____

Chapter 17

SOCIAL CHANGE AND COLLECTIVE BEHAVIOR

Day 173

Day 5 of 10

Content:	Ch. 17, Sec. 3: Collective Behavior (pp. 581-589)
Objective:	Students will analyze social problems within and across groups.
Act. Type:	Class Discussion, Class Activity, Independent Practice, Cooperative Learning, Role-playing, Presentation
Introduction:	Begin with Role Play (TWE p. 581).
Instruction:	Discuss Using the Section Preview (TWE p. 581).
	Use Teaching Strategy (TWE p. 583).
	Have students do On-Demand Writing (TWE pp. 586-587).
Close:	Read and discuss Sociology Today (TWE p. 584).
	Ask students to read Sec. 4: Social Movements – The Nature of Social Movements; Primary Types of Social Movements (pp. 590-593).

Notes and Comments: _____

_____

_____

_____

_____

_____

_____

_____

_____

_____

_____

Chapter 17

SOCIAL CHANGE AND COLLECTIVE BEHAVIOR

Day 174

Week of _____

Day 6 of 10

Content:	Ch. 17, Sec. 4: Social Movements – The Nature of Social Movements; Primary Types of Social Movements (pp. 590-593)
Objective:	Students will identify types of social movements.
Act. Type:	Class Discussion, Class Activity, Independent Practice, Cooperative Learning
Introduction:	Read and discuss Tech Trends (TWE p. 590).
Instruction:	Have students do Using Decision-Making Skills (TWE pp. 590-591).
	Review and discuss Working with the Data (TWE p. 592).
	Discuss Reinforcing Vocabulary (TWE p. 592).
	Use Teaching Strategy (TWE p. 593).
Close:	Assign students to prepare questions for guest speakers from Working with the Data (TWE p. 594).
	Ask students to read Sec. 4: Social Movements – Theories of Social Movements (pp. 593-596).

Notes and Comments: _____

_____

_____

_____

_____

_____

_____

_____

_____

_____

SOCIAL CHANGE AND COLLECTIVE BEHAVIOR

Day 175

Week of _____

Day 7 of 10

Content:	Ch. 17, Sec. 4: Social Movements – Theories of Social Movements (pp. 593-596)
Objective:	Students will compare and contrast theories of social movements.
Act. Type:	Class Discussion, Class Activity, Independent Practice, Cooperative Learning, Demonstration, Experiment, Debate, Role-playing, Presentation
Introduction:	Discuss Working with the Data (TWE p. 594)
Instruction:	Invite guest speakers from above to lead presentation/discussion.
Close:	Remind students that chapter presentations are due the following class session.

Notes and Comments: _____

_____

_____

_____

_____

_____

_____

_____

_____

_____

_____

_____

_____

_____

_____

PLANNING GUIDE

Day 176

Week of _____

Day 8 of 10

Content:	Chapter 17 (pp. 566-596)
Objective:	Students will present projects and activities summarizing objective/s learned in the chapter.
Act. Type:	Class Activity and Presentation
Introduction:	Have students interpret the map in Snapshot of America (TWE p. 595).
Instruction:	Have students do presentations (See TWE, Chapter Assessment: Sociology Projects and Technology Activities, pp. 598-599).
Close:	Assign Chapter 17 Learning Goals Outline (see *Unit 5 Booklet,* TRB), due the day of the chapter evaluation.

Notes and Comments: _____

_____

_____

_____

_____

_____

_____

_____

_____

_____

_____

_____

_____

318

SOCIAL CHANGE AND COLLECTIVE BEHAVIOR

Day 177   Week of _____

Day 9 of 10

Content:	Ch. 17, Assessment (pp. 597-599)
Objective:	Students will review for evaluation of the concepts learned in this chapter.
Act. Type:	Class Discussion, Class Activity, Independent Practice, Cooperative Learning, Demonstration, Experiment, Debate, Role-playing, Presentation
Introduction:	Review Chapter 17 Vocabulary Activity homework (see *Unit 5 Booklet,* TRB).
Instruction:	Do Chapter Assessment as needed (TWE pp. 597-599).
Close:	Remind students to study for the chapter evaluation.

Notes and Comments: _____

_____

_____

_____

_____

_____

_____

_____

_____

_____

_____

_____

_____

_____

_____

Day 178   Week of _____

Day 10 of 10

Evaluate: To evaluate the students' comprehension of the chapter, administer Chapter 17
Test A or B. You may want to use the Alternative Assessment found in the TRB.
There is also a final exam for your use, in the TRB.

Close: Discuss Enrichment Reading (TWE pp. 600-601). Remind students that final
presentations are due to begin the following class session.

Notes and Comments: _____

_____

_____

_____

_____

_____

_____

_____

_____

_____

_____

_____

_____

_____

_____

_____

_____

_____

Chapter 17

SOCIAL CHANGE AND COLLECTIVE BEHAVIOR

Day 179

Week of _____

SPECIAL PROJECT PRESENTATION DAY

Content:	*Doing Sociology: Focus on Research*
Objective:	Students will present results of research projects.
Act. Type:	Class Discussion, Class Activity, Independent Practice, Cooperative Learning, Demonstration, Experiment, Debate, Role-playing, Presentation
Introduction:	Discuss reading from Culture Studies: The Sociological Perspective (see TRB).
Instruction:	Allow time for students to present research projects.
Close:	Give feedback on presentations.

Notes and Comments: _____

_____

_____

_____

_____

_____

_____

_____

_____

_____

_____

_____

_____

_____

Chapter 17

SOCIAL CHANGE AND COLLECTIVE BEHAVIOR

Day 180

Week of _____

SPECIAL PROJECT PRESENTATION DAY

Content: *Doing Sociology: Focus on Research*

Objective: Students will present results of research projects.

Act. Type: Class Discussion, Class Activity, Independent Practice, Cooperative Learning, Demonstration, Experiment, Debate, Role-playing, Presentation

Introduction: Discuss reading from Culture Studies: The Sociological Perspective (see TRB).

Instruction: Allow time for students to present research projects.

Close: Give feedback on presentations.

Notes and Comments: _____

_____

_____

_____

_____

_____

_____

_____

_____

_____

_____

_____

_____

_____

Planning Guide
Sociology and You

Year-long course – Block (18 weeks – 90 days)

Resource Key

TWE   Teacher's Wrap Edition
TRB   Teacher's Resource Box

Select the activities best suited to your students' needs and abilities.

Chapter 1

AN INVITATION TO SOCIOLOGY

Day 1   Block Schedule   Week of _____

Day 1 of 4

Content:	Unit 1 Intro., Ch. 1 Intro., and Sec. 1: The Sociological Perspective (pp. 2-13)
Objective:	Students will understand the importance of the sociological imagination and will describe uses of the sociological perspective.
Act. Type:	Demonstration, Class Discussion, Class Activity, Independent Practice
Introduction:	Use one of the strategies described in the Ch. 1 Lead-Off Activity (TWE pp. 4-5).
Instruction:	Have students read and discuss Using Your Sociological Imagination (TWE p. 5).
	Discuss More About...C. Wright Mills (TWE p. 11).
	Do Demonstration-Sociological Imagination (TWE p. 12).
	Ask students to answer the questions in Another Time – Native American's Speech (TWE p. 10).
Close:	Assign chapter project (see Chapter Assessment: Sociology Projects and Technology Activities, pp. 33-34) to be presented to the class prior to final chapter evaluation.
	Assign Chapter 1 Vocabulary Activity (see *Unit 1 Booklet, TRB*), due the day of the chapter review.
	Ask students to read Sec. 2: The Origins of Sociology (pp. 14-22).

Notes and Comments: _____

_____

_____

_____

_____

_____

_____

_____

Day 2   Block Schedule   Week of _____

Day 2 of 4

Content:	Ch. 1, Sec. 2: The Origins of Sociology (pp. 14-22)
Objective:	Students will outline the contributions of the major pioneers of sociology.
Act. Type:	Class Discussion, Class Activity, Independent Practice, Cooperative Learning, Role-playing, Presentation
Introduction:	Do Using the Section Preview (TWE p. 14)
Instruction:	Discuss More About...August Comte (TWE p. 14).
	Ask students to do Interdisciplinary Activity – Current Events (TWE p. 14).
	Discuss More About...Emile Durkheim (TWE p. 16).
	Discuss More About...Sociology in America (TWE p. 15)
	Ask students to complete Ch. 1 Graphic Organizer (*Unit 1 Booklet, TRB*). Discuss More About...Jane Addams (TWE p. 19).
	Ask students to do activity described in Biography-W.E.B. DuBois (TWE p. 22).
	Read and discuss Focus on Research (pp. 20-21).
Close:	Ask students to read Sec. 3: Theoretical Perspectives (pp. 23-31).
	Remind students that chapter presentations are due the following class session.

Notes and Comments: _____

_____

_____

_____

_____

_____

_____

_____

_____

Day 3	**Block Schedule**	**Week of** _____

Day 3 of 4

Content: Ch. 1, Sec. 3: Theoretical Perspectives (pp. 23-31), Chapter 1 Presentations (pp. 4-31)

Objective: Students will understand the theoretical perspective of the historic interpretations of human social development and will present projects and activities summarizing objective/s learned in the chapter.

Act. Type: Class Discussion, Class Activity, Independent Practice, Cooperative Learning, Demonstration, Presentations

Introduction: Have students do Demonstration-The Chairs Game (TWE p. 24).

Introduce the terms *perception* and *perspective* as in Using the Illustration (TWE p. 23).

Instruction: Ask students to interpret the map in World View (TWE p. 24).

Have students answer questions about Working with the Data-Fig. 1.2: Focus on Theoretical Perspectives and do Using Problem-Solving Skills-Conflict Perspective (TWE p. 27).

Have students do presentations (See TWE, Chapter Assessment: Sociology Projects and Technology Activities, pp. 33-34).

Close: Discuss and have students answer questions in Tech Trends (TWE pp. 28-29).

Assign Chapter 1 Learning Goals Outline (see *Unit 1 Booklet, TRB*), due the day of the chapter evaluation.

Remind students to study for the chapter evaluation.

Notes and Comments: _____

_____

_____

_____

_____

_____

_____

An Invitation to Sociology

Day 4

Block Schedule   **Week of** _____

Day 4 of 4

Content: Ch. 1, Assessment (pp. 32-34) and Evaluation

Objective: Students will review for evaluation of the concepts learned in this chapter.

Act. Type: Class Discussion, Class Activity, Independent Practice, Cooperative Learning, Demonstration, Experiment, Debate, Role-playing, Presentation

Introduction: Review Chapter 1 Vocabulary Activity homework (see *Unit 1 Booklet, TRB*).

Instruction: Do Chapter Assessment as needed (TWE pp. 32-34).

Evaluate: To evaluate the students' comprehension of the chapter, administer Chapter 1 Test A or B. You may want to use the Alternative Assessment found in the Teacher's Edition.

Close: Discuss Enrichment Reading (pp. 35).

Assign Chapter 2 Intro, (pp. 36-37) and Sec. 1: Research Methods (pp. 38-49).

Notes and Comments: _____

_____

_____

_____

_____

_____

_____

_____

_____

_____

_____

Chapter 2 SOCIOLOGISTS DOING RESEARCH

Day 5   Block Schedule   Week of _____

Day 1 of 4

Content:	Ch. 2 Intro. (pp. 36-37) and Ch. 2, Sec. 1: Research Methods (pp. 38-49)
Objective:	Students will understand the importance of sociological research and will describe the major quantitative and qualitative research methods used by sociologists.
Act. Type:	Class Discussion, Class Activity, Independent Practice, Demonstration
Introduction:	Have students do Lead-Off Activity (TWE pp. 36-37).
Instruction:	Read and discuss Using Your Sociological Imagination (TWE p. 37).
	Discuss Using the Section Preview (TWE p. 38)
	Do Demonstrations-Quantitative Research (TWE p. 38) and Qualitative Research (TWE p. 39).
Close:	Ask students to do On-Demand Writing (TWE p. 44).
	Assign Chapter 2 Vocabulary Activity (see *Unit 1 Booklet, TRB*), due the day of the chapter review.
	Assign chapter project (see Chapter Assessment: Sociology Projects and Technology Activities, TWE pp. 64-65) to be presented to the class prior to final chapter evaluation.
	Ask students to read Sec. 2: Causation in Science (pp. 50-55).

Notes and Comments: _____

_____

_____

_____

_____

_____

_____

_____

_____

Day 6   Block Schedule   Week of _____

Day 2 of 4

Content: Ch. 2, Skills at a Glance (pp. 46-49) and Ch. 2, Sec. 2: Causation in Science (pp. 50-55)

Objective: Students will use geographic and other tools to collect, analyze, and interpret sociological data and will discuss basic research concepts, including variables and correlations and the standards for proving a cause-and-effect relationship.

Act. Type: Class Discussion, Class Activity, Independent Practice, Cooperative Learning, Demonstration

Introduction: Discuss More About the Census (TWE p. 46).

Discuss Addressing Current Social Issues (TWE p. 42).

Have students do Cooperative Learning Activity-School Census Survey (TWE pp. 42-43).

Instruction: Introduce Working with the Data-Skills at a Glance (TWE p. 46) and have students do Skills at a Glance, (pp. 46-49, answers in TWE pp. 47, 49).

Ask students to interpret the map in World View (TWE p. 51).

Ask students to do Paired Learning Activity (TWE p. 52) and Cooperative Learning Activity (TWE p. 53).

Assign Doing Sociology: Focus on Research (see TRB).

Close: Read and answer questions for Another Time – Reason and Science (TWE p. 54.

Ask students to read Sec. 3: Procedures and Ethics in Research (pp. 56-61).

Remind students that chapter presentations are due the following class session.

Notes and Comments: _____

_____

_____

_____

_____

_____

Chapter 2 SOCIOLOGISTS DOING RESEARCH

Day 7   **Block Schedule**   **Week of** _____

Day 3 of 4

Content:	Ch. 2, Sec. 3: Procedures and Ethics in Research (pp. 56-61), and Chapter 2 Presentations (pp. 36-62)
Objective:	Students will discuss ethics in sociological research and will present projects and activities summarizing objective/s learned in the chapter.
Act. Type:	Class Discussion, Class Activity, Independent Practice, Cooperative Learning, and Presentations
Introduction:	Discuss Focus on Research (pp. 56-57, see TWE p. 56 for Teaching Strategy).
	*Optional - Invite a psychologist in to do Encouraging Citizenship Activity (TWE p. 57).
Instruction:	Assign groups to do Encouraging Citizenship Activity (TWE pp. 58-59).
	Ask students to do Ch. 2 Student Journal Prompts (*see Unit 1 Booklet, TRB*).
	Have students do presentations (See TWE, Chapter Assessment: Sociology Projects and Technology Activities, pp. 64-65).
Close:	Discuss Tech Trends (p. 60).
	Assign Chapter 2 Learning Goals Outline (see *Unit 1 Booklet, TRB*), due the day of the chapter evaluation.
	Remind students to study for the chapter evaluation.

Notes and Comments: _____

_____

_____

_____

_____

_____

_____

_____

Chapter 2   SOCIOLOGISTS DOING RESEARCH

Day 8   Block Schedule   Week of _____

Day 4 of 4

Content:	Ch. 2, Assessment (pp. 63-65) and Evaluation
Objective:	Students will review for evaluation of the concepts learned in this chapter.
Act. Type:	Class Discussion, Class Activity, Independent Practice, Cooperative Learning
Introduction:	Review Chapter 2 Vocabulary Activity homework (see *Unit 1 Booklet, TRB*).
Instruction:	Do Chapter Assessment as needed (TWE pp. 63-65).
Evaluate:	To evaluate the students' comprehension of the chapter, administer Chapter 2 Test A or B. You may want to use the Alternative Assessment found in the TRB. A test for Unit 1 is also available in the TRB.
Close:	Discuss Sociology Today (TWE p. 62).
	Read and discuss Enrichment Reading (TWE pp. 66-67).
	Assign Unit 2, Chapter 3 Intro. (pp. 68-71) and Sec. 1: The Basis of Culture.

Notes and Comments: _____

_____

_____

_____

_____

_____

_____

_____

_____

_____

_____

_____

Chapter 3

CULTURE

Day 9	Block Schedule	Week of _____

Day 1 of 6

Content: Unit 2 Intro, Ch. 3 Intro., (pp. 68-71) and Ch. 3, Sec. 1: The Basis of Culture (pp. 72-75)

Objective: Students will understand the importance of culture in society and will name the essential components of culture.

Act. Type: Class Discussion, Class Activity, Independent Practice, Cooperative Learning, Debate, Role-playing

Introduction: Ask students to do Lead-Off Activity (TWE pp. 70-71).

Read and discuss Using Your Sociological Imagination (TWE p. 71).

Instruction: Introduce Using the Section Preview (TWE p. 72).

Do activity in Using Conflict Resolution Skills (TWE p. 72).

Lead students in informal debate in Using Problem-Solving Skills (TWE p. 73).

Close: Assign Chapter 3 Vocabulary Activity (see *Unit 2 Booklet, TRB*), due the day of the chapter review.

Assign chapter project (see Chapter Assessment: Sociology Projects and Technology Activities, pp. 104-105) to be presented to the class prior to final chapter evaluation.

Ask students to read Sec. 2: Language and Culture (pp. 77-78)

Notes and Comments: _____

_____

_____

_____

_____

_____

_____

Day 10   Block Schedule   Week of _____

Day 2 of 6

Content:	Ch. 3, Sec. 2: Language and Culture (pp. 76-80)
Objective:	Students will describe how language and culture are related and will explain the hypothesis of linguistic relativity.
Act. Type:	Class Discussion, Class Activity, Independent Practice, Demonstration
Introduction:	Discuss Another Time (TWE p. 76).
	Ask students to do On-Demand Writing (TWE p. 76).
Instruction:	Introduce Using the Section Preview (TWE p. 77).
	Do Demonstration-Knowing Your Culture (TWE p. 77).
	Review and discuss Working with the Data, Fig. 3.1 (TWE p. 78).
	Discuss Working with the Quote (TWE p. 78).
	Do Demonstration-Keeping the Time (TWE p. 78).
	Discuss Teaching Strategy (TWE p. 79).
	Read and discuss Sociology Today-Cultural Relativism (TWE p. 80).
Close:	Discuss Making Connections to Other Cultures (TWE p. 80).
	Ask students to read Sec. 3: Norms and Values (pp. 81-91).

Notes and Comments: _____

_____

_____

_____

_____

_____

_____

_____

_____

Chapter 3 — CULTURE

Day 11	**Block Schedule**	**Week of** _____

Day 3 of 6

Content: Ch. 3, Sec. 3: Norms and Values (pp. 81-91)

Objective: Students will identify various types of norms and how conformity to those norms is encouraged and will understand that cultural values vary in different locations.

Act. Type: Class Discussion, Class Activity, Independent Practice, Cooperative Learning, Demonstration, Experiment, Debate, Role-playing

Introduction: Do Using the Section Preview (TWE p. 81).

Instruction: Discuss Working with the Data-Fig. 3.2 (TWE p. 82).

*Optional - Use Teaching Strategy-*The Gods Must Be Crazy* (TWE p. 82).

Ask students to do Learning Styles-Bodily-Kinesthetic (TWE p. 84).

Ask students to interpret the map in World View (TWE p. 85) and discuss Working with the Data-Fig. 3.3 (TWE p. 86).

Ask students to do Cooperative Learning Activity (TWE pp. 86-87).

Ask students to do the writing described in Pulling It All Together (TWE p. 91).

Close: Ask students to read Sec. 4: Beliefs and Material Culture (pp. 92-94) and Ch. 3, Sec. 5: Cultural Diversity and Similarity – Cultural Change; Cultural Diversity (pp. 95-98).

Ask students to do Learning Styles-Interpersonal/Linguistic (TWE p. 85).

Notes and Comments: _____

_____

_____

_____

_____

_____

Day 12   Block Schedule   Week of _____

Day 4 of 6

Content:	Ch. 3, Sec. 4: Beliefs and Material Culture (pp. 92-94) and Ch. 3, Sec. 5: Cultural Diversity and Similarity – Cultural Change; Cultural Diversity (pp. 95-98)
Objective:	Students will distinguish between nonmaterial, material, ideal, and real culture and will discuss how cultural diversity is promoted within a society.
Act. Type:	Class Discussion, Class Activity, Independent Practice, Cooperative Learning, Experiment
Introduction:	Discuss student-designed projects from Learning Styles-Interpersonal/Linguistic (TWE p. 85).
Instruction:	Have students do Paired-Learning Activity (TWE p. 92).
	Discuss Observation – Ideal and Real Culture (TWE p. 94).
	Present and discuss Using Problem-Solving Skills (TWE p. 95).
	Discuss and do Survey (TWE pp. 96-97 and/or TWE p. 98).
	Read and discuss Focus on Research-How Do Schools and Parents Fail Teens? (TWE pp. 96-97).
Close:	As needed, have students do the Ch. 3 Increasing Your Reading Comprehension worksheet in the *Unit 2 Booklet, TRB*.
	Ask students to read Sec. 5: Cultural Diversity and Similarity – Ethnocentrism; Cultural Universals (pp. 98-102).
	Remind students that chapter presentations are due the following class session.

Notes and Comments: _____

_____

_____

_____

_____

_____

CULTURE

Day 13   Block Schedule   Week of _____

Day 5 of 6

Content:	Ch. 3, Sec. 5: Cultural Diversity and Similarity – Ethnocentrism; Cultural Universals (pp. 98-102), and Chapter 3 Presentations (pp. 70-102)
Objective:	Students will compare and contrast cultural norms among subculture groups and will present projects and activities summarizing objective/s learned in the chapter.
Act. Type:	Class Discussion, Class Activity, Independent Practice, Cooperative Learning, Debate, and Presentations
Introduction:	Discuss Reinforcing Vocabulary-Ethnocentrism (TWE p. 100).
Instruction:	Ask students to do Cooperative Learning Activity (TWE p. 100).
	Have students interpret the map in Snapshot of America (TWE p. 101).
	Discuss and have students analyze the graph in Working with the Data-Fig. 3.5 (TWE p. 102).
	Read and discuss Tech Trends-Star Wars and the Internet (TWE p. 99).
	Have students do presentations (See TWE, Ch. Review: Projects and Activities, pp. 104-105).
Close:	Assign Chapter 3 Learning Goals Outline (see *Unit 2 Booklet, TRB*), due the day of the chapter evaluation.
	Remind students to study for the chapter evaluation.

Notes and Comments: _____

_____

_____

_____

_____

_____

_____

_____

Day 14   **Block Schedule**   **Week of** _____

Day 6 of 6

Content:	Ch. 3, Assessment (pp. 103-105) and Evaluation
Objective:	Students will review for evaluation of the concepts learned in this chapter.
Act. Type:	Class Discussion, Class Activity, Independent Practice, Cooperative Learning, Demonstration, Experiment, Debate, Role-playing, Presentation
Introduction:	Review Chapter 3 Vocabulary Activity homework (see *Unit 2 Booklet, TRB*).
Instruction:	Do Chapter Assessment as needed (TWE pp. 103-105).
Evaluate:	To evaluate the students' comprehension of the chapter, administer Chapter 3 Test A or B. You may want to use the Alternative Assessment found in the TRB.
Close:	Discuss Enrichment Reading (TWE pp. 106-107).
	Assign Chapter 4 intro. (pp. 108-109) and Sec. 1: The Importance of Socialization (pp. 110-114).

Notes and Comments: _____

_____

_____

_____

_____

_____

_____

_____

_____

_____

_____

_____

Chapter 4

SOCIALIZATION

Day 15	Block Schedule	Week of _____

Day 1 of 5

Content: Ch. 4 Intro. (pp. 108-109) and Ch. 4, Sec. 1: The Importance of Socialization (pp. 110-114)

Objective: Students will understand the importance of socialization and the role socialization plays in human development.

Act. Type: Class Discussion, Class Activity, Independent Practice, Cooperative Learning, Demonstration, Debate, Presentation

Introduction: Do Lead-Off Activity (TWE pp. 108-109).

Read and discuss Using Your Sociological Imagination (TWE p. 109).

Instruction: Do demonstration in Using the Section Preview (TWE p. 110).

Ask students to do Interdisciplinary Activity-Animal Research Debate (TWE p. 111).

Read and discuss Tech Trends (TWE p. 112).

Ask students to do Learning Styles-Logical-Mathematical (TWE p. 112).

Close: Assign Chapter 4 Vocabulary Activity (see *Unit 2 booklet*), due the day of the chapter review.

Assign chapter project (see TWE pp. 134-135, Chapter Assessment: Sociology Projects and Technology Activities) to be presented to the class prior to final chapter evaluation.

Ask students to read Sec. 2: Socialization and the Self (pp. 115-119).

Notes and Comments: _____

_____

_____

_____

_____

_____

_____

_____

Day 16   Block Schedule   Week of _____

Day 2 of 5

Content:	Ch. 4, Sec. 2: Socialization and the Self (pp. 115-119)
Objective:	Students will compare and contrast the functionalist, conflict, and symbolic interactionist perspectives on socialization.
Act. Type:	Class Discussion, Class Activity, Independent Practice, Cooperative Learning, Experiment
Introduction:	Do Using the Section Preview (TWE p. 115).
Instruction:	Discuss Points to Stress (TWE p. 116).
	Ask students to do On-Demand Writing-Self-Concept (TWE p. 116).
	Ask students to do Working with the Table -Fig. 4.1 (TWE p. 117).
	Do Learning Styles-Musical/Interpersonal (TWE p. 118).
	Discuss Points to Stress (TWE p. 118).
	Use Reteaching (TWE p. 118) for emphasis.
Close:	Discuss Pulling It All Together (TWE p. 119).
	Ask students to read Sec. 3: Agents of Socialization (pp. 120-127).

Notes and Comments: _____

_____

_____

_____

_____

_____

_____

_____

_____

Day 17   **Block Schedule**   Week of _____

Day 3 of 5

Content: Ch. 4, Sec. 3: Agents of Socialization (pp. 120-127)

Objective: Students will analyze the roles of the family and school in socializing young people and will evaluate mass media techniques used to influence perceptions, attitudes, and behaviors of individuals and groups.

Act. Type: Class Discussion, Class Activity, Demonstration, Cooperative Learning, Presentation

Introduction: Read and discuss Another Time (TWE p. 120).

Instruction: Introduce Using the Section Preview (TWE p. 121).

     Share Making Connections to Other Cultures (TWE p. 123).

     Ask students to do Cooperative Learning Activity (TWE p. 121).

     Ask students to interpret the map in World View (TWE p. 125).

     Do Interdisciplinary Activity-Culture Studies (TWE pp. 124-125).

Close: Introduce "Writing on the Wall" described in Learning Styles-Visual (TWE pp. 122-123).

     Ask students to read Sec. 4: Processes of Socialization (pp. 128-132).

     Remind students that chapter presentations are due the following class session.

Notes and Comments: _____

_____

_____

_____

_____

_____

_____

_____

_____

SOCIALIZATION

Day 18

Block Schedule   **Week of** _____

Day 4 of 5

Content: Ch. 4, Sec. 4: Processes of Socialization (pp. 128-132), and Ch. 4 Presentations (pp. 108-132)

Objective: Students will discuss processes for socialization in adulthood and will present projects and activities summarizing objective/s learned in the chapter.

Act. Type: Class Discussion, Class Activity, Independent Practice, Role Play Presentations

Introduction: Follow-up on Interdisciplinary Activity-Culture Studies (TWE pp. 124-125) from previous session.

Instruction: Read and discuss Sociology Today-Struggling Through the Teen Years (TWE pp. 126-127).

Ask students to interpret the map in Snapshot of America (TWE p. 129).

Read and do Focus on Research (TWE p. 130-131).

Ask students to do Role Play (TWE p. 131).

Have students do presentations (See TWE, Chapter Assessment: Sociology Projects and Technology Activities, pp. 134-135).

Have students do On-Demand Writing (TWE p. 130).

Close: Assign Chapter 4 Learning Goals Outline (see *Unit 2 Booklet, TRB*), due the day of the chapter evaluation.

Remind students to study for the chapter evaluation.

Notes and Comments: _____

_____

_____

_____

_____

_____

_____

Chapter 4

SOCIALIZATION

Day 19   **Block Schedule**   **Week of** _____

Day 5 of 5

Content:	Ch. 4, Assessment (pp. 133-135) and Evaluation
Objective:	Students will review for evaluation of the concepts learned in this chapter.
Act. Type:	Class Discussion, Class Activity, Independent Practice, Cooperative Learning, Demonstration, Experiment, Debate, Role-playing, Presentation
Introduction:	Review Chapter 4 Vocabulary Activity homework (see *Unit 2 Booklet, TRB*).
Instruction:	Do Chapter Assessment as needed (TWE pp. 133-135).
Evaluate:	To evaluate the students' comprehension of the chapter, administer Chapter 4 Test A or B. You may want to use the Alternative Assessment found in the TRB.
Close:	Discuss Enrichment Reading (TWE pp. 136-137).
	Assign Chapter 5, intro. (pp. 138-139) and Ch. 5, Sec. 1: Social Structure and Status (pp. 140-143).

Notes and Comments: _____

_____

_____

_____

_____

_____

_____

_____

_____

_____

_____

Chapter 5 SOCIAL STRUCTURE AND SOCIETY

Day 20	**Block Schedule**	**Week of** _____

Day 1 of 6

Content: Ch. 5 Intro. (pp. 138-139) and Ch. 5, Sec. 1: Social Structure and Status (pp. 140-143)

Objective: Students will understand the effects of social structure and will explain what sociologists mean by social structure and how statuses are related to that social structure.

Act. Type: Class Discussion, Class Activity, Independent Practice, Cooperative Learning, Demonstration, Role-playing, Presentation

Introduction: Direct students in Lead-Off Activity (TWE p. 138).

Read and discuss Using Your Sociological Imagination (TWE p. 139).

Instruction: Discuss Using the Section Preview (TWE p. 140).

Do Demonstration (TWE p. 140).

Have students do Role Play activity (TWE p. 141).

Close: Introduce and assign Teaching Strategy-Act.#5 from Ch. Assessment (TWE p. 167).

Assign Chapter 5 Vocabulary Activity (see *Unit 2 Booklet, TRB*), due the day of the chapter review.

Assign chapter project (see TWE pp. 166-167, Chapter Assessment: Sociology Projects and Technology Activities) to be presented to the class prior to final chapter evaluation.

Ask students to read Sec. 2: Social Structure and Roles (pp. 144-151).

Notes and Comments: _____

_____

_____

_____

_____

_____

_____

344

Chapter 5 SOCIAL STRUCTURE AND SOCIETY

Day 21	**Block Schedule**	**Week of** _____

Day 2 of 6

Content: Ch. 5, Sec. 2: Social Structure and Roles (pp. 144-151)

Objective: Students will discuss how roles are related to social structure and will define and explain how to manage role conflict and role strain.

Act. Type: Class Discussion, Class Activity, Independent Practice, Cooperative Learning, Demonstration, Role-playing, Presentation

Introduction: Follow up on Teaching Strategy-Act.#5 from Ch. Assessment.

Instruction: Read and discuss Focus on Research (TWE pp. 144-145).

Ask students to do On-Demand Writing (TWE p. 145).

Ask students to do Demonstration (TWE p. 146).

Discuss Using the Section Preview (TWE p. 146).

Ask students to do Role Play (TWE p. 149).

Ask students to interpret the map in Snapshot of America (TWE p. 149).

Conduct Survey (TWE p. 150).

Read and discuss *Sociology Today* (TWE p. 152).

Close: Assign Learning Styles-Linguistic/Spatial (TWE p. 147).

Ask students to read Sec. 3: Preindustrial Societies (pp. 153-157).

Notes and Comments: _____

_____

_____

_____

_____

_____

_____

_____

Day 22   Block Schedule   Week of _____

Day 3 of 6

Content:	Ch. 5, Sec. 3: Preindustrial Societies (pp. 153-157)
Objective:	Students will describe the means of subsistence in preindustrial societies.
Act. Type:	Class Discussion, Class Activity, Demonstration, Presentation, Independent Practice, Cooperative Learning
Introduction:	Show video as described in Using the Section Preview (TWE p. 153).
Instruction:	Do Demonstration (TWE p. 153).
	*Optional - Do Interdisciplinary Activity (TWE p. 154).
	Discuss Using the Illustration-Timeline (TWE p. 155).
	Ask students to do Paired Learning Activity (TWE p. 156).
	Discuss Pulling It All Together (TWE p. 156).
Close:	Assign Learning Styles-Artistic (TWE p. 155) as appropriate.
	Ask students to read Sec. 4: Industrial and Postindustrial Societies – Basic Features of Industrial Societies; A Conversation with Two Sociologists (pp. 158-162).

Notes and Comments: _____

_____

_____

_____

_____

_____

_____

_____

_____

Chapter 5 — SOCIAL STRUCTURE AND SOCIETY

Day 23

Block Schedule   **Week of** _____

Content:	Ch. 5, Sec. 4: Industrial and Postindustrial Societies – Basic Features of Industrial Societies; A Conversation with Two Sociologists (pp. 158-162)
Objective:	Students will describe changes that take place when agricultural societies become industrial societies and will explain the contributions of early sociologists who wrote about preindustrial and industrial societies.
Act. Type:	Class Discussion, Class Activity, Cooperative Learning, Role-playing, Presentation
Introduction:	Read and discuss Another Place (TWE p. 158).
Instruction:	Ask students to do Role Play (TWE p. 160).
	Discuss and do activity in Using Decision-Making Skills (TWE p. 162).
	Discuss and ask students to do Learning Styles-Bodily/Kinesthetic (TWE p. 159).
Close:	Discuss World View (TWE p. 161).
	Ask students to read Sec. 4: Industrial and Postindustrial Societies – Major Features of Postindustrial Society; Social Instability in Postindustrial Society (pp. 162-163).
	Remind students that chapter presentations are due the following class session.

Notes and Comments: _____

_____

_____

_____

_____

_____

_____

_____

Day 24   **Block Schedule**   **Week of** _____

Day 5 of 6

Content:	Ch. 5, Sec. 4: Industrial and Postindustrial Societies – Major Features of Postindustrial Society; Social Instability in Postindustrial Society (pp. 162-163) and Ch. 5 Presentations (pp. 138-164)
Objective:	Students will analyze changes resulting from industrialization and will present projects and activities summarizing objective/s learned in the chapter.
Act. Type:	Class Discussion, Class Activity, Cooperative Learning, and Presentation
Introduction:	Discuss Pulling It All Together (TWE p. 163).
Instruction:	Share information in Points to Stress (TWE p. 162).
	Use Reteaching suggestion (TWE p. 162) as needed.
	*Optional - Do Encouraging Citizenship activity (TWE p. 163).
	Read and discuss Tech Trends (TWE p. 164).
	Have students do Cooperative Learning Activity (TWE p. 164).
	Have students do presentations (See TWE Chapter Assessment: Sociology Projects and Technology Activities, pp. 166-167).
Close:	Assign Chapter 5 Learning Goals Outline (see *Unit 2 Booklet, TRB*), due the day of the chapter evaluation.
	Remind students to study for the chapter evaluation.

Notes and Comments: _____

_____

_____

_____

_____

_____

_____

_____

Day 25   Block Schedule   Week of _____

Day 6 of 6

Content:	Ch. 5, Assessment and Evaluation
Objective:	Students will review for evaluation of the concepts learned in this chapter.
Act. Type:	Class Discussion, Class Activity, Independent Practice, Cooperative Learning, Demonstration, Experiment, Debate, Role-playing, Presentation
Introduction:	Review Chapter 5 Vocabulary Activity homework (see *Unit 2 Booklet, TRB*).
Instruction:	Do Chapter Assessment as needed (TWE pp. 165-167)
Evaluate:	To evaluate the students' comprehension of the chapter, administer Chapter 5 Test A or B. You may want to use the Alternative Assessment found in the TRB.
Close:	Discuss Enrichment Reading (TWE pp. 168-169).
	Assign Chapter 6, intro. (pp. 170-171) and Ch. 6, Sec. 1: Primary and Secondary Groups – Groups, Categories, and Aggregates; Primary Groups (pp. 172-174).

Notes and Comments: _____

_____

_____

_____

_____

_____

_____

_____

_____

_____

_____

_____

Chapter 6

GROUPS AND FORMAL ORGANIZATIONS

Day 26

Block Schedule   **Week of** _____

Day 1 of 5

Content: Ch. 6 Intro. (pp. 170-171) and Ch. 6, Sec. 1: Primary and Secondary Groups – Groups, Categories, and Aggregates; Primary Groups (pp. 172-174)

Objective: Students will understand the effects of group membership and will compare the roles of group membership in primary groups.

Act. Type: Class Discussion, Class Activity, Independent Practice

Introduction: Introduce Lead-Off Activity (TWE p. 170).

Read and discuss Using Your Sociological Imagination (TWE p. 171).

Introduction: Introduce Using the Section Preview (TWE p. 172).

Ask students to do On-Demand Writing (TWE p. 172).

Discuss Using the Illustration (TWE p. 172).

Share and discuss More About...Gender Interaction (TWE p. 173).

Close: Assign Chapter 6 Vocabulary Activity (see *Unit 2 Booklet, TRB*), due the day of the chapter review.

Assign chapter project (see TWE pp. 198-199, Chapter Assessment: Sociology Projects and Technology Activities) to be presented to the class prior to final chapter evaluation.

Ask students to read Sec. 1: Primary and Secondary Groups – Secondary Groups (pp. 174-175) and Sec. 2: Other Groups and Networks (pp. 177-179).

Notes and Comments: _____

_____

_____

_____

_____

_____

_____

_____

Chapter 6 GROUPS AND FORMAL ORGANIZATIONS

Day 27   Block Schedule   Week of _____

Day 2 of 5

Content:	Ch. 6, Sec. 1: Primary and Secondary Groups – Secondary Groups (pp. 174-175) and Ch. 6, Sec. 2: Other Groups and Networks (pp. 177-179)
Objective:	Students will compare the roles of group membership in secondary groups and will explain the purposes of reference groups and social networks.
Act. Type:	Class Discussion, Class Activity, Independent Practice, Cooperative Learning, Demonstration, Presentation
Introduction:	Do activity as described in Making Connections to Other Cultures (TWE p. 174).
Instruction:	Ask students to do Observation (TWE p. 174).
	Conduct Survey-Primary and Secondary Groups (TWE p. 175).
	Brainstorm as in Using the Section Preview (TWE p. 177).
	Discuss Using the Illustration (TWE p. 178).
	Facilitate students in doing Cooperative Learning Activity (TWE p. 177).
	Do Observation (TWE p. 178).
Close:	Ask students to read Sec. 3: Types of Social Interaction (pp. 180-186).

Notes and Comments: _____

_____

_____

_____

_____

_____

_____

_____

_____

Chapter 6

GROUPS AND FORMAL ORGANIZATIONS

Day 28   Block Schedule   Week of _____

Day 3 of 5

Content:	Ch. 6, Sec. 3: Types of Social Interaction (pp. 180-186)
Objective:	Students will discuss how these interactions affect the members of groups and will compare and contrast coercion and conformity.
Act. Type:	Class Discussion, Class Activity, Independent Practice, Cooperative Learning, Demonstration, Experiment, Debate
Introduction:	Do Using Problem-Solving Skills (TWE p. 179).
Instruction:	Ask students to do Cooperative Learning Activity (TWE p. 181).
	Discuss Controversy and Debate (TWE p. 182).
	Lead students in doing the Encouraging Citizenship Activity (TWE p. 183).
	Have students do Demonstration (TWE p. 184).
	Discuss Using the Illustration (TWE p. 185).
	Share and discuss information in Working with the Data-Fig. 6.2 (TWE p. 186).
	Discuss Sociology Today (TWE p. 180).
Close:	Assign Learning Styles-Intrapersonal/Linguistic (TWE p. 186).
	Ask students to read Sec. 4: Formal Organizations (pp. 190-196).
	Remind students that chapter presentations are due the following class session.

Notes and Comments: _____

_____

_____

_____

_____

_____

_____

_____

Day 29 — Block Schedule — Week of _____

Day 4 of 5

Content:	Ch. 6, Sec. 4: Formal Organizations (pp. 190-196) and Ch. 6 Presentations (pp. 170-196)
Objective:	Students will discuss the use of power and its effect on the roles of group membership in formal organizations and will present projects and activities summarizing objective/s learned in the chapter.
Act. Type:	Class Discussion, Class Activity, Independent Practice, Demonstration, and Presentations
Introduction:	Read and discuss Tech Trends (TWE p. 187).
Instruction:	Lead Observation (TWE pp. 190-191).
	Review and discuss Working with the Data-Fig. 6.3 (TWE p. 191).
	With students, do Demonstration (TWE p. 193).
	Read and discuss Focus on Research (TWE pp. 188-189).
	Have students do presentations (See TWE, Chapter Assessment: Sociology Projects and Technology Activities, pp. 198-199).
Close:	Discuss Snapshot of America (TWE p. 193).
	Assign Chapter 6 Learning Goals Outline (see *Unit 2 Booklet, TRB*), due the day of the chapter evaluation.
	Remind students to study for the chapter evaluation.

Notes and Comments: _____

_____

_____

_____

_____

_____

_____

Chapter 6

GROUPS AND FORMAL ORGANIZATIONS

Day 30
Block Schedule   Week of _____

Day 5 of 5

Content: Ch. 6, Assessment (pp. 197-199) and Evaluation

Objective: Students will review for evaluation of the concepts learned in this chapter.

Act. Type: Class Discussion, Class Activity, Independent Practice, Cooperative Learning, Demonstration, Experiment, Debate, Role-playing, Presentation

Introduction: Review Chapter 6 Vocabulary Activity homework (see *Unit 2 Booklet, TRB*).

Instruction: Do Chapter Assessment as needed (TWE pp. 197-199).

Evaluate: To evaluate the students' comprehension of the chapter, administer Chapter 6 Test A or B. You may want to use the Alternative Assessment found in the TRB.

Close: Discuss Enrichment Reading (TWE pp. 200-201).

Assign Chapter 7, intro. (pp. 202-203) and Ch. 7, Sec. 1: Deviance and Social Control (pp. 204-208).

Notes and Comments: _____

_____

_____

_____

_____

_____

_____

_____

_____

_____

_____

Day 31   Block Schedule   Week of _____

Day 1 of 6

Content: Ch. 7 Intro. (pp. 202-203) and Ch. 7, Sec. 1: Deviance and Social Control (pp. 204-208)

Objective: Students will identify the major types of social control.

Act. Type: Class Discussion, Class Activity, Independent Practice, Demonstration, Debate

Introduction: Have students do Lead-Off Activity (TWE pp. 202-203).

Read and discuss Using Your Sociological Imagination (TWE p. 203).

Introduction: Review and discuss Working with the Data-Fig. 7.1 (TWE p. 204).

Discuss and do activity/s in Using Conflict-Resolution Skills (TWE pp. 204-205) or Observation (TWE p. 207).

Ask students to interpret the map in Snapshot of America (TWE p. 206).

Close: Discuss Another Time (TWE p. 208).

Assign Chapter 7 Vocabulary Activity (see *Unit 2 booklet*), due the day of the chapter review.

Assign chapter project (see TWE pp. 235, Chapter Assessment: Sociology Projects and Technology Activities) to be presented to the class prior to final chapter evaluation.

Ask students to read Sec. 2: Functionalism and Deviance (pp. 209-212).

Notes and Comments: _____

_____

_____

_____

_____

_____

_____

_____

Day 32

Block Schedule   **Week of** _____

Day 2 of 6

Content:	Ch. 7, Sec. 2: Functionalism and Deviance (pp. 209-212)
Objective:	Students will explain the positive and negative consequences of deviance and will differentiate the major functional theories of deviance.
Act. Type:	Class Discussion, Class Activity, Cooperative Learning, Independent Practice, Debate, Role-playing
Introduction:	Introduce Using the Section Preview (TWE p. 209).
Instruction:	Ask students to do Role Play (TWE p. 209).
	Share More About Strain Theory (TWE p. 210).
	Share and discuss Controversy and Debate (TWE p. 210).
	Review and discuss Working with the Data-Fig. 7.2 (TWE p. 211).
	Ask students to do On-Demand Writing (TWE p. 210).
Close:	Ask students to read Sec. 3: Symbolic Interactionism and Deviance (pp. 213-217) and Ch. 7, Sec. 4: Conflict Theory and Deviance (pp. 218-221).

Notes and Comments: _____

_____

_____

_____

_____

_____

_____

_____

_____

_____

_____

DEVIANCE AND SOCIAL CONTROL

Day 33   Block Schedule   Week of _____

Day 3 of 6

Content:	Ch. 7, Sec. 3: Symbolic Interactionism and Deviance (pp. 213-217) and Ch. 7, Sec. 4: Conflict Theory and Deviance (pp. 218-221)
Objective:	Students will compare and contrast cultural transmission theory and labeling theory, will discuss the conflict theory view of deviance, and will discuss the relationship between minorities, white-collar crime, and the judicial system.
Act. Type:	Class Discussion, Class Activity, Independent Practice, Cooperative Learning, Debate, Demonstration, Experiment
Introduction:	Read and discuss Sociology Today (TWE p. 213).
Instruction:	Share More About...Deviance and Labeling Theory (TWE p. 215).
	Use Teaching Strategy-the Labeling Game (TWE p. 216).
	Discuss and assign Controversy and Debate (TWE p. 219).
	Facilitate Cooperative Learning Activity (TWE p. 218).
	Ask students to do Reinforcing Vocabulary (TWE p. 220).
	Discuss and do Paired Learning Activity (TWE p. 220).
Close:	Assign Interdisciplinary Activity-Creative Writing (TWE p. 217).
	Ask students to read Sec. 5: Crime and Punishment (pp. 222-232).

Notes and Comments: _____

_____

_____

_____

_____

_____

_____

_____

Day 34   Block Schedule   Week of _____

Day 4 of 6

Content:	Ch. 7, Sec. 5: Crime and Punishment (pp. 222-232)
Objective:	Students will identify the meaning of crime statistics, especially as related to juvenile delinquency and will describe four approaches to crime control.
Act. Type:	Class Discussion, Class Activity, Independent Practice, Demonstration, Cooperative Learning, Presentation
Introduction:	Read and discuss Focus on Research (TWE pp. 222-223).
Instruction:	Introduce Using the Section Preview (TWE p. 224).
	Do Demonstration (TWE pp. 224-225).
	Review and discuss Working with the Data-Fig.7.6 (TWE p. 225).
	Facilitate Cooperative Learning Activity (TWE p. 226).
	Read and discuss Making Connections to Other Cultures (TWE p. 227).
	If possible, use Teaching Strategy (TWE p. 228) or Careers in Sociology (TWE p. 229) to invite a guest speaker to visit your class.
	Read and discuss Tech Trends (TWE p. 228).
	Have students do On-Demand Writing (TWE p. 227).
Close:	Remind students that chapter presentations are due the following class session.

Notes and Comments: _____

_____

_____

_____

_____

_____

_____

_____

Day 35   Block Schedule   Week of _____

Day 5 of 6

Content:	Ch. 7 (pp. 202-232) Presentations
Objective:	Students will present projects and activities summarizing objective/s learned in the chapter.
Act. Type:	Class Activity, Role-playing, and Presentation
Introduction:	Ask students to Role Play (TWE p. 231).
Instruction:	Have students do presentations (See TWE Chapter Assessment: Sociology Projects and Technology Activities, p. 235.)
Close:	Assign Chapter 7 Learning Goals Outline (see *Unit 2 Booklet, TRB*), due the day of the chapter evaluation.
	Remind students to study for the chapter evaluation.

Notes and Comments: _____

_____

_____

_____

_____

_____

_____

_____

_____

_____

_____

_____

_____

Chapter 7 — DEVIANCE AND SOCIAL CONTROL

Day 36   **Block Schedule**   **Week of** _____

Day 6 of 6

Content:	Ch. 7 Assessment (pp. 233-235) and Evaluation
Objective:	Students will review for evaluation of the concepts learned in this chapter.
Act. Type:	Class Discussion, Class Activity, Independent Practice, Cooperative Learning, Demonstration, Experiment, Debate, Role-playing, Presentation
Introduction:	Review Chapter 7 Vocabulary Activity homework (see *Unit 2 Booklet, TRB*).
Instruction:	Do Chapter Assessment as needed (TWE pp. 233-235).
Evaluate:	To evaluate the students' comprehension of the chapter, administer Chapter 7 Test A or B. You may want to use the Alternative Assessment found in the TRB. A test for Unit 2 is also available in the TRB.
Close:	Discuss Enrichment Reading (TWE pp. 236-237).
	Assign Unit 3, Chapter 8 Intro. (pp. 238-241) and Ch. 8, Sec. 1: Dimensions of Stratification (pp. 242-249).

Notes and Comments: _____

_____

_____

_____

_____

_____

_____

_____

_____

_____

_____

SOCIAL STRATIFICATION

Day 37   **Block Schedule**   **Week of** _____

Day 1 of 6

Content:	Unit 3, Chapter 8 Intro. (pp. 238-241) and Ch. 8, Sec. 1: Dimensions of Stratification (pp. 242-249).
Objective:	Students will understand how the economic dimension of social stratification affects human motivation and will analyze the relationships among social class and other culture group membership and political power.
Act. Type:	Class Discussion, Class Activity, Independent Practice, Demonstration, Cooperative Learning, Debate
Introduction:	Use Lead-Off Activity (TWE p. 240-241).
	Read and discuss Using Your Sociological Imagination (TWE p. 241).
Instruction:	Do activity found in Learning Styles-Bodily-Kinesthetic/Interpersonal (TWE p. 242).
	Ask students to interpret the map in World View (TWE p. 243).
	Facilitate Cooperative Learning Activity (TWE p. 246-247).
	Review and discuss Working with the Data-Fig.8.3 (TWE p. 247).
Close:	Discuss and assign Another Time (TWE p. 249).
	Assign Chapter 8 Vocabulary Activity (see *Unit 3 booklet*), due the day of the chapter review.
	Assign chapter project (see TWE p. 271, Chapter Assessment: Sociology Projects and Technology Activities) to be presented to the class prior to final chapter evaluation.
	Ask students to read Sec. 2: Explanations of Stratification (pp. 250-253).

Notes and Comments: _____

_____

_____

_____

_____

Chapter

8

SOCIAL STRATIFICATION

Day 38   Block Schedule   Week of _____

Day 2 of 6

Content:	Ch. 8, Sec. 2: Explanations of Stratification (pp. 250-253)
Objective:	Students will state the differences between the functionalist, conflict, and symbolic interactionist approaches to social stratification.
Act. Type:	Class Discussion, Class Activity, Debate, Role-playing
Introduction:	Share Using the Section Preview (TWE p. 250).
Instruction:	Ask students to Role Play (TWE p. 250).
	Share and discuss Controversy and Debate (TWE p. 251).
	Review and discuss Working with the Data-Fig. 8.4 (TWE p. 252).
Close:	Discuss Focus on Research and Using Problem-Solving Skills (TWE p. 253).
	Ask students to read Sec. 3: Social Classes in America (pp. 254-257).

Notes and Comments: _____

_____

_____

_____

_____

_____

_____

_____

_____

_____

_____

_____

Day 39	Block Schedule	Week of _____

Day 3 of 6

Content: Ch. 8, Sec. 3: Social Classes in America (pp. 254-257)

Objective: Students will compare cultural values associated with socioeconomic stratification of the upper, middle, working, and underclasses.

Act. Type: Class Discussion, Class Activity, Independent Practice, Cooperative Learning, Demonstration

Introduction: Do activity/demonstration described in Using the Section Preview (TWE p. 254).

Instruction: Ask students to conduct a Survey (TWE p. 254).

Share More About...Social Mobility (TWE p. 255).

Assign Increasing Your Reading Comprehension (see TRB) as needed.

Share Points to Stress (TWE p. 256).

If possible, use Teaching Strategy (TWE p. 256).

Have students do Using Decision-Making Skills activity (TWE p. 258).

Close: Assign On-Demand Writing (TWE p. 257).

Ask students to read Sec. 4: Poverty in America (pp. 258-264).

Notes and Comments: _____

_____

_____

_____

_____

_____

_____

_____

_____

Day 40

Block Schedule   **Week of** _____

Day 4 of 6

Content:	Ch. 8, Sec. 4: Poverty in America (pp. 258-264)
Objective:	Students will discuss the measurement and extent of poverty in the United States and will evaluate commitment to poverty programs in the United States.
Act. Type:	Class Discussion, Class Activity, Independent Practice, Cooperative Learning, Debate
Introduction:	Use the Internet to do Using the Section Preview (TWE p. 259).
Instruction:	Ask the students to do Paired Learning Activity (TWE p. 259).
	Discuss Points to Stress (TWE p. 259).
	Discuss and do Using Problem-Solving Skills activity (TWE pp. 260-261).
	Lead discussion in Controversy and Debate (TWE p. 260).
	Ask students to do Encouraging Citizenship Activity (TWE p. 263).
Close:	Discuss and assign Sociology Today – Parenting Across Class Lines (TWE p. 258).
	Ask students to read Sec. 5: Social Mobility (pp. 265-268).
	Remind students that chapter presentations are due the following class session.

Notes and Comments: _____

_____

_____

_____

_____

_____

_____

_____

_____

Chapter

8

SOCIAL STRUCTURE

Day 41	**Block Schedule**	Week of _____

Day 5 of 6

Content:	Ch. 8, Sec. 5: Social Mobility and Ch. 5 Presentations (pp. 242-268)
Objective:	Students will analyze the influence of motivation on socioeconomic consequences and will present projects and activities summarizing objective/s learned in the chapter.
Act. Type:	Class Discussion, Class Activity, Independent Practice, Cooperative Learning, Demonstration, and Presentations
Introduction:	Do demonstration in Using the Section Preview (TWE p. 265).
Instruction:	Facilitate Cooperative Learning Activity (TWE p. 268).
	Read and discuss Tech Trends (TWE p. 264).
	Have students do presentations (See TWE, Chapter Assessment: Sociology Projects and Technology Activities, p. 271).
Close:	Assign Learning Styles-Intrapersonal/Spatial (TWE p. 265).
	Assign Chapter 8 Learning Goals Outline (see *Unit 3 Booklet, TRB*), due the day of the chapter evaluation.
	Remind students to study for the chapter evaluation.

Notes and Comments: _____

_____

_____

_____

_____

_____

_____

_____

_____

Day 42   Block Schedule   Week of _____

Day 6 of 6

Content:	Ch. 8, Assessment (pp. 269-271) and Evaluation
Objective:	Students will review for evaluation of the concepts learned in this chapter.
Act. Type:	Class Discussion, Class Activity, Independent Practice, Cooperative Learning, Demonstration, Experiment, Debate, Role-playing, Presentation
Introduction:	Review Chapter 8 Vocabulary Activity homework (see *Unit 3 Booklet, TRB*).
Instruction:	Do Chapter Assessment as needed (TWE pp. 269-271).
Evaluate:	To evaluate the students' comprehension of the chapter, administer Chapter 8 Test A or B. You may want to use the Alternative Assessment found in the TRB.
Close:	Discuss Enrichment Reading (TWE pp. 272-273).
	Assign Chapter 9, intro. (pp. 274-275) and Sec. 1: Minority, Race, and Ethnicity (pp. 276-279).

Notes and Comments: _____

_____

_____

_____

_____

_____

_____

_____

_____

_____

_____

Chapter 9

INEQUALITIES OF RACE AND ETHNICITY

Day 43	**Block Schedule**	**Week of** _____

Day 1 of 5

Content: Ch. 9 Intro. (pp. 274-275) and Sec. 1: Minority, Race, and Ethnicity (pp. 276-279)

Objective: Students will compare various U.S. subculture groups such as ethnic and national origin and will describe what sociologists mean by minority, race, and ethnicity.

Act. Type: Class Discussion, Class Activity, Independent Practice, Demonstration, Cooperative Learning

Introduction: Use Lead-Off Activity (TWE p. 274-275).

Read and discuss Using Your Sociological Imagination (TWE p. 275).

Introduction: Ask students to do Survey (TWE p. 276).

Ask Open-Response Question (TWE p. 277).

Review and discuss Working with the Data (TWE p. 278).

Close: Do Making Connections to Other Cultures (TWE p. 278).

Assign chapter project (see TWE p. 305, Chapter Assessment: Sociology Projects and Technology Activities) to be presented to the class prior to final chapter evaluation.

Assign Chapter 9 Vocabulary Activity (see *Unit 3 Booklet, TRB*), due the day of the chapter review.

Ask students to read Sec. 2: Racial and Ethnic Relations (pp. 280-283).

Notes and Comments: _____

_____

_____

_____

_____

_____

_____

Chapter 9

INEQUALITIES OF RACE AND ETHNICITY

Day 44   Block Schedule   Week of _____

Day 2 of 5

Content:	Ch. 9, Sec. 2: Racial and Ethnic Relations
Objective:	Students will discuss patterns of racial and ethnic relations.
Act. Type:	Class Discussion, Class Activity, Independent Practice, Cooperative Learning, Demonstration
Introduction:	Read and discuss Another Place – The Travelling People (TWE p. 279).
Instruction:	Discuss Using the Section Preview (TWE p. 280).
	Ask students to do Using Problem-Solving Skills (TWE pp. 280-281).
	Do Pulling It All Together activity (TWE p. 282).
Close:	Read and discuss Sociology Today – Bridging the Digital Divide (TWE p. 283).
	Ask students to read Sec. 3: Theories of Prejudice and Discrimination (pp. 284-289).

Notes and Comments: _____

_____

_____

_____

_____

_____

_____

_____

_____

_____

_____

_____

Chapter 9

INEQUALITIES OF RACE AND ETHNICITY

Day 45   Block Schedule   Week of _____

Day 3 of 5

Content:	Ch. 9, Sec. 3: Theories of Prejudice and Discrimination (pp. 284-289)
Objective:	Students will discuss the difference between prejudice and discrimination and will compare and contrast the perspectives of the three theories.
Act. Type:	Class Discussion, Class Activity, Independent Practice, Cooperative Learning, Debate
Introduction:	Read and debate Using the Section Preview (TWE p. 284).
Instruction:	Discuss Open-Response Question (TWE p. 284).
	Have students do the Survey (TWE p. 284).
	Do Learning Styles-Visual Spatial activity (TWE pp. 286-287).
	Ask students to interpret the map in Snapshot of America (TWE p. 287).
	Share information in Teaching Strategy (TWE p. 287).
	Review and discuss Working with the Data (TWE p. 288).
Close:	Read and discuss Tech Trends-Spinning a Web of Hate (TWE p. 289).
	Ask students to read Sec. 4: Minority Groups in the United States (pp. 290-301).

Notes and Comments: _____

_____

_____

_____

_____

_____

_____

_____

_____

INEQUALITIES OF RACE AND ETHNICITY

Day 46   Block Schedule   Week of _____

Day 4 of 5

Content: Ch. 9, Sec. 4: Minority Groups in the United States (pp. 290-301)

Objective: Students will compare cultural socialization, norms, values, motivation, and communication between subculture groups.

Act. Type: Class Discussion, Class Activity, Independent Practice, Cooperative Learning, Demonstration, Experiment, Debate, Role-playing, Presentation

Introduction: Do demonstration activity in Using the Section Preview (TWE p. 290).

Instruction: Ask students to do Demonstration (TWE p. 290).

    Review and discuss Working with the Data (TWE p. 292 and TWE p. 294).

    Introduce and assign Learning Styles – Interpersonal (TWE pp. 292-293).

    Have students research and debate Controversy and Debate-Casinos and Gambling (TWE p. 296).

    Review and discuss Working with the Data (TWE p. 300).

Close: Read and discuss Focus on Research (TWE pp. 298-299).

    Assign Chapter 9 Learning Goals Outline (see *Unit 3 booklet*), due the day of the chapter evaluation.

    Remind students that chapter presentations are due the following class session.

    Also remind students to study for the chapter evaluation.

Notes and Comments: _____

_____

_____

_____

_____

_____

_____

INEQUALITIES OF RACE AND ETHNICITY

Day 47	**Block Schedule**	**Week of** _____

Day 5 of 5

Content: Ch. 9 Presentations (pp. 274-301), Assessment (pp. 302-305) and Evaluation

Objective: Students will present projects and activities summarizing objective/s learned and will review for evaluation of the concepts learned in this chapter.

Act. Type: Class Activity and Presentation

Introduction: Review Chapter 9 Vocabulary Activity homework (see *Unit 3 Booklet, TRB*).

Instruction: Have students do presentations (See TWE, Chapter Assessment: Sociology Projects and Technology Activities, p. 305).

Do Chapter Assessment as needed (TWE pp. 302-305).

Evaluate: To evaluate the students' comprehension of the chapter, administer Chapter 9 Test A or B. You may want to use the Alternative Assessment found in the TRB.

Close: Discuss Enrichment Reading (TWE pp. 306-307).

Assign Chapter 10, intro. (pp. 308-309) and Sec. 1: Sex and Gender Identity (pp. 310-315).

Notes and Comments: _____

_____

_____

_____

_____

_____

_____

_____

_____

_____

_____

Chapter 10 INEQUALITIES OF GENDER AND AGE

Day 48 — Block Schedule — Week of _____

Day 1 of 6

Content: Ch.10 Intro. (pp. 308-309) and Ch.10, Sec.1: Sex and Gender Identity (pp. 310-315)

Objective: Students will compare various U.S. subculture groups such as gender and age, distinguish the concepts of sex, gender, and gender identity, and discuss the research findings regarding gender and behavior.

Act. Type: Class Discussion, Class Activity, Independent Practice, Cooperative Learning, Demonstration, Experiment, Presentation

Introduction: Use Lead-Off Activity (TWE p. 308).

Do Demonstration (TWE p. 309).

Read and discuss Using Your Sociological Imagination (TWE p. 309).

Instruction: Use Teaching Strategy to make assignment (TWE p. 310).

Have students do Cooperative Learning Activity (TWE pp. 310-311).

Close: Assign chapter project (see TWE pp. 340-341, Chapter Assessment: Sociology Projects and Technology Activities) to be presented to the class prior to final chapter evaluation.

Assign Chapter 10 Vocabulary Activity (see *Unit 3 Booklet, TRB*), due the day of the chapter review.

Ask students to read Sec.2: Theoretical Perspectives on Gender (pp. 316-320).

Notes and Comments: _____

_____

_____

_____

_____

_____

Chapter 10 INEQUALITIES OF GENDER AND AGE

Day 49	Block Schedule	Week of _____

Day 2 of 6

Content: Ch.10, Sec.2: Theoretical Perspectives on Gender (pp. 316-320)

Objective: Students will outline the perspectives on gender taken by the three theories.

Act. Type: Class Discussion, Class Activity, Independent Practice, Demonstration

Introduction: Read and discuss Another Time-Manly Hearted Woman (TWE p. 315).

Do Demonstration-Gender Roles (TWE p. 318-319).

Discuss Using the Section Preview (TWE p. 316).

Instruction: Ask students to do On-Demand Writing (TWE p. 316).

Ask students to do Demonstration (TWE p. 317).

Ask students to interpret the map in World View (TWE p. 318).

Review and discuss Working with the Data (TWE p. 319).

Close: Use Teaching Strategy (TWE p. 319).

Ask students to read Sec.3: Gender Inequality (pp. 320-329).

Assign Observation (TWE p. 322).

Notes and Comments: _____

_____

_____

_____

_____

_____

_____

_____

_____

_____

_____

Chapter 10

INEQUALITIES OF GENDER AND AGE

Day 50   Block Schedule   Week of _____

Day 3 of 6

Content: Ch.10, Sec.3: Gender Inequality (pp. 320-329)

Objective: Students will describe the occupational, economic, legal, and political status of women in the United States.

Act. Type: Class Discussion, Class Activity, Independent Practice, Cooperative Learning, Debate, Role-playing

Introduction: Discuss results from Observation assignment (TWE p. 322).

Instruction: Read and discuss Sociology Today-Gender-Based Hierarchy (TWE p. 321).

     Review and discuss Working with the Data (TWE p. 323-325).

     Use activity in Controversy and Debate (TWE p. 324).

     Review and discuss Working with the Data (TWE p. 326) and (TWE p. 327).

     Have students do role-plays as in Teaching Strategy (TWE p. 327).

     Ask students to do Paired-Learning Activity (TWE p. 328).

Close: Read and discuss Tech Trends-Men, Women, and the Internet (TWE p. 329).

     Ask students to read Sec. 4: Ageism (pp. 330-332) and Ch.10, Sec.5: Inequality in America's Elderly Population – Elderly People as a Minority Group; Economics of the Elderly (pp. 333-336).

Notes and Comments: _____

_____

_____

_____

_____

_____

_____

_____

Chapter 10 INEQUALITIES OF GENDER AND AGE

Day 51	**Block Schedule**	**Week of** _____

Day 4 of 6

Content:	Ch.10, Sec.4: Ageism (pp. 330-332) and Ch.10, Sec.5: Inequality in America's Elderly Population – Elderly People as a Minority Group; Economics of the Elderly (pp. 333-336)
Objective:	Students will distinguish between age stratification and ageism and will describe the economic status of the elderly in the United States.
Act. Type:	Class Discussion, Class Activity, Independent Practice, Cooperative Learning
Introduction:	Ask students to do Cooperative Learning Activity (TWE p. 329).
Instruction:	Do the activity in Using the Section Preview (TWE p. 330).
	Review and discuss Working with the Data (TWE p. 331).
	Do Internet activity in Using the Section Preview (TWE p. 333).
	Read and discuss Focus on Research (TWE pp. 334-335).
	Discuss and ask students to do On-Demand Writing (TWE pp. 334-335).
Close:	Discuss and assign Using Problem-Solving Skills (TWE p. 332).
	Discuss and assign Learning Styles-Musical/Interpersonal (TWE p. 337).
	Ask students to read Sec. 5: Inequality in America's Elderly Population – Political Power and the Elderly (pp. 337-338).
	Remind students that chapter presentations are due the following class session.

Notes and Comments: _____

_____

_____

_____

_____

_____

_____

Day 52   Block Schedule   Week of _____

Day 5 of 6

Content:	Ch.10, Sec.5: Inequality in America's Elderly Population – Political Power and the Elderly (pp. 337-338) and Ch.10 Presentations (pp. 308-338)
Objective:	Students will describe the legal and political status of the elderly in the United States and will present projects and activities summarizing objective/s learned in the chapter.
Act. Type:	Class Discussion, Class Activity, Independent Practice, Demonstration, and Presentations
Introduction:	Discuss results from Learning Styles-Musical/Interpersonal activity (TWE p. 337).
Instruction:	Discuss Open-Response Question (TWE p. 336).
	Ask students to interpret the map in Snapshot of America (TWE p. 337).
	Ask students to do On-Demand Writing (TWE p. 336).
	Review and discuss Working with the Data (TWE p. 338).
	Have students do presentations (See TWE, Chapter Assessment: Sociology Projects and Technology Activities, pp. 340-341).
Close:	Assign Chapter 10 Learning Goals Outline (see *Unit 3 Booklet, TRB*), due the day of the chapter evaluation.
	Remind students to study for the chapter evaluation.

Notes and Comments: _____

_____

_____

_____

_____

_____

_____

_____

_____

Chapter 10 INEQUALITIES OF GENDER AND AGE

Day 53
Block Schedule   **Week of** _____

Day 6 of 6

Content: Ch.10 Assessment (pp. 339-341) and Evaluation

Objective: Students will review for evaluation of the concepts learned in this chapter.

Act. Type: Class Discussion, Class Activity, Independent Practice, Cooperative Learning, Demonstration, Experiment, Debate, Role-playing, Presentation

Introduction: Review Chapter 10 Vocabulary Activity homework (see *Unit 3 Booklet, TRB*).

Instruction: Do Chapter Assessment as needed (TWE pp. 339-341).

Evaluate: To evaluate the students' comprehension of the chapter, administer Chapter 10 Test A or B. You may want to use the Alternative Assessment found in the TRB.

Close: Discuss Enrichment Reading (TWE pp. 342-343).

Ask students to do On-Demand Writing (TWE p. 313).

Assign Unit 4 Intro., Chapter 11 intro. (pp. 344-347) and Sec.1: Family and Marriage Across Cultures – Defining the Family; Two Basic Types of Families; Patterns of Family Structure (pp. 348-351).

Notes and Comments: _____

_____

_____

_____

_____

_____

_____

_____

_____

_____

_____

Day 54   Block Schedule   Week of _____

Day 1 of 5

Content: Ch.11 Intro. (pp. 344-347) and Ch.11, Sec.1: Family and Marriage Across Cultures – Defining the Family; Two Basic Types of Families; Patterns of Family Structure (pp. 348-351)

Objective: Students will understand how the social institution of family meets basic needs in society and will summarize the functions of the social institution of the family.

Act. Type: Class Discussion, Class Activity, Independent Practice, Presentation

Introduction: Use Lead-Off Activity (TWE p. 346).

           Read and discuss Using Your Sociological Imagination (TWE p. 347).

Instruction: Ask students to do Cooperative Learning Activity (TWE p. 348).

           Ask students to do research project/bulletin board in Making Connections to Other Cultures (TWE p. 349 and TWE p. 350.)

Close: Do Learning Styles-Visual (TWE p. 350).

           Assign chapter project (see Chapter Assessment: Sociology Projects and Technology Activities) to be presented to the class prior to final chapter evaluation.

           Assign Chapter 11 Vocabulary Activity (see *Unit 4 Booklet, TRB*), due the day of the chapter review.

           Ask students to read Sec.1: Family and Marriage Across Cultures – Marriage Arrangements; Choosing a Mate (pp. 351-355) and Ch.11, Sec.2: Theoretical Perspectives and the Family (pp. 356-361)

Notes and Comments: _____

_____

_____

_____

_____

_____

_____

Chapter 11

THE FAMILY

Day 2 of 5

Content:	Ch.11, Sec.1: Family and Marriage Across Cultures – Marriage Arrangements; Choosing a Mate (pp. 351-355); and Ch.11, Sec.2: Theoretical Perspectives and the Family (pp. 356-361)
Objective:	Students will describe norms for marriage arrangements and will compare and contrast views of the family proposed by the three major perspectives.
Act. Type:	Class Discussion, Class Activity, Independent Practice, Cooperative Learning, Demonstration, Experiment, Debate
Introduction:	Use Teaching Strategy (TWE p. 351).
Instruction:	Ask students to interpret the map in World View (TWE p. 353).
	Review and discuss Working with the Data (TWE p. 354).
	Have students do Cooperative Learning Activity (TWE pp. 354-355).
	Do Demonstration (TWE pp. 358-359).
	Read and discuss Another Time-Courtship and Marriage Among the Hopi (TWE p. 356).
Close:	Assign On-Demand Writing (TWE p. 353).
	Ask students to read Sec.3: Family and Marriage in the United States (pp. 362-369) and Ch.11, Sec.4: Changes in Marriage and Family – Blended Families; Single-Parent Families; Childless Marriages; Dual-Employed Marriages (pp. 370-375).

Notes and Comments: _____

_____

_____

_____

_____

_____

_____

Chapter 11

THE FAMILY

Day 56   Block Schedule   Week of _____

Day 3 of 5

Content: Ch.11, Sec.3: Family and Marriage in the United States (pp. 362-369) and Ch.11, Sec.4: Changes in Marriage and Family – Blended Families; Single-Parent Families; Childless Marriages; Dual-Employed Marriages (pp. 370-375)

Objective: Students will outline the extent and cause of divorce and family violence in the United States and will describe alternatives to the traditional nuclear family structure.

Act. Type: Class Discussion, Class Activity, Independent Practice, Cooperative Learning, Demonstration, Debate, Role-playing

Introduction: Have students do Using Decision-Making Skills (TWE pp. 360-361).

Instruction: Read and discuss Sociology Today (TWE p. 362).

     Do Demonstration (TWE p. 369).

     Review and discuss Working with the Data (TWE p. 364) and (TWE p. 368).

     Ask students to interpret the map in Snapshot of America (TWE p. 365).

     Read and discuss Tech Trends-Technology and the Family (TWE p. 370).

     Review and discuss Working with the Data (TWE p. 373).

Close: Do Cooperative Learning Activity (TWE p. 374).

     Ask students to read Sec. 4: Changes in Marriage and Family – Cohabitation; Same Sex Domestic Partners; Single Life; Boomerang Kids; Looking Forward (pp. 375-380).

     Remind students that chapter presentations are due the following class session.

Notes and Comments: _____

_____

_____

_____

_____

| **Day 57** | **Block Schedule** | **Week of** _____ |

Day 4 of 5

Content: Ch.11, Sec.4: Changes in Marriage and Family – Cohabitation; Same Sex Domestic Partners; Single Life; Boomerang Kids; Looking Forward (pp. 375-380) and Ch.11 Presentations (pp. 346-380)

Objective: Students will evaluate the importance of the social institution of the family in the United States and will present projects and activities summarizing objective/s learned in the chapter.

Act. Type: Class Discussion, Class Activity, Independent Practice, Cooperative Learning, Debate, and Presentations

Introduction: Have students do Learning Styles activity (TWE p. 375).

Instruction: Share More About...Lasting Marriages and More About...Happy Marriages (TWE p. 378)

Ask students to do On-Demand Writing (TWE pp. 378-379).

Read and discuss Focus on Research (TWE pp. 376-377).

Have students do presentations (See TWE, Chapter Assessment: Sociology Projects and Technology Activities, pp. 382-383).

Close: Assign Chapter 11 Learning Goals Outline (see *Unit 4 Booklet, TRB*), due the day of the chapter evaluation.

Remind students to study for the chapter evaluation.

Notes and Comments: _____

_____

_____

_____

_____

_____

_____

_____

Chapter 11

THE FAMILY

Day 58   Block Schedule   Week of _____

Day 5 of 5

Content:	Ch.11, Assessment (pp. 381-383)
Objective:	Students will review for evaluation of the concepts learned in this chapter.
Act. Type:	Class Discussion, Class Activity, Independent Practice, Cooperative Learning, Demonstration, Experiment, Debate, Role-playing, Presentation
Introduction:	Review Chapter 11 Vocabulary Activity homework (see *Unit 4 Booklet, TRB*).
Instruction:	Do Chapter Assessment as needed (TWE pp. 381-383).
Evaluate:	To evaluate the students' comprehension of the chapter, administer Chapter 11 Test A or B. You may want to use the Alternative Assessment found in the TRB.
Close:	Discuss Enrichment Reading (TWE pp. 384-385).
	Assign Chapter 12, intro. (pp. 386-387) and Sec.1: Development and Structure of Education.

Notes and Comments: _____

_____

_____

_____

_____

_____

_____

_____

_____

_____

_____

_____

Chapter 12

EDUCATION

Day 59	Block Schedule	Week of _____

Day 1 of 4

Content: Ch.12 Intro. (pp. 386-387) and Sec.1: Development and Structure of Education (pp. 388-395)

Objective: Students will understand how the social institution of education meets basic needs in society, will discuss schools as bureaucracies, and alternative forms of education.

Act. Type: Class Discussion, Class Activity, Independent Practice, Cooperative Learning, Demonstration, Debate, Presentation

Introduction: Use Lead-Off Activity (TWE pp. 386-387).

Read and discuss Using Your Sociological Imagination (TWE p. 387) with guest speaker, if possible.

Instruction: Ask students to do the Survey (TWE p. 389).

Do Controversy and Debate (TWE p. 390).

Read and discuss Another Time-Understanding Freedom and Education in America (TWE p. 392).

Have students do the Cooperative Learning Activity (TWE p. 393).

Close: Assign students to do the Paired-Learning Activity (TWE p. 392).

Assign chapter project (see Chapter Assessment: Sociology Projects and Technology Activities) to be presented to the class prior to final chapter evaluation.

Ask students to read Sec.2: Functionalist Perspective (pp. 396-399) and Sec.3: Conflict Perspective.

Notes and Comments: _____

_____

_____

_____

_____

_____

Day 60

Block Schedule   **Week of** _____

Day 2 of 4

Content:	Ch.12, Sec.2: Functionalist Perspective (pp. 396-399) and Ch.12, Sec.3: Conflict Perspective (pp. 400-407)
Objective:	Students will summarize the functions of the social institution of education, evaluate the merit-based nature of public education, and educational equality.
Act. Type:	Class Discussion, Class Activity, Independent Practice, Experiment, Debate, Presentation
Introduction:	Do the activity in Using the Section Preview (TWE p. 396).
Instruction:	Read and discuss Sociology Today-Educating Yourself for the Future (TWE p. 399).
	Show video as described in Using the Section Preview (TWE p. 400).
	Review and discuss Working with the Data (TWE p. 401-402).
	Ask students to do Using Conflict Resolution Skills (TWE pp. 400-401).
	Conduct the debate in Learning Styles-Linguistic/Bodily-Kinesthetic (TWE pp. 402-403).
	Ask students to interpret the map in Snapshot of America-School Expenditures (TWE p. 404).
Close:	Assign On-Demand Writing (TWE pp. 398-399).
	Assign Chapter 12 Vocabulary Activity (see *Unit 4 Booklet, TRB*), due the day of the chapter review.
	Ask students to read Sec.4: Symbolic Interactionism (pp. 409-415).
	Remind students that chapter presentations are due the following class session.

Notes and Comments: _____

_____

_____

_____

_____

384

EDUCATION

Day 61   **Block Schedule**   **Week of** _____

Day 3 of 4

Content:	Ch.12, Sec.4: Symbolic Interactionism (pp. 409-415) and Ch.12 Presentations (pp. 386-415)
Objective:	Students will evaluate the importance of the social institution of education in the United States and will present projects and activities summarizing objective/s learned in the chapter.
Act. Type:	Class Discussion, Class Activity, Independent Practice, Demonstration, Experiment, Debate, and Presentations
Introduction:	Introduce research project in Using the Section Preview (TWE p. 409).
Instruction:	Do Demonstration (TWE pp. 410-411).
	Review and discuss Working with the Data (TWE p. 411).
	Read and discuss Focus on Research (TWE pp. 414-415).
	Read and discuss Tech Trends (TWE p. 408).
	Have students do presentations (See TWE, Chapter Assessment: Sociology Projects and Technology Activities, pp. 418-419).
Close:	Have students do On-Demand Writing (TWE p. 412).
	Assign Chapter 12 Learning Goals Outline (see *Unit 4 booklet,* TRB), due the day of the chapter evaluation.
	Remind students to study for the chapter evaluation.

Notes and Comments: _____

_____

_____

_____

_____

_____

385

Day 62   Block Schedule   Week of _____

Day 4 of 4

Content:	Ch.12 Assessment (pp. 416-419) and Evaluation
Objective:	Students will review for evaluation of the concepts learned in this chapter.
Act. Type:	Class Discussion, Class Activity, Independent Practice, Cooperative Learning, Demonstration, Experiment, Debate, Role-playing, Presentation
Introduction:	Review Chapter 12 Vocabulary Activity homework (see *Unit 4 booklet,* TRB).
Instruction:	Do Chapter Assessment as needed (TWE pp. 416-419).
Evaluate:	To evaluate the students' comprehension of the chapter, administer Chapter 12 Test A or B. You may want to use the Alternative Assessment found in the TRB.
Close:	Discuss Enrichment Reading (TWE pp. 420-421).
	Assign Chapter 13, Intro. (pp. 422-423) and Sec.1: Power and Authority.

Notes and Comments: _____

_____

_____

_____

_____

_____

_____

_____

_____

_____

_____

_____

_____

Chapter 13

POLITICAL AND ECONOMIC INSTITUTIONS

| **Day 63** | **Block Schedule** | **Week of** _____ |

Day 1 of 6

Content: Ch.13 Intro. (pp. 422-423) and Sec.1: Power and Authority (pp. 424-431)

Objective: Students will understand how the political and economic social institutions meet basic needs in society, will identify three forms of authority, and will discuss differences among democracy, totalitarianism, and authoritarianism.

Act. Type: Class Discussion, Class Activity, Independent Practice, Role-playing, Debate, Presentation, Simulation, Cooperative Learning, Demonstration

Introduction: Use Lead-Off Activity (TWE pp. 422-423).

Read and discuss Using Your Sociological Imagination (TWE p. 423).

Instruction: Do Demonstration (TWE pp. 424-425).

Do Learning Styles activity (TWE pp. 426-427).

Have students write and share On-Demand Writing (TWE p. 429).

Close: Review and discuss Working with the Data (TWE p. 430).

Assign Another Place-China's One-Child Policy (TWE p. 432).

Assign Chapter 13 Vocabulary Activity (see *Unit 4 Booklet*, TRB), due the day of the chapter review.

Assign chapter project (see Review: Projects and Activities) to be presented to the class prior to final chapter evaluation.

Ask students to read Sec.2: Political Power in American Society (pp. 433-439).

Notes and Comments: _____

_____

_____

_____

_____

_____

_____

Chapter 13

POLITICAL AND ECONOMIC INSTITUTIONS

Day 64   Block Schedule   Week of _____

Day 2 of 6

Content: Ch.13, Sec.2: Political Power in American Society (pp. 433-439)

Objective: Students will explain how voting is an exercise of power and will evaluate the importance of political social institutions in the United States.

Act. Type: Class Discussion, Class Activity, Independent Practice, Cooperative Learning, Presentation

Introduction: Discuss assignment Another Place-China's One-Child Policy (TWE p. 432).

Instruction: Discuss Using the Section Preview (TWE p. 433).

         Review and discuss Working with the Data (TWE p. 435).

         Have students do Net Worthy activities (TWE p. 434).

         Review and discuss Working with the Data (TWE p. 437-438).

         Use Teaching Strategy (TWE p. 437).

         Do Interdisciplinary Activity (TWE pp. 436-437).

Close: Ask students to interpret the map in Snapshot of America (TWE p. 436).

         Ask students to read Sec. 3: Economic Systems (pp. 440-444) and Sec.4: The Modern Corporation (pp. 446-449).

Notes and Comments: _____

_____

_____

_____

_____

_____

_____

_____

_____

POLITICAL AND ECONOMIC INSTITUTIONS

Day 65   **Block Schedule**   Week of _____

Day 3 of 6

Content: Ch.13, Sec.3: Economic Systems (pp. 440-444) and Sec.4: The Modern Corporation (pp. 446-449)

Objective: Students will list characteristics of capitalism and socialism and will analyze the influence of corporations on economic decisions.

Act. Type: Class Discussion, Class Activity, Independent Practice, Cooperative Learning

Introduction: Pre-assess by Using the Section Preview (TWE p. 440).

Instruction: Review and discuss Working with the Data (TWE p. 442).

Share More About...Socialism (TWE p. 442).

Have students do Cooperative Learning Activity (TWE p. 446).

Compare results from above with Making Connections to Other Cultures (TWE p. 447).

Review and discuss Working with the Data (TWE p. 447).

Close: Assign Sociology Today-Employee Rights (TWE p. 448).

Ask students to read Sec.5: Work in the Modern Economy (pp. 450-456).

Notes and Comments: _____

_____

_____

_____

_____

_____

_____

_____

Day 66   Block Schedule   Week of _____

Day 4 of 6

Content:	Ch.13, Sec.5: Work in the Modern Economy (pp. 450-456)
Objective:	Students will analyze the influence of cultural values on economic behavior and will evaluate the importance of economic social institutions in the United States.
Act. Type:	Class Discussion, Class Activity, Independent Practice, Demonstration, Cooperative Learning, Presentation
Introduction:	Discuss assignment Sociology Today-Employee Rights (TWE p. 448).
Instruction:	Discuss Using the Section Preview (TWE p. 450).
	Get student participation using Teaching Strategy (TWE p. 450).
	Read and discuss Focus on Research (TWE pp. 452-453).
	Do Demonstration (TWE p. 456).
	Have students do Observation (TWE pp. 452-453).
	Discuss Pulling It All Together (TWE p. 456).
Close:	Review and discuss Working with the Data (TWE p. 451).
	Ask students to do Survey (TWE pp. 450-451).
	Remind students that chapter presentations are due the following class session.

Notes and Comments: _____

_____

_____

_____

_____

_____

_____

_____

Chapter 13 — POLITICAL AND ECONOMIC INSTITUTIONS

Day 67	**Block Schedule**	**Week of** _____

Day 5 of 6

Content: Chapter 13 Presentations (pp. 422-455)

Objective: Students will present projects and activities summarizing objective/s learned in the chapter.

Act. Type: Class Activity and Presentation

Introduction: Read and discuss Tech Trends (TWE p. 445).

Instruction: Have students do presentations (See TWE, Chapter Assessment: Sociology Projects and Technology Activities, p. 459.)

Close: Assign Chapter 13 Learning Goals Outline (see *Unit 4 booklet,* TRB), due the day of the chapter evaluation.

Remind students to study for the chapter evaluation.

Notes and Comments: _____

_____

_____

_____

_____

_____

_____

_____

_____

_____

_____

_____

_____

Chapter 13

POLITICAL AND ECONOMIC INSTITUTIONS

Day 68   Block Schedule   Week of _____

Day 6 of 6

Content:	Ch. 13 Assessment (pp. 457-459) and Evaluation
Objective:	Students will review for evaluation of the concepts learned in this chapter.
Act. Type:	Class Discussion, Class Activity, Independent Practice, Cooperative Learning, Demonstration, Experiment, Debate, Role-playing, Presentation
Introduction:	Review Chapter 13 Vocabulary Activity homework (see *Unit 4 booklet,* TRB).
Instruction:	Do Chapter Assessment as needed (TWE pp. 457-459).
Evaluate:	To evaluate the students' comprehension of the chapter, administer Chapter 13 Test A or B. You may want to use the Alternative Assessment found in the TRB.
Close:	Discuss Enrichment Reading (TWE pp. 460-461).
	Assign Chapter 14 Intro. (pp. 462-463) and Sec.1: Religion and Society.

Notes and Comments: _____

_____

_____

_____

_____

_____

_____

_____

_____

_____

_____

_____

_____

Chapter 14

RELIGION

Day 69	Block Schedule	Week of _____

Day 1 of 5

Content: Ch.14 Intro. (pp. 462-463) and Sec.1: Religion and Society (pp. 464-466)

Objective: Students will understand how social institutions of religion meet basic needs in society and will explain the sociological meaning of religion.

Act. Type: Class Discussion, Class Activity, Independent Practice, Demonstration, Debate

Introduction: Use Lead-Off Activity (TWE pp. 462-463).

Read and discuss Using Your Sociological Imagination (TWE p. 463).

Introduction: Do Demonstration (TWE p. 464).

Discuss More About...Studying Religion (TWE p. 464).

Have students do Demonstration (TWE p. 465).

Close: Read and discuss Another Place-Religion at War (TWE p. 466).

Assign chapter project (see Chapter Assessment: Sociology Projects and Technology Activities) to be presented to the class prior to final chapter evaluation.

Assign Chapter 14 Vocabulary Activity (see *Unit 4 Booklet*, TRB), due the day of the chapter review.

Ask students to read Sec.2: Theoretical Perspectives (pp. 467-473).

Notes and Comments: _____

_____

_____

_____

_____

_____

_____

_____

Day 70　　　　　　**Block Schedule**　　　　**Week of** _____

Day 2 of 5

Content:	Ch.14, read Sec.2: Theoretical Perspectives (pp. 467-473)
Objective:	Students will describe the sociological functions of religion and will analyze the relationship between cultural values and religion.
Act. Type:	Class Discussion, Class Activity, Independent Practice, Cooperative Learning, Demonstration
Introduction:	Discuss Careers in Sociology (TWE pp. 466-467).
Instruction:	Ask students to do On-Demand Writing (TWE pp. 468-469).
	Discuss and compare Working with the Data (TWE p. 468) and World View (TWE p. 469).
	Introduce Demonstration (TWE p. 472).
	Share and discuss More About...Marx (TWE p. 470).
	Discuss both Open-Response Questions (TWE p. 472).
	Have students do Cooperative Learning Activity (TWE p. 473).
Close:	Assign Tech Trends (TWE p. 474).
	Ask students to read Sec. 3: Religious Organization and Religiosity (pp. 475-480); and Sec.4: Religion in the United States.

Notes and Comments: _____

_____

_____

_____

_____

_____

_____

_____

　　　　　　　　　　　　　　394

Chapter 14

RELIGION

Day 71   **Block Schedule**   Week of _____

Day 3 of 5

Content:	Ch.14, Sec.3: Religious Organization and Religiosity (pp. 475-480); and Sec.4: Religion in the United States (pp. 481-488)
Objective:	Students will discuss the meaning and nature of religiosity and will analyze the relationship between secularization and religion in the United States.
Act. Type:	Class Discussion, Class Activity, Independent Practice, Cooperative Learning, Demonstration, Role-playing
Introduction:	Discuss Tech Trends (TWE p. 474).
Instruction:	Ask students to do On-Demand Writing (TWE pp. 474-475).
	Have students do Encouraging Citizenship Activity (TWE p. 476).
	Read and discuss Sociology Today (TWE pp. 476-477).
	Have students do Demonstration (TWE p. 481).
	Review and discuss Working with the Data (TWE p. 482-483).
	Share More About...Church Attendance (TWE p. 483).
	Review and discuss Working with the Data (TWE p. 485-486).
	Discuss Addressing Current Social Issues (TWE p. 485).
Close:	Assign On-Demand Writing (TWE p. 477).
	Remind students that chapter presentations are due the following class session.

Notes and Comments: _____

_____

_____

_____

_____

_____

Chapter 14

RELIGION

Day 72   Block Schedule   Week of _____

Day 4 of 5

Content:	Chapter 14 Presentations (pp. 462-488)
Objective:	Students will present projects and activities summarizing objective/s learned in the chapter.
Act. Type:	Class Activity and Presentation
Introduction:	Read and discuss Focus on Research (TWE p. 484).
Instruction:	Have students do presentations (See TWE, Chapter Assessment: Sociology Projects and Technology Activities, p. 491).
Close:	Assign Chapter 14 Learning Goals Outline (see *Unit 4 booklet,* TRB), due the day of the chapter evaluation.
	Remind students to study for the chapter evaluation.

Notes and Comments: _____

_____

_____

_____

_____

_____

_____

_____

_____

_____

_____

_____

_____

Day 73	**Block Schedule**	**Week of** _____

Day 5 of 5

Content: Ch.14 Assessment (pp. 489-491) and Evaluation

Objective: Students will review for evaluation of the concepts learned in this chapter.

Act. Type: Class Discussion, Class Activity, Independent Practice, Cooperative Learning, Demonstration, Experiment, Debate, Role-playing, Presentation

Introduction: Review Chapter 14 Vocabulary Activity homework (see *Unit 4 booklet,* TRB).

Instruction: Do Chapter Assessment (TWE p. 491).

Evaluate: To evaluate the students' comprehension of the chapter, administer Chapter 14 Test A or B. You may want to use the Alternative Assessment found in the TRB.

Close: Discuss Enrichment Reading (TWE p. 492-493).

Assign Chapter 15, Intro. (pp. 494-495) and Ch.15, Sec.1: The Nature of Sport (pp. 496-501).

Notes and Comments: _____

_____

_____

_____

_____

_____

_____

_____

_____

_____

_____

_____

Chapter 15

SPORT

Day 1 of 3

Content: Ch.15 Intro. (pp. 494-495) and Ch.15, Sec.1: The Nature of Sport (pp. 496-501)

Objective: Students will understand how the social institution of sport meets basic needs in society and will justify sport as an American institution.

Act. Type: Class Discussion, Class Activity, Independent Practice, Cooperative Learning, Experiment

Introduction: Use Lead-Off Activity (TWE pp. 494-495).

                   Read and discuss Using Your Sociological Imagination (TWE p. 495).

Instruction: Discuss Using the Section Preview and Using the Illustration (TWE p. 496).

                   Discuss and graph Open-Response Questions (TWE p. 497-498).

                   Discuss Addressing Current Social Issues (TWE p. 500).

Close: Assign Using Decision-Making Skills (TWE pp. 500-501).

                   Assign chapter project (see Chapter Assessment: Sociology Projects and Technology Activities) to be presented to the class prior to final chapter evaluation.

                   Ask students to read Ch.15, Sec. 2: Theoretical Perspectives and Sport (pp. 502-511) and Sec.3: Social Issues in Sport (pp. 512-518).

Notes and Comments: _____

_____

_____

_____

_____

_____

_____

_____

Chapter 15 · SPORT

Day 2 of 3

Content:	Ch.15, Sec. 2: Theoretical Perspectives and Sport (pp. 502-511) and Sec.3: Social Issues in Sport (pp. 512-518).
Objective:	Students will compare and contrast sport in America from a functionalist, conflict, and symbolic interactionist perspective, define the relationship between American sport and social mobility and cite evidence of sexism and racism in American sport.
Act. Type:	Class Discussion, Class Activity, Independent Practice, Cooperative Learning, Debate
Introduction:	Discuss assignment Using Decision-Making Skills (TWE pp. 500-501).
Instruction:	Review and discuss Working with the Data (TWE p. 504-508).
	Have students do Controversy and Debate (TWE p. 504).
	Have students do Cooperative Learning Activity (TWE pp. 510-511).
	Have students take the Survey (TWE pp. 512-513).
	Review and discuss Working with the Data (TWE p. 513-514).
	Share Making Connections to Other Cultures (TWE p. 517).
Close:	Read and discuss Sociology Today (TWE p. 519).
	Assign Chapter 15 Learning Goals Outline or Chapter 15 Vocabulary Activity (see *Unit 4 Booklet*, TRB), due the day of the chapter evaluation.
	Remind students to study for the chapter evaluation.
	Also remind students that chapter presentations are due the following class session.

Notes and Comments: _____

_____

_____

_____

_____

Chapter 15

SPORT

Day 76 **Block Schedule** **Week of** _____

Day 3 of 3

Content:	Ch.15, Presentations (pp. 494-519), Assessment (pp. 520-523), and Evaluation
Objective:	Students will present projects and activities summarizing objective/s learned in the chapter and will review for evaluation of the concepts learned in this chapter.
Act. Type:	Class Discussion, Class Activity, Independent Practice, Cooperative Learning, Demonstration, Experiment, Debate, Role-playing, Presentations
Introduction:	Review Chapter 15 homework (see *Unit 4 Booklet*, TRB).
	Read and discuss Tech Trends-Mass Media and Sports (TWE p. 502).
	Do Chapter Assessment as needed (TWE pp. 520-523).
Instruction:	Have students do presentations (See TWE, Chapter Assessment: Sociology Projects and Technology Activities, pp. 522-523).
Evaluate:	To evaluate the students' comprehension of the chapter, administer Chapter 15 Test A or B. You may want to use the Alternative Assessment found in the TRB.
Close:	Read and discuss Careers in Sociology (TWE pp. 518-519).

Notes and Comments: _____

_____

_____

_____

_____

_____

_____

_____

_____

_____

400

Chapter 15

Day 77 **Block Schedule** Week of _____

SPECIAL PROJECT PLANNING DAY

Content: *Doing Sociology: Focus on Research*

Objective: Students will plan and carry out a complete research project, including presentation of results.

Act. Type: Class Discussion, Class Activity, Independent Practice, Cooperative Learning, Demonstration, Experiment, Debate, Role-playing, Presentation

Introduction: Assign student research projects. (See TRB, *Doing Sociology: Focus on Research),* Research Projects 10-15.

Instruction: Allow students to work with partners/groups to plan research projects.

Close: Discuss timeline for research project presentation-students will make presentations the last class session.

Notes and Comments: _____

_____

_____

_____

_____

_____

_____

_____

_____

_____

_____

_____

_____

Chapter
15

Day 78 **Block Schedule** **Week of** _____

SPECIAL PROJECT PLANNING DAY

Content: *Doing Sociology: Focus on Research*

Objective: Students will plan and carry out a complete research project, including presentation of results.

Act. Type: Class Discussion, Class Activity, Independent Practice, Cooperative Learning, Demonstration, Experiment, Debate, Role-playing, Presentation

Introduction: Discuss reading from Culture Studies: The Sociological Perspective (seeTRB).

Instruction: Allow students to work with partners/groups to plan research projects.

Close: Assign Unit 5, Chapter 16, Intro, (pp. 526-529).

Notes and Comments: _____

_____

_____

_____

_____

_____

_____

_____

_____

_____

_____

_____

_____

402

Chapter 16 POPULATION AND URBANIZATION

Day 1 of 6

Content:	Ch.16 Intro. (pp. 526-529)
Objective:	Students will understand the importance of urbanization resulting in changes in American institutions.
Act. Type:	Class Discussion, Class Activity, Independent Practice
Introduction:	Use Lead-Off Activity (TWE pp. 528-529).
Instruction:	Discuss Key Terms (TWE p. 530).
	Read and discuss Using Your Sociological Imagination (TWE p. 529).
	Assign chapter project (see Chapter Assessment: Sociology Projects and Technology Activities) to be presented to the class prior to final chapter evaluation.
Close:	Ask students to read Sec.1: The Dynamics of Demography (pp. 530-535).

Notes and Comments: _____

_____

_____

_____

_____

_____

_____

_____

_____

_____

_____

_____

Day 80   Block Schedule   Week of _____

Day 2 of 6

Content:	Ch.16, Sec.1: The Dynamics of Demography (pp. 530-535)
Objective:	Students will evaluate cause and effect on American institutions due to population and urbanization changes.
Act. Type:	Class Discussion, Class Activity, Independent Practice, Cooperative Learning, Demonstration
Introduction:	Discuss Using the Section Preview (TWE p. 530).
Instruction:	Share and have students draw graphic representations of information in Teaching Strategy (TWE p. 530).
	Ask students to do Demonstration (TWE pp. 530-531).
	Ask students to interpret the map in Snapshot of America (TWE p. 532).
	Conduct a Survey (TWE pp. 532-533).
	Read and discuss Another Place (TWE p. 535).
Close:	Assign Chapter 16 Vocabulary Activity (see *Unit 5 Booklet*, TRB), due the day of the chapter review.
	Ask students to read Sec.2: World Population (pp. 536-546).

Notes and Comments: _____

_____

_____

_____

_____

_____

_____

_____

_____

_____

Day 81	**Block Schedule**	**Week of** _____

Day 3 of 6

Content:	Ch.16, Sec.2: World Population (pp. 536-546)
Objective:	Students will evaluate cause and effect on global institutions due to population and urbanization changes and will predict world population trends.
Act. Type:	Class Discussion, Class Activity, Independent Practice, Cooperative Learning, Demonstration
Introduction:	Do activity in Using the Section Preview (TWE p. 536).
Instruction:	Have students do Demonstration (TWE pp. 536-537).
	Review and discuss Working with the Data (TWE p. 537-538).
	Do Demonstration (TWE pp. 538-539).
	Use demonstration in Teaching Strategy (TWE p. 541).
	Have students do Using Conflict-Resolution Skills (TWE pp. 540-541).
	Ask students to do Cooperative Learning Activity (TWE pp. 542-543).
	Share More About...Population Control (TWE p. 543).
Close:	Have students do On-Demand Writing (TWE pp. 544-545).
	Ask students to read Sec. 3: The Urban Transition (pp. 547-554) and Ch.16, Sec.4: Urban Ecology (pp. 556-560).

Notes and Comments: _____

_____

_____

_____

_____

_____

_____

_____

Day 82

Block Schedule   **Week of** _____

Day 4 of 6

Content:	Ch.16, Sec.3: The Urban Transition (pp. 547-554) and Ch.16, Sec.4: Urban Ecology (pp. 556-560)
Objective:	Students will trace the development of preindustrial and modern cities and will compare and contrast four theories of city growth.
Act. Type:	Class Discussion, Class Activity, Independent Practice, Demonstration, Role-playing, Presentation, Cooperative Learning
Introduction:	Read and discuss Sociology Today (TWE p. 547).
Instruction:	Have students do Role Play (TWE pp. 548-549).
	Ask students to interpret the map in World View (TWE p. 550).
	Review and discuss Working with the Data (TWE p. 551) and (TWE p. 553).
	Ask students to do On-Demand Writing (TWE pp. 554-555).
	Do transparency activity in Using the Section Preview (TWE pp. 556).
	Have students do Learning Styles (TWE pp. 556-557).
	Use Teaching Strategy (TWE p. 559).
Close:	Discuss Careers in Sociology (TWE pp. 552-553).
	Assign Tech Trends (TWE p. 555).
	Remind students that chapter presentations are due the following class session.

Notes and Comments: _____

_____

_____

_____

_____

_____

_____

406

Day 83	**Block Schedule**	**Week of** _____

Day 5 of 6

Content: Chapter 16 (pp. 528-560) Presentations

Objective: Students will present projects and activities summarizing objective/s learned in the chapter.

Act. Type: Class Activity and Presentation

Introduction: Read and discuss Focus on Research (TWE p. 558).

Instruction: Have students do presentations (See TWE, Chapter Assessment: Sociology Projects and Technology Activities pp. 562-563).

Close: Assign Chapter 16 Learning Goals Outline (see *Unit 5 booklet,* TRB), due the day of the chapter evaluation.

Remind students to study for the evaluation.

Notes and Comments: _____

_____

_____

_____

_____

_____

_____

_____

_____

_____

_____

_____

_____

Day 84

Block Schedule Week of _____

Day 6 of 6

Content:	Ch.16 Assessment (pp. 561-563) and Evaluation
Objective:	Students will review for evaluation of the concepts learned in this chapter.
Act. Type:	Class Discussion, Class Activity, Independent Practice, Cooperative Learning, Demonstration, Experiment, Debate, Role-playing, Presentation
Introduction:	Review Chapter 16 Vocabulary Activity homework (see *Unit 5 booklet*, TRB).
Instruction:	Do Chapter Assessment as needed (TWE pp. 561-563).
Evaluate:	To evaluate the students' comprehension of the chapter, administer Chapter 16 Test A or B. You may want to use the Alternative Assessment found in the TRB.
Close:	Discuss Enrichment Reading (TW pp. 564-565).
	Assign Chapter 17 Intro. (pp. 566-567) and Ch.17, Sec.1: Social Change (pp. 568-575).

Notes and Comments: _____

_____

_____

_____

_____

_____

_____

_____

_____

_____

_____

_____

Day 85   Block Schedule   Week of _____

Day 1 of 5

Content:	Ch.17 Intro. (pp. 566-567) and Ch.17, Sec.1: Social Change (pp. 568-575)
Objective:	Students will understand the relevance and importance of social change, basic sociological principles related to social change, and the impact of scientific and technological discoveries evidenced by social change.
Act. Type:	Class Discussion, Class Activity, Independent Practice, Cooperative Learning, Role-playing
Introduction:	Introduce Lead-Off Activity (TWE pp. 566-567).
	Read and discuss Using Your Sociological Imagination (TWE p. 567).
Instruction:	Discuss results of Lead-Off Activity (TWE pp. 566-567).
	Review and discuss Working with the Data (TWE p. 569).
	Introduce and have students do Learning Styles (TWE p. 568).
	Ask students to interpret map in World View (TWE p. 574).

Close: Assign chapter project (see Chapter Assessment: Sociology Projects and Technology Activities) to be presented to the class prior to final chapter evaluation.

Assign Chapter 17 Vocabulary Activity (see *Unit 5 Booklet*, TRB), due the day of the chapter review.

Ask students to read Sec.2: Theoretical Perspectives on Social Change (pp. 576-580) and Sec.3: Collective Behavior (pp. 581-589).

Introduce and assign Paired Learning Activity (TWE pp. 574-575).

Notes and Comments: _____

_____

_____

_____

_____

_____

Day 86   Block Schedule   Week of _____

Day 2 of 5

Content:	Ch.17, Sec.2: Theoretical Perspectives on Social Change (pp. 576-580) and Ch.17, Sec.3: Collective Behavior (pp. 581-589)
Objective:	Students will describe social change as viewed by the functionalist, conflict, and symbolic interactionist perspective and will analyze social problems within and across groups.
Act. Type:	Class Discussion, Class Activity, Independent Practice, Cooperative Learning, Demonstration, Role-playing, Presentation
Introduction:	Discuss results from Paired Learning Activity (TWE pp. 574-575).
Instruction:	Discuss Focus on Research (TWE pp. 576-577).
	Ask students to do On-Demand Writing (TWE pp. 576-577).
	Review and discuss Working with the Data (TWE p. 579).
	Have students do Role Play (TWE p. 581).
Close:	Do Demonstration (TWE p. 580).
	Read and discuss Sociology Today (TWE p. 584).
	Ask students to read Sec.4: Social Movements (pp. 590-596).
	Assign students to prepare questions for guest speakers from Working with the Data (TWE p. 594).

Notes and Comments: _____

_____

_____

_____

_____

_____

_____

_____

PLANNING GUIDE   410

Chapter 17

SOCIAL CHANGE AND COLLECTIVE BEHAVIOR

Day 87   Block Schedule   Week of _____

Day 3 of 5

Content: Ch.17, Sec.4: Social Movements (pp. 590-596)

Objective: Students will identify types of social movements and will compare and contrast theories of social movements.

Act. Type: Class Discussion, Class Activity, Independent Practice, Cooperative Learning, Presentation

Introduction: Read and discuss Tech Trends (TWE p. 590).

Instruction: Have students do Using Decision-Making Skills (TWE pp. 590-591).

Review and discuss Working with the Data (TWE p. 592).

Discuss Reinforcing Vocabulary (TWE p. 592).

Use Teaching Strategy (TWE p. 593).

Discuss Working with the Data (TWE p. 594).

Invite guest speakers from above to lead presentation/discussion.

Close: Remind students that chapter presentations are due the following class session.

Notes and Comments: _____

_____

_____

_____

_____

_____

_____

_____

_____

Chapter 17

SOCIAL CHANGE AND COLLECTIVE BEHAVIOR

Day 88   Block Schedule   Week of _____

Day 4 of 5

Content:	Chapter 17 (pp. 566-596) Presentations
Objective:	Students will present projects and activities summarizing objective/s learned in the chapter.
Act. Type:	Class Activity and Presentation
Introduction:	Have students interpret the map in Snapshot of America (TWE p. 595).
Instruction:	Have students do presentations (See TWE, Chapter Assessment: Sociology Projects and Technology Activities, pp. 598-599).
Close:	Assign Chapter 17 Learning Goals Outline (see *Unit 5 booklet,* TRB), due the day of the chapter evaluation.
	Remind students to study for the chapter evaluation.

Notes and Comments: _____

_____

_____

_____

_____

_____

_____

_____

_____

_____

_____

_____

_____

Chapter 17

SOCIAL CHANGE AND
COLLECTIVE BEHAVIOR

Day 89   Block Schedule   Week of _____

Day 5 of 5

Content:	Ch.17, Assessment (pp. 597-599) and Evaluation
Objective:	Students will review for evaluation of the concepts learned in this chapter.
Act. Type:	Class Discussion, Class Activity, Independent Practice, Cooperative Learning, Demonstration, Experiment, Debate, Role-playing, Presentation
Introduction:	Review Chapter 17 Vocabulary Activity homework (see *Unit 5 booklet,* TRB).
Instruction:	Do Chapter Assessment as needed (TWE pp. 597-599).
Evaluate:	To evaluate the students' comprehension of the chapter, administer Chapter 17 Test A or B. You may want to use the Alternative Assessment found in the TRB. There is also a final exam for your use, in the TRB.
Close:	Discuss Enrichment Reading (TWE pp. 600-601).
	Remind students that final presentations are due the following class session.

Notes and Comments: _____

_____

_____

_____

_____

_____

_____

_____

_____

_____

_____

_____

Chapter 17

SOCIAL CHANGE AND COLLECTIVE BEHAVIOR

Day 90   **Block Schedule**   Week of _____

SPECIAL PROJECT PRESENTATION DAY

Content:	*Doing Sociology: Focus on Research*
Objective:	Students will present results of research projects.
Act. Type:	Class Discussion, Class Activity, Independent Practice, Cooperative Learning, Demonstration, Experiment, Debate, Role-playing, Presentation
Introduction:	Discuss reading from Culture Studies: The Sociological Perspective (see TRB).
Instruction:	Allow time for students to present research projects.
Close:	Give feedback on presentations.

Notes and Comments: _____

_____

_____

_____

_____

_____

_____

_____

_____

_____

_____

_____

_____